GW01605958

ALLABOUT

COLOUR

JANICE LINDSAY

Library and Archives Canada Cataloguing in Publication

Lindsay, Janice
All about colour / Janice Lindsay.

ISBN 978-0-7710-5150-0

1. Color – History. 2. Colors – History. I. Title.

QC495.L46 2008 535.609 C2007-905911-7

We acknowledge the financial support of the Government of Canada through the Book Publishing Industry Development Program and that of the Government of Ontario through the Ontario Media Development Corporation's Ontario Book Initiative. We further acknowledge the support of the Canada Council for the Arts and the Ontario Arts Council for our publishing program.

Typeset in Scala by M&S, Toronto
Printed and bound in China

McClelland & Stewart Ltd.
75 Sherbourne Street
Toronto, Ontario
M5A 2P9
www.mcclelland.com

1 2 3 4 5 12 11 10 09 08

To Molly Lindsay-Kent,
my Mum and the most colourful person I know.

ALL ABOUT COLOUR CONTAINS

I BEFORE COLOUR WAS COLOUR

MAKE

C O
L O
U R

Why is choosing a colour so tricky?
It is only colour!
Surface, skin.
No big deal.

I know I like my bedroom white,
my clothes black, my car silver.
My favourite colour is red.
But that is no help with choosing the right colour
for this,
for here,
for now.
And if I get it wrong,
I will waste money,
Feel foolish,
Be unhappy.
Why can something so apparently trifling, feel so immensely important?
Why does something so simple seem so hard?
How can something so obvious be so mysterious?

Dave, Caroline, and Red: A Love Story

Colour is my job. It is also my passion. My daughter seems to have acquired this predisposition. She was reading a draft of this book and, being a copious writer of journals and letters, she penned a short response to my colour ramblings. Here it is, just as she wrote it, a little love story that reveals the power, the pleasure, and the significance of colour. In a page, she conveys what I take this book to explain.

To set the scene, I should mention that Caroline studied at Queen's University in Kingston, Ontario, and, in her first week, she met Dave. Both were living in residence at the time and they became chums. The next year, like most students, they moved out of res and into their respective shared rental houses in the student ghetto. They remained friends.

In student houses, aesthetics are never the landlord's priority; often they are not the students' either, especially not guys'. But there are exceptions. There are those who take pleasure in arranging their possessions and colouring their space so that even the most ramshackle digs become a place of comfort and a reflection of who they are and what they love. In their last year of university, Caroline discovered that Dave had the knack. And their friendship took a romantic turn.

Mom, as I was reading your book I started thinking about Dave and me when we started going out. We would hang out a lot in his room, talking and listening to music and watching movies. I always felt comfy there and really liked his room. The thing is his room was tiny and totally crammed with his bed, desk, dog, and all the junk that he had accumulated over his years at university. It was a really shitty little room but I loved the way it felt. His blinds were maroon but somehow they didn't clash with his walls, which were red; they made them look better.

I seriously think the colour of his room had something to do with my decision to give him a try. The fact that he painted his room a deep red signalled to me the type of guy he was – passionate, creative, sensual, and bold. It had some mystery. I was drawn to that room and it somehow didn't feel claustrophobic. And it reminded me of our home. Because we were both red lovers, I felt at home there – with him and with his red.

This year he had to move. His new room is much bigger. He has some hardwood floor and room to move around. But I don't like this one nearly as much. The walls are purpley grey–white. His same furniture looks more random and mismatched against it. The clutter is more noticeable. I don't like being in the room the way I did in the other one but I love him now enough to put up with the wall colour (which he didn't choose). But had I met him in this new room, I am not sure I would have been as confident in giving us a try. I know that sounds silly but it is true. Now we spend more time in his living room, which has salmon walls, red curtains, and a red lamp. It feels more us.

This book is not for Dave or Caroline and it's not for kids. They don't need it. They are already fluent with colour. They are not confused by its unpredictable ways or put off by its endless possibilities. For them colour comes from the heart. Anything else – rules, theories, and other people's opinions – just gets in the way.

This book is not for academics because there aren't footnotes, and they have done the in–depth research into original sources. (A big thank you to them for laying the foundation upon which I have built.) The book will annoy literary types who might be put off by my lack of consistent style and formality. My chatty desire to share all the neat things I discover doesn't always lend itself to tidy structure. Artists and decorators might pine for more images. Readers wanting only a quick romp through colour can stick to the short pieces located between meatier chapters. (You can always come back for more.) And for sticklers who will say white and black are not colours, I say that when it comes to painting and pigments, they are.

This book is for anyone who comes home to a room that needs a fix but hasn't bought a gallon of colour to make it work. It is for anyone who lives in a perfectly nice place that doesn't feel like home because they haven't expressed themselves there – yet. It is for those who spend their days in buildings that sap their energy and want to find out if "non-essentials," like being surrounded by good colour and design, might actually make them want to get up and go to work or to school each morning. It is for anyone who loves colour or thinks they might if they could just figure out how it works.

This is a pretty crazy colour journey – one of millions of possible journeys – back into our evolutionary past and up to our present, into the ways of artists, architects, and a colour designer, me. It covers the uselessness of colour theory and the helpfulness of intuition. It is a journey that looks at colour from inside and out, from backstage – our head – and from the only place where it makes sense – our heart.

WHAT IS IT ABOUT COLOUR ANYWAY?

When I say that colour is my job, I know what most people think. Oh, how nice. And do I help with picking clothes in colours that suit a person's complexion? Am I a decorator of sorts? Whatever I do, it must be a fluffy kind of occupation, a girl–job, because it is colour and colour can seem like the least important of attributes. A car will handle the road just as easily if it is silver, black, or red. Walls hold up the roof whether or not they are white. A floor will function as a floor regardless of hue.

Colour, like comfort, is something we take for granted, something we notice more in its absence and more when it is wrong than when it is right. Surrounded by colours that please us, we are more ourselves, but get one wrong and it is like a constant bickering that eats away at the edges of our being.

I have always been overly aware of colour's persistent conversation. For example, white ceilings. Stark white ceilings in coloured rooms are such a common mistake that I sometimes think they will drive me crazy. I can be sitting in a beautifully coloured room trying to have a perfectly nice time, but if the walls are coloured and the ceiling is hovering above like a bright white lid, it really bothers me. The white keeps saying, "Look at me, look at me." Much as I'd rather not, I do. Some people are better at ignoring colour's conversation than others. I have never been one of those people.

I am not alone and so colour, my passion, became colour, my career. Everyone needs objective colour advice; they just don't always know it. In fact, it is those who know and care a lot about colour who usually realize they could use some help. And so my clients include artists, architects, and graphic designers, as well as people who begin by saying they never use designers because they do not usually feel the need of help. I just nod.

One such client was a group of lawyers, Chris, Russell, and Stephen, three confident and opinionated men who had no trouble deciding on client issues, office location and layout, and every other aspect of their practice but were going in circles when it came to wall colour. Their new offices were in a historic warehouse building. The normal corporate neutrals seemed inappropriate but alternatives were difficult to agree on. They were getting frustrated with themselves and each other so they called me in.

I decided it was best to begin with their individual offices so I could understand their taste and they could each exercise some control. That relaxed them into the process. By the time we moved on to colour planning the common areas, I had a good idea of their tastes and their interpersonal dynamics and they found themselves quite enjoying our process. I developed a palette drawn from existing colours and textures in the building but with an intensity level set by them. Where the space did not dictate how the colour should look, the desired psychological effect of colour did. The boardroom would be red because they wanted it to feel powerful and active rather than a place of contemplation. It was also windowless and needed colour to compensate for the lack of natural light. As we built the plan, the lawyers found that appropriate colour choices suddenly seemed easy. It was all so logical. Thanks to the right colours their rented space reflected who they were individually and as a firm.

Barbara, another client, had just built a country retreat. She collaborated with an architect in the design of every detail but when it came to choosing wall colours she was lost. Being a savvy and opinionated professional, she had no difficulty deciding on all the expensive and permanent aspects of her house. But when it came to something as "simple" and alterable as wall colour, she felt paralyzed.

We can look at a scale model of a house and have a solid idea of what we are in for. Shape is predictable. Colour is a trickster because colour is energy, something we can judge only when we experience it. Unlike scale and proportion, only experienced colourists can accurately predict colour's psychological and physiological effects from a model or a paint chip. For most, predicting the experience of colour feels like guesswork.

Barbara decided to play it safe and just paint everything white. It didn't work. The white walls contrasted too starkly against the pine ceilings, trim, and floors. She called for help. Together we chose a medley of straw yellows and soft oranges, a few touches of deep red. The walls blended into the warm hues of the pine woodwork. Views of nature through large wood–trimmed windows became the main colour. The palette drawn from the tones in wood and dried grasses made the place look built of natural materials, not drywall and paint. Substituting warm for white let everything relax.

I didn't find colour. It found me but it took its time. It was only after three careers and several decades that colour's calling became impossible to ignore. At an age when most people are settled in to long–established careers, colour became what I had to do.

I was always keen on colour, which is probably why, like many people, my memories are often linked to it. There are green ones: my friend Mary and I lying on our backs in the garden on a hot summer day, chatting lazily and looking up at the shimmering leaf canopy. Green comes with the sound of cicadas, the drone of lawn mowers, and the green smell of freshly cut grass.

As a teenager, I painted a large room in our basement black, turning it into my retreat. Black let me hear my music better and think better. Surrounded by black, I contentedly contemplated life and love or what outfit to sew up for the Saturday dance. Black was calming and quiet and seriously beautiful.

My first "party shoes" were red patent leather with one strap and a little gold buckle. I felt like a storybook princess or Dorothy in *The Wizard of Oz* every time I wore them. As a teenager I made red velvet bell bottoms for Garth, my second boyfriend and the lead singer in a local band. I felt really chuffed watching him perform in those pants. In grade school I had a winter jacket that I loved. It was red with a white fake–fur trimmed hood, the sort of jacket Saint Nicholas wears in embossed Victorian Christmas cards. When I put it on, I felt like "me" and happy. It seemed magical that just putting on a silly red jacket had this special power. Some clothes still have that transformative effect. So does being in a room dressed in just the right colour.

White is crisp–winter walks home from school, the neighbourhood sparkling in the low afternoon sunlight as if it were dusted with sequins. The pristine white expanses between the shovelled walks seemed like an invitation to lie down, look up at the sky, and make angel wings. Pure white beckons or taunts. Whether it is fresh snow, a blank page, or a white wall, it begs to be defiled. Its perfection can seem arrogant, superior. When I see big expanses of white wall, I feel the pull of a deep–seated graffiti urge.

White is a call to action, a beginning, the "once upon a time" place where a story can unfold. Walking home on those white winter days, the summer and all its vivid colours seemed worlds away.

And now, in a world of too many white walls, I make a career of helping others use colour to imprint their individuality on their often impersonal spaces. I help them use colour to tell their stories, to match their rooms to their personality, make them feel like I did when I put on that red jacket, happy and themselves.

I came to colour design along a circuitous route. I grew up in Stratford, Ontario, a small town with big theatres. Every summer actors and musicians from across the country or England blew into town. I went from being a teenager writing "Car wash fifty–cents" in the dust on Alan Bates's red mustang to a design assistant deciding with Maggie Smith what hat pin was the most appropriate for her as Masha in Chekhov's *Three Sisters*. (Maggie always got her way.) When I did four years of art history at university, the theatre consumed my summers. I began as a props maker and soon discovered my specialty was adding the finishing patinas. Using paints, glazes, brushes, and sponges, I dabbled, dribbled, and speckled interesting patinas on to newly made props. Paint made King John's crown aged, paint weathered Lear's. Paint made King Henry's armour battered and bloodied and Portia's three caskets look tarnished but magnificently expensive. Sir Andrew Aguecheek and his cronies could hide behind huge garden urns that looked damp and mossy, all thanks to a bit of paint.

I wanted to do a post–graduate degree in theatre design but the real thing called. Why study theatre when I could work in one? So I did a short stint as a fabric dyer because, they said, I was "good with colour." Then I became assistant designer and, after that, a designer.

There is no better place than theatre to learn about colour. I lost any fear of using it on a big scale, and I learned how to use it expressively. In technical rehearsals I also learned how important light was to the overall effect of what I had designed.

Theatre taught me the language of colour and that no choice is arbitrary. A costume's colour tells the audience about a character's personality and his or her importance. The star often wears the brightest or boldest clothes. The less important the characters, the more they blend into the background – a principle I now use all the time: decide what to highlight and what to play down and make the distinction with colour.

The first costumes I designed were for August Strindberg's *Miss Julie*. I was terrified. The Stratford Festival was such an important theatre and I had been given a design deadline that preceded the hiring of the director! I designed the costumes but left the colours to be decided later. Robin Phillips, the artistic director, called to say he had seen the designs and they were looking good but he wanted to know what colour I had in mind for Julie's frock.

The play is set in the kitchen of a country estate. It is the summer solstice, and the servants are staying up all night celebrating. Miss Julie, the daughter of the landowner, makes an unexpected appearance down in the kitchen. By the end of the evening Jean, the chauffeur, has seduced her but refuses to run away with her.

So what colour for the frock? Reds? Pinks? Robin listened as I mumbled about the colours of passion and love. Then he said it would be good to remember that during Jean's seduction, he holds and toys with fragrant lilacs. It was suddenly so obvious! The play was set in Strindberg's time, the end of the nineteenth century. Mauve, the colour of lilacs, was all the rage, and Miss Julie, a fashionable young woman, would want to wear it. But more importantly, when Miss Julie ventures into the rustic, earthy kitchen, the pastel colour would have a ghost–like appearance. She would look like a vision from another world, out of place among the servants. Mauve would suggest pale innocence, the refinement and fragility of a porcelain doll. Miss Julie does not arrive in the kitchen in love and lusting for Jean as a red dress would suggest. Dressed in mauve, an ambivalent colour, we watch as Jean arouses the passion in her. The colour would speak volumes. And so I confidently tinted the drawing of her dress with the colour of lilacs.

Theatre taught me how to use colour to establish time, place, and mood. For Chekhov's *The Seagull* or *The Three Sisters,* the colours would not be bright and lively. Masha tells us she wears black "because I am in mourning for my life." The setting would be cold and damp. A few characters, including Masha, would have drunk too much vodka. Greys, browns, and muddy colours would set the tone. Accent colours would be dark or dulled. If a red were used, it would be a maroon or dark and bloodless red.

But if the play were Noel Coward's *Private Lives,* a comedy set in 1930s France, Amanda's art deco apartment in Paris would sparkle. Light and bright colours, mirrored details and accents in black, silver, or gold would set the tone. Whites were fashionable in the deco period after Somerset Maugham's wife, Syrie, decorated their living room entirely in white. Any red accents would be a juicy orange–red, the kind that Diaghilev's Ballets Russe had popularized at the time. Light colours with bright accents and sparkle would be historically accurate and emotionally perfect. Whether the audience knows the historical references is not essential. They read colour's emotional content intuitively.

After my second child arrived, I gave up the nomadic life of a theatre designer for the more stable and profitable job of stylist for photographers and for television. Ten years later, I was a colour designer. The transition was not as big as it might seem. Houses and offices were not so different from stage and film sets. Good colour was still not about running off into great flights of fancy. It was not about designer likes and dislikes. It was about finding the most appropriate colours for the circumstance. It was collaboration. In theatre the play sets the stage; the director adds an interpretation; and the designer works with both to bring the piece to life for the audience. It requires attention to details – clues such as lilacs. Colour unites the emotional and physical demands of a production into a cohesive whole. In a home or workplace, colour must suit the architecture or physical setting, the materials and objects already in place, and the purpose and personality of the people who spend their days there.

I began a quest to learn all I could about colour. I read voraciously and wrote a monthly colour column for a design magazine. Readers sought me out, and my colour career began. Colour was how I would help others to decorate, or so I thought. Clients taught me that colour is decoration but also transformation. Changing a colour completely changes our experience of a place.

Beth, a single mum, came home from work the week the colours were done and found her teenaged daughter sitting in the living room smiling. She looked up and said, "You know, Mum, the new colours make even our old furniture look really good. It is as if we moved out and someone with great taste moved in."

My sister felt her grey front room looked tired and drab and in desperate need of a fix. I suggested pumpkin orange. Her cleaning lady came in the week it was done and asked if she had had her furniture reupholstered. My sister started entertaining again.

The right colours make people feel energized, empowered, and happy. Colour is more than paint, more than surface. To understand why, I needed to go deeper into the guts of colour, to get behind the scenes, and to find out if there were rules and codes underlying the professional application of colour. I made three trips to San Diego for a brief but intense colour course offered by the International Association of Color Consultants.

We were a group of about twelve from around the world, sequestered for several days at a time in a less than interesting hotel room overlooking the highways of San Diego, learning about colour and architecture, colour and light, colour history, colour and emotion, colour and psycho–physiological responses. The course was less about new information than reinforcing what I knew and strengthening my conviction that colour is not to be treated lightly.

Next I joined the Color Marketing Group, a colour trend forecasting organization. Its thousand–odd members, mostly American, are people who make colour decisions in their field. Twice a year a few hundred of us meet at conferences to discuss what colour shifts are happening in our industry and why. Trend forecasting is not about making trends so much as seeing them coming, being aware.

I also began to explore what was foreign territory for me – psychology, science, biology, and the ways of the brain. The deeper I went, the more fascinating colour became. But no book put all the different sides of colour together for me. If I wanted the diverse parts of colour sewn together, I was going to have to try to do it myself. Then I might be able to answer the basic and baffling question: What is colour?

To find out if others already knew the answer I asked around. A watercolour class in Montreal answered the question this way:

"The opposite of darkness."

"Life, mood, and vibration."

"A reflection of a joie de vivre – gaiety."

"Peaches, bold birds, South America, my mother's living room – I miss her."

"Emotion. Access to the soul."

"Colour is being alive. It is content."

I asked a house painter and he replied, "That's a difficult question. Let me see. It's tones. It's red, blue, green. It's the tints that go in white (paint) base to make all your wall colours."

My mother said, "It is something deep and vibrant that makes the world come alive from black and white. It is something ephemeral juxtaposed with something permanent, like on these tiles."

An artist friend of mine who uses colour sparingly in her work said, "Colour is light. It is variety. It is confusion, joy, exuberance and can sometimes wear us out."

My husband, perhaps because he has been around me and my colour musings for a long time, said, "It is interpretations of light. The way we perceive light through the material world."

The answer reveals more about the person than about colour. Many define colour by what it *does* or how it makes them *feel* rather than by what it is. Or, like the painter, colour is described as something like, well, you know, *colour.* Colour seems mysterious, something to do with pigments and light but that is deeply hooked to our emotions. It is hard to describe, hard to remember accurately, hard to pin down. As it turns out, there are very good reasons why colour is never as easy as we think it should be. But they are not understood by coming at colour from just one direction. Thinking we know what it is because we study art, or read colour theory or design, is like saying we know Europe, a continent that stretches from Sicily to Spitsbergen and from Ireland to the Bosphorus and the Urals, because we have lived in Paris or Prague or Rome. To begin to know Europe or colour requires going to a variety of places.

Our colour destinations on this journey are historical, biological, and personal. Some are popular hot spots – red, blue, green, and yellow – and some are off the beaten track – wabi–sabi and why beauty is a little bit ugly. Some places you might never have gone to on your own and will never want to go back to again. Other places are where you might wish we had stayed longer. You will have to go back on your own and take them at your own pace. Every journey through colour is really an exploration of self, the positive feeling of a red jacket, the benefits to be had from a pleasing room, and an exploration of the nature of happiness.

BEFORE COL

OUR WAS
COLOUR

PRIVATE
PARKING
ONLY
24 HOURS
ENFORCED
23

TESTING THE LIMITS

When I was starting up my colour consulting business, I didn't know there was no such thing as too much colour, and I went about exploring the limits of colour tolerance, beginning with my own. I would be my own colour guinea pig within the confines of my studio. Red was out because I have a high red tolerance. My dining room is two reds, my kitchen has upper cabinets in five shades of red; the ceiling is a sixth. I was already getting a good daily dose of red and there was no limit in sight. Green, red's opposite, was the way to go.

I had no interest in easy, tasteful, decorator grey–greens or sages. No celadon for me. Blue–greens were not energetic enough. I wanted the colour of leaves full of sunshine. I began paying attention to this colour wherever I found it. My timing was good. It was spring and a really bright yellow–green was everywhere in abundance. Even the maple tree outside the studio window was a profusion of the lime green leaf buds. "My green" was the colour of new growth and suddenly it was everywhere I looked. It was as if nature were telling me to go ahead. Just do it! But how well would nature's sunshine green translate into a wall colour? (Ask the world a question and sooner or later it will present the answer – always. I got mine in a matter of days.)

My husband and I took the kids to the art gallery to see an Andy Warhol exhibit. We had already wandered through a few rooms when I turned a corner and there it was, My green. One great big gallery wall of it! Opposite this wall, Warhol's photo–lithographs of Marilyn Monroe, Liz Taylor, James Dean, and Chairman Mao hung on a tomato red wall. Beyond it was a black one. I loved the way the three colours played off each other. My green was divine. It felt as if I were not just seeing the colour but drinking it in, receiving it with my entire body. I decided on the spot that if it looked and felt that good on a big wall, there would be no problem using it in my studio.

I kept the ceiling, trim, and my work zone neutral. The green went on the walls of the lounge area. Inspired by the gallery, I put tomato red on a short wall at the entrance. And then to really push myself, I used high–gloss black on the tall baseboards and the trim around an interior stained–glass window.

Was it too much colour? Not at all! I don't know if I was surprised or disappointed. It didn't feel the least bit pushy. There was no regret, no panic, no would–have–could–have–should–have. The green was terrific. The black, however, was a shock. Around my stained–glass window it was good. It made all the colours glow like stars in the night. I hadn't really noticed how much of "my green" was in the glass already until the green walls brought it out and the black set it off. But on the baseboard, black shifted the balance in the room. It seemed to weigh it down, as if I had put Doc Martens on my elegant walls. My housekeeper came in and loved the black. It reminded her of home in Barbados. (Black on baseboards is a very old idea, popular because it didn't show dirt.) The walls took no time to love; the baseboards took a week or two. Now I would hate them to be light. (I recently went to a party in a very modern and neutrally coloured condo where all the doors were high–gloss black. The effect was so stunningly beautiful, strong, dramatic, and classy that I decided I will copy the idea.)

The problem with my new colour is that it isn't new any more. The green has been with me for years. As a colour designer, I think I should keep trying new things and have another go at finding my limits – maybe a shocking yellow would push me. The furniture in the room is neutral to allow for change. But I cannot part with that green. When I am asked how often you need to paint walls, I say to wait until either the paint gets damaged or you feel the need of a change but that might be never. My green has helped many colour–fearful clients push their limits. When they hesitate over a subtle tone, I show them my wild hue. Their colour usually looks very tame by comparison.

LEAVING HOME

THE BEGINNING

I say what I do is colour design but what I really do is try to make people feel happy with where they are. So when good friends were moving and I was heading out the door on my way to see their new house, my husband, who is not prone to colour commentary (he gets enough of it from me), called after me, "I hope you will encourage them to use some colour." I stopped in my tracks. What?! "Yes. Their old house never felt like a home. I think it was because all the walls were white. Somehow it always had the feel of a rental property." How would colour have made their house feel like a home? They obviously didn't want colour. Why had the place needed it? Why was I embarking on a career based on helping people to understand colour and use it and enjoy it when, through most of history, colour was not a home essential. Why would it matter now?

Home can be anything from a roof and a few walls to the palace of Versailles. For a baby, home is being held against her mother's chest. For kids, it's wherever their family is. Home is a place we like to share with those who matter to us. Home is so many different things because it is not a place, it is a feeling – a feeling of safety, comfort, and support.

Home is a place where we can be ourselves. The more I worked with colour, the more I came to understand that my primary goal was not to make rooms look pretty but to make them feel like home.

I became less interested in decor magazines full of see–what–money–can–buy rooms, rooms that seemed over–designed and in the designer's signature style – usually elegant, traditional with a modern infusion, neutral in colour, and expensive, very expensive. These rooms were attractive but in a predictable way. They seemed to be showing off and were not as individual as the people who live in them. When I am asked if I wouldn't rather design the entire room than just the colour, the answer is yes. And I do but only for clients whose taste I understand and can embrace so we collaborate as a unit.

Colour is different. I will design colour plans for anybody, anywhere, with any kind of taste or style because I am more of a translator, a coach, or a therapist. I listen, empathize, and advise, understanding that each of us is our own colour expert and it is our differences that make things, including colour, interesting.

If I am faced with a room that has objects in a palette that seems unappealing, my challenge is to select a wall colour that will make it gorgeous. As Thelonious Monk once said: There are no bad notes, just bad combinations. Like theatre, my job requires getting into character and seeing things from the client's perspective so I can refine and finesse their ideas. I am a guide clearing the path, they are finding their way home.

But if home is so varied, what is it that triggers the feeling? What is at the root of home? As it turns out, the journey home takes us back over five million years to our original home, the savannah grasslands of East Africa, the one we started leaving about sixty thousand years ago. In evolutionary terms this was only a moment ago. Subliminally, we have pined for it ever since.

Nature, and specifically the savannahs, is the home that resonates with our inner being because we were built by it and for it. I discovered this the year my husband suggested we spend the month of August in a rented cottage on an island in Georgian Bay, a few hours north of Toronto. Our children were little at the time and he knew my idea of a holiday was a few days off, going somewhere exciting like New York, London, or Paris. He added that the cottage he had in mind would have no running water or electricity and, in that pre-cellphone era, no easy contact with the outside world. Transportation would be mainly by canoe. Would it not be fun, he asked. I imagined exactly how much fun it would be to be stranded on a little island up north in the middle of nowhere dealing with two small children, one of whom was a non-swimmer and still in diapers. My husband prevailed. He was starting a novel set in the area. It seemed unreasonable not to be a good sport, not to try it – once.

That was seventeen years ago and we have never missed an August holiday up north since. What occurred on that small, forested island with its granite shoreline and little back bays took me completely by surprise. I had no idea I would feel so at home. I felt reborn. Everything came into balance. I felt an unexpected contentment and experienced a feeling of benign power. Freed from technologies beyond my control, I felt I was participating in my daily life as I never had before. Things became simple and straightforward. Technical solutions were as complex as a bang, a poke, or a prod. I stopped wearing a watch; time was determined by the position of the sun. The sky was full of information.

There was a colour unity too. I don't think I had ever been so free of the colour interruptions caused by man-made attention-grabbing colour – the billboard in the farmer's field, road signs and factories and shopping malls. If these colours were harmonious, they would blend into nature's beauty and defeat their look-at-me purpose. The island was relaxing because it was free of the staccato interruptions of man-made colour. Nature's colours are comfortable and useful, a helpful dialogue, not an abusive monologue.

I felt a connection, a oneness, even as I hauled water, kneaded bread, tinkered with the wood stove, or spread ash and peat in the outhouse, and made my peace with a fox snake who liked to sunbathe on "my" rock. This initiation took place during the rainiest August anyone could remember.

A few years later I was listening to a lecture given by environmental scientist James A. Wise, CEO of Eco–Integrations Inc., a consulting firm specializing in integrating people, technology, and the environment, and I understood the reason for my island euphoria. According to Wise, we respond to our physical settings with programming rooted in our evolution on the savannah grasslands of East Africa. Built environments don't resemble the savannahs but our ancient responses haven't changed. At the northern cottage I had experienced a setting and a lifestyle that were as close as I had ever come to those I had evolved to fit. This fit, I came to realize, sits at the heart of what looks good and what feels right. There is a relaxing beauty in a place without aesthetic mistakes. Nature, our original home, is the right from which we judge wrong, and is at the core of all good design. It is something that I think about during every colour consultation I do.

Even the most inveterate condo dwellers have the savannahs encoded as "home" in their DNA. We never stop craving traces of it. To prove it, environmental psychologists Judith H. Heerwagen and Gordon H. Orians showed people of all ages and cultures from all parts of the world photographs of diverse natural and urban settings. Nearly all chose the most savannah–like one as the favourite. Given a choice, they preferred a banal image of nature to a variety of urban settings, a flat farmer's field over a spiffy city setting. The savannahs moved into second place only when an adult's life experience had bonded them with a more familiar setting. For children the savannah landscape is always the favourite.

Anyone who buys a house plant is putting a bit of savannah into their home. We look for a picnic spot or a campsite that resembles a savannah. The characteristics of our universal home, the one we carry in our DNA are these: wide, open space that is bordered by trees, and long views that let us see what is coming and escape if necessary. Clustered trees border the open space, giving us shade and shelter, hiding places and food. (Environmental psychologists have discovered that we still have a preference for trees that we could climb should the need arise.) Today neighbourhoods and city streets lined with trees look better to us than those without. Even land developers who mow down every tree and shrub call their developments Georgian Glen, Glen Manor, Riverdale, to suggest landscapes full of trees and hills. Their sales brochures show houses surrounded by tall trees that are no longer there.

Home is not flat. Undulating berms, hills, and outcroppings give us prospects and refuge, lookouts and landmarks. They also create mystery, a characteristic that, according to the findings of Drs. Stephen and Rachel Kaplan, researchers in environmental psychology, University of Michigan (1974), is surprisingly important to us. Mystery is the promise of new information. Being curious to know what was over the hills or around the next bend encouraged us to explore. Not knowing if it would be Eden or a pack of predators added interest, suspense, and excitement and kept us alert and engaged. We like winding roads, curving beaches, and L-shaped rooms. We are dulled by long, flat paths, highways, and hallways.

Home has water because our survival depends on it. Clouds, foliage, and flowers enhance a setting because they all indicate the presence of water. With a pond, lake, or river present we relax because we do not need to be constantly on the lookout for water. On the savannahs, water was not always easy to find so our peripheral vision evolved to be alerted by and attracted to shiny things. Fountains, waterfalls, and swimming pools are surrogate water bodies. Great cities almost always have a river running through them.

At home we are not alone. Cows grazing, birds singing, fish jumping, butterflies fluttering, and the presence of other people make a place "lived in." If no one else is around, we get anxious. The presence of others acts as an all–clear signal. We feel at home in a busy restaurant, a street where others are walking, and parks with dog walkers and parents with kids because subliminally they are backup for sensing, spotting, or dealing with a threat. Plants and pets bring with them the comfort of having other living things around. (A study of 4,300 Americans performed by the Minnesota Stroke Institute at the University of Minnesota revealed that risk of heart attacks was reduced by almost 30 per cent for those who lived with a cat. Another of their studies indicated that one twelve–minute visit from a dog improved the heart and lung function of people with heart conditions.)

In high–rises, apartments at the height of tree branches are the most ideal. From the second to the seventh floor we feel safe from predators but not cut off from life on the ground.

Home has no straight lines. Curves and undulations relax us. The curving patterns of waves, grasses swaying, fish swimming, birds in flight, and cumulous clouds are nature's relaxation tools. Studies reveal that we perceive straight lines to be finite, logical, or dead while curves are living, spiritual, and infinite. NASA research has shown that even looking at curved patterns relaxes us. Smart airline companies have curves in the woven patterns of the seat upholstery we have to stare at for interminable hours.

Home is full of meaningful colour; very little of it is white.

The essential characteristics of our first home are the same ones that made British landscape painter John Constable (1776–1837) one of the most successful landscape painters. He put savannah characteristics into landscapes even though his preparatory sketches show they were not always in the original setting. We put the essential features of our savannah home into parks, golf courses, and our own backyard. They have been handed down through the history of landscape design.

In the nineteenth century when American landscape designer Frederick Law Olmstead (1822–1903) and his partner, architect Calvert

Vaux (1824–1895), were putting meadows, lakes, and groves into their design for Central Park and Prospect Park in New York City, they were influenced by eighteenth-century English park designs. These English gardens, planned by British landscape designer Humphrey Repton (1752–1818), were derived from medieval deer parks which in turn were based on Roman designs. The Roman designs were derived from the landscapes of Persia considered to be like the Garden of Eden. According to many scholars, Eden was like the savannahs of East Africa.

We are willing to pay a high price to get traces of our ancestral home on the savannahs – the house that backs onto a ravine, sits across from a park, or has a garden and climbable trees. Houses with big windows or the condo with high ceilings and an open plan are preferred. We will pay for a view of nature but especially one with trees and water. In restaurants, hotels, and apartment buildings we all want the room or table with the best view.

Outdoor cafés attract our business if they are edged with packaged bits of nature – a boxwood hedge, flower boxes, or potted palms. Floral arrangements are put into hotel lobbies to make us feel at home – the fresher the flowers and the bigger the bouquet, the more expensive the rooms. The floral welcome is extended with floral carpets, upholstery, and landscape paintings. In the courtyard restaurant of the chic and expensive Pershing Hall Hotel in Paris there is a thirty-metre tall vertical garden with three hundred types of plants by French botanist and green wall guru Patrick Blanc.

Seeing nature makes us feel better. Windowless intensive care units deprive patients of information about time, weather, and season so they become unsettled and disoriented. Their blood pressure elevates and their immune function declines. Sterile hospital rooms lacking colour, natural materials, and views depress patients and caregivers alike.

That even tenuous connections to our natural home make us better was indicated in over a hundred studies by Robert Ulrich, director of

Health Systems and Design at Texas A & M University. In a Pennsylvania hospital, he studied patients recovering from surgery. Some were given a room with a view of a stand of trees. The others had the same room but with a view of a brown brick wall. The patients were of similar age, weight, and general health. In the room with the natural view, patients consistently healed faster, required fewer and milder pain killers, were less demanding of staff, and had fewer post–operative complications. He found that even looking at pictures of trees can lower blood pressure and release muscle tension.

The fit between the savannahs and ourselves took millions of years to finesse.

> **It is hard to imagine how long this was. Evolutionary biologist Richard Dawkins, in *Unweaving the Rainbow*, puts our evolution into a time perspective like this. He suggests we think of the expanse of time as the span of outstretched arms. If you go from the fingertips of your right hand all the way across your chest to your left elbow, we are still in the bacteria stage of development. Dinosaurs make an appearance at the lowest joint of the index finger of your left hand. *Homo sapiens* spans the thickness of one fingernail. Not the length of that nail, the thickness. The ten thousand years since we left the life of nomads in nature and started to build our own homes can be swept away with one passing of a nail file.**

All that time to iron out our kinks, to polish up our design, improve and modify our size and shape and all our mechanisms. Millions of years of finessing so that to this very day we are born into the world built perfectly for life as nomadic hunters and gatherers on the savannah grasslands of East Africa! Our eyes developed to handle nature's colours and forms, our ears, her sounds. Light set the schedule: work, sleep, mate, and hibernate. We became skilful interpreters of nature's signals.

And we would have lived happily ever after if it hadn't been that our brain took an evolutionary leap forward a few million years ago. It got very big very fast. Intellect started to get the upper hand over instinct and emotion. Eventually we thought we didn't need to fit into nature any more. We could improve it and we could control it. Why roam around looking for food if you could grow your own? Only ten thousand years ago we gave up our nomadic life and became farmers. We put a roof over our heads and moved home inside.

But we didn't immediately require colour. Even without it a house felt like home when it was built with our own hands and the help of friends, when it was made out of local materials and carefully shaped to meet the demands of the climate, the setting, and our personal needs. It felt like home in places like Bali, where a house was built using a set of measurements taken from the body of the owner. Even though many of us still measure in feet (the length of a man's foot), inches (the tip of the thumb to the first knuckle), and yards (the length of one stride or of the walking stick used to facilitate striding), we often live and work in places that seem to have been made according to a very foreign set of measurements.

As houses multiplied into villages and villages grew into cities and cities spread, trampling nature, economics replaced ergonomics. Speed replaced diligence, and machine-made anonymity replaced craftsmanship. Houses lost personal meaning and individuality. *This* was why my husband was right about our friends' house needing colour. Now we need colour to bring signs of life into spaces that have lost their connection to both our original home and so to ourselves.

And so, a few years ago, when my mother moved into a banal little apartment that she hated, colour came to the rescue. Mum is one of those people with a knack for making wherever she is seem like home but this apartment thwarted even her experienced nesting skills. She would tell you that the place isn't important. It is the people that matter. That was why it was easy for her to leave Britain when my sisters and I were little and make Canada her home. It was good for Dad's work. The people were friendly. She settled in and didn't look back.

When my father died suddenly after forty–six years of marriage, Mum visited her hometown and her old chums in Wales. A year later she married Fred, her first boyfriend. (His wife, one of Mum's best friends, had died the year before too.) For several years his home became her home. Then Fred died and it didn't feel good any more. Mum moved back to Stratford, Ontario, the town where she and Dad had raised six of us in a big old house on a hill. In my memory, home was full of sunshine, kids, chaos, friends, and music.

Mum has always been a glass–half–full kind of person but try as she might to be positive, it was very sad to be coming back to Stratford and moving – alone – into a small apartment. The building was a rather ordinary structure, built in the early sixties but in a great location overlooking a river with a view of the old town centre across the way. It should have been ideal because it met all the savannah conditions – long view edged with willow trees, water, other living things – swans, dog walkers, joggers, paddle boats. The problem was that the windows were so parsimoniously small and set so unintelligently high that if you sat down you were cut off from the view. It felt bad not to see the beauty on the other side of the wall. It was worse than if there had been nothing attractive there at all. (Such bad architecture makes my blood boil. It would have taken so little for the developers to build a place that would feel good to anyone living there every single day of their lives. A few dollars and a bit more thought and this cramped box would have seemed magnificent. They would have recouped any extra costs many times over because of the premium we are willing to pay for our savannah characteristics.)

Mum was despondent when I went to help her choose paint colours. She wondered if she should have stayed in Wales. She thought, at the very least, she should consider moving out.

Mum has always loved greens so we chose a soft apple green for her bedroom. Colour accents here and there added architectural interest and made the place look more like her. When the paint was on, we added mirrors to catch light and the view as best we could.

It worked. She said that in the mornings in her bedroom she felt like she was waking up in a sunny field. Each room began to feel more pleasing. Mum can sometimes be given to a bit of hyperbole but she called me after the painting was done and said, "Janice, with the colour on the walls, it feels like I have come out of the grave and into the sunshine." She continued, "It is funny. I mean, I have heard your stories about doing people's colours and what a difference it makes. But I never realized how much! I feel like I should be running door to door and saying to people, "Get your colours done! Get your colours done!"

Too often where we need colour most – apartments, schools, offices, auditoriums, hospitals, mega mansions, or basement flats – is where we have it least. When we live inside places built without our unique selves and tastes in mind, colour is how we can make them speak to us. We aren't going to go back to live in nature but with colour we can put back some of what we have lost. Colour can help us find our way home.

GREEN, THE FOURTH PRIMARY

There was a time when green was my least favourite colour, especially the primary green of kid's crayons, the jock colour of Astroturf, billiard tables, and the alligator on a golf shirt.

When I was a kid, my girlfriends' parents all seemed to have living rooms in pale celadon verging on institutional green. These rooms had crisp and unfriendly furniture, family photographs professionally done that made everyone look stiff and unpleasant, and a few carefully poised don't–touch knick–knacks. Sheers bordered by drapes kept sunlight at bay. There was no air, only stillness, in these pale green rooms. They were waiting for someone more important than I, royalty perhaps. Somewhere a clock ticked like the room's intransigent pulse.

When I was a teen in home ec class, sewing up miniskirts for myself in bold colours – purple with yellow flowers – the conservative girls chose green. They wore sage green cardigans, green tartan skirts, and hunter green woollen knee socks that defied gravity. Green attire was especially favoured by my red–headed chum, Patty, who thought it suited her colouring, not realizing that, because it was the complementary colour, it made her look a bit florid.

It was years later that my studio's lime green helped me realize there are greens for every personality.

More recently I had another green epiphany. I was going to a colour conference in Prague and it was time to put together my "hot, new, up–and–coming hues." Normally participants take a few colours with them but for the first time ever I was taking only one – green. Not just green but greens, greenness with nothing tame about it.

Green was avoided by early Christians because it was the pagan colour associated with fertility. It has been linked to inertia, indecisiveness, and envy. Oscar Wilde wore a green carnation to signal his homosexuality. As a pigment, green couldn't compete with blue or red, colours made of rare materials that took a lot of work to prepare and cost a packet of money to use. Vermilion and lapis lazuli were as expensive as gold. Unlike a good red or blue, greens tended to fade. Vivid and affordable synthetic greens, Scheele's Green and emerald green, were invented in the nineteenth century and became the most popular wallpaper colour of the Victorian era. Unfortunately, they were made with arsenic, which gave off toxic fumes. These greens were banned for use in wallpapers by the end of the century because they were killing people, especially children, as they slept in their newly decorated bedrooms.

Red and blue team up with yellow as the three primaries that make all colour but green always looked like a primary to me. If you didn't know you could make a pure green by mixing blue and yellow, you wouldn't see blue and yellow in it. For centuries no one realized that blue and yellow could be mixed to make green.

Green is categorized as a secondary colour when it comes to paint but not light. Light's three primaries are blue (short wavelength), red (long wavelength), and green (medium wavelength).

In many ways green is the most perfect colour: the colour of balance and harmony. Aristotle thought green was the midpoint between darkness and light and that was why it was relaxing to the eye. He positioned green in the centre of his white–to–black colour scale. He was right about it being easy on the eye. Centuries later, we learned that our eyes can relax when they look at green because the green wavelength is the perfect length to fit our eyeball. It lands smack on the retina without any focusing effort or adjustment. Red light waves are too long so the colour advances. Blues are too short so blue recedes.

Green is neither masculine nor feminine. It is neither warm nor cool but poised between the two. It is often classed as a cool colour for the sake of keeping the colour wheel symmetrical.

Green is calming so schools, hospitals, and all manner of institutions have used it pervasively over the years – usually in weak, insipid, pale–mint tones. "Institutional green" can be hard to disassociate from a negative association with places of illness or control. Green has always been too ubiquitous to seem special. It was the main colour of our original savannah home where it was encoded in our genes as good background, nature's wallpaper. Green is the colour against which more interesting things catch our eye. We evolved to know it was there but not to pay it close attention, at least not the way we must pay attention to, say, red. I think of green as always the wife and never the mistress – supportive, comfortable, always around but lacking mystery, magic, and exotic passion; enjoyed but rarely an obsession.

The impediment to green getting attention has always been red, green's nemesis. Red constantly upstages green. Green gets stuck with red because of the ill–conceived and outdated notion that *complementary* colours are *complimentary* – which they are not. Red is the extrovert, noisy, and passionate. Green is laid back, quiet, and restful. Mixed together in equal amounts, they cancel out each other's personality. Green can always use a bit of red to stir the pot, keep the party happening, but a little goes a long way. At the Prague conference, I said the time had come for green to divorce her overbearing partner.

Greens are chromatic peacekeepers, getting along well with any colour. But they can be overwhelmed unless, as in nature, they are allowed to predominate. Consequently, greens love the company of other greens. No greens clash. Other colours can join in as long as they are in the minority or quiet, or tinted with green – complex greys, black greens, olives and avocadoes and khaki.

Without the competition of red, green looked fresh. Used in unexpected places – high–end Italian furniture companies put it on expensive sofas and chairs – it looked exciting. Even primary greens started to look sophisticated. Acid green–yellow or citrus yellow–green of Japanese grasses replaced red as the punchy accent. Together green's sum became greater than its parts. Green, I said to my group at the conference, was about to become a star.

We want green for the very reasons we used to shun it. In a chaotic world, green's flaw becomes its feature. When wars and environmental devastation are front–page news, we start to want the comfort colour, the colour that is always connected with positive values, things clean and fresh and healthy. In North America, green begins to resonate like a Norman Rockwell painting or an Aaron Copland suite. We want it because it *is* uncomplicated and because it *is* common. We want it because it is the main colour of nature – from which we feel cut off. It is the nothing–special colour of familiar things – crayons and Christmas, the backyard. Greenness feels like sunshine photosynthesized into things that are good for us. Green feels like home.

RED, BLUE, AND THE BARKING OF THE DOGS

PRIMITIVE MAN

The power went out late one August afternoon at a cottage on an island in the middle of Lake Temagami. Power outages are not uncommon in Ontario's cottage country so I didn't think much about it. In any case, it was time to head off to the marina to pick up my husband, who was coming up from the city, a six–hour drive away. The kids and I reached the marina as the sun began to drop. It did not take long for us to realize that something was wrong. Usually people lounge about, calmly waiting for cars bearing family or friends to come down the gravel road. Instead everyone seemed rushed. There was a lineup at the only phone booth. Few cars came down the side road. News filtered out from boaters with shortwave radios that the power outage was not a local affair. This was 2003, the summer of the blackout that ran up the eastern seaboard from New York and across Quebec and swaths of Ontario. Cellphones were out of commission. So too were gas pumps. David's arrival would depend on whether he'd fuelled up in time.

As we grew more anxious, the sun seemed to sink faster. Should we head back and leave David stranded? I imagined him pulling up just as we disappeared on the horizon. We began calculating how much daylight was left. How long could we hang on before aborting our mission? The light was disappearing quickly now. Suddenly the sun was a red sliver on the horizon. We would have to leave or risk life, limb, and boat propeller getting back to the island. That was when I noticed another boat about to set off. I rushed over and begged a ride from the accommodating cottager so we could leave our boat behind for David, should he make it. He did not. He spent the night in a dark hotel in a dark city an hour away.

Back on the island with only minutes of precious light left to get organized, we cursed ourselves for not being better prepared but who ever is? Not having light made light the one thing we wanted. With only candlelight, our day was cut short. We reverted to a more primitive state, and headed early to bed.

Most people who call me up for help with colour make this distinction. White is light. Colour, which is not as light, must be varying degrees of darkness. White, which is light, is a good thing, and colour, which takes away light, is feared. It sometimes occurs to me as I am working with clients that this is a colour attitude that links us to our most primitive ancestors.

Light was prehistoric society's lifeline and animator. It made the world safe and activities possible. Darkness put on the brakes. Light brought back the colour that darkness took away. Light, not colour, was important. Colour was not particularly interesting because it seemed inert, a fixed characteristic of substance. Leaves were green, the sky was blue, things were the colour they were and that was that. To this day most primitive cultures have no word for colour. Instead of colour they had materials. Ochre was yellow or red. It wasn't its yellow or redness that held power but ochre, the material. And if the material were shiny, a catcher of light, so much the better.

Many of the people I help today are the opposite. They see paint as colour but materials – their brick fireplace, their wooden floor, the marble fireplace surround – as not part of the palette. When picking trim for exteriors, some people don't see the colour of their brick as the biggest and most important colour of all. Sometimes I colour-match "real" materials to a paint chip and put these in the mix to hold the place of the real materials and help clients see how our choices have to harmonize with them. Even a white needs to be coordinated.

So how did we view colour when colour as we know it did not exist? We imagine colour as a circle or a wheel, but through most of history it was black and white, a two-colour system that extended from darkness to light. Instead of sorting it by *hue,* colour was sorted by *value* or brightness. The only difference between my clients' two-colour system and primitive society's is what they put on either side of the great divide. For my clients, white fills one side of the equation. It is so valued and so widely used that it and pale neutrals stand on their own; all colour is situated on the other side.

To most primitive cultures, warm colours – yellow, orange, and red – were light. Red sat next to white as the lightest colour of all, lighter and brighter than all yellows put together. What was bright was what was visible, and, against nature's greens, red stood out like a beacon. Cool colours, blues and greens, were on the dark side. The blue sky, at the end of the day, shifted to indigo and then to the black canopy of night, so blues were shades of black. Greens were shades of blue. In many languages, including Welsh and Japanese, blue and green are put into the same colour category.

Dividing colour into brightness – *value* and not *hue* – made sense. The rising sun was the great energizer, its power godlike. The brighter or shinier a colour, the more light it radiated and so the more powerful and godlike it was. To add the appearance of light to paintings, primitive people added parallel wiggly white lines along the edges of their shapes. To get light's "quiver" or shimmer they added rows of tiny white dots. Australian aboriginal artists still do.

It takes a power outage to experience the vulnerability of not having light on demand. It can take the passing of a day in a sickbed to understand how light connects us to the world around us. When we are still, immobilized, and sunlight comes into the room, it is a welcome visitor, filling the space with energy and news. It moves about, shifting across surfaces, changing positions, flickering and dancing, constantly marking the passage of time with its angles and the phases of a day with its colour. It notes shifts of weather. Its shadows keep the rhythm of the breezes through the trees, track the flight path of birds, and note the passing of clouds.

As the sun lowers in the sky, it fires up the leaves that border the window or sections of the trees beyond, with alternating patterns of bright chartreuse and deep green. As the day winds down, in comes the brief warm intense light that signals the end is close. This light is not from above. It comes in sideways. The sun has come down to our level, close and intimate, to bathe everything in its most dramatic amber chiaroscuro. Ordinary objects become golden–edged still lifes – carpet, chair, slippers. Its warmth presses against the side of things as the chill of night moves in from the opposite direction.

If light's amber finale weren't killed with the flick of a switch, it would be savoured as we focused nostalgically on the last strands of a day where so many things were possible before the night's blindness moved in. Finally everything must pause until light and life, in full colour, can begin again.

Ironically we have always been and always will be very bad judges of lightness and darkness. Photographers use light meters. Cameramen have someone hold up a white card so they can set the light level. Colour designers move the colour around and hold it next to other surfaces: the floor, the fabrics, the furniture, the north wall, the south wall, with lights on and lights off so we can compare, compare, compare. Only by giving the colour sample this quick tour of comparisons do we know how dark or light it really is in that particular setting.

Because lightness and darkness are comparative, I wear black when I colour–consult because this is what happens. I open my large paint kit, and my client and I choose colours from the almost two thousand possibilities. It seems like a lot but we very quickly zero in on which colour or hue works. It is so much easier than which value of that colour, the tone or shade. I hold up a few candidates so the client can stand back and look at them. Most of the time the colours are held up against white walls. Against white, any colour looks its darkest and to this the client responds, "Oh, that would be too dark." This is when I hold the colour against my black clothing and it looks its lightest. "Oh, maybe it isn't too dark." Then we compare the colour to objects in the room until we become capable judges of how dark or light it really is.

Hue is easier to judge but black and white, dark or light, have no internal reference. They don't exist except as fluctuating comparisons. The page you are reading gets brighter outside and darker inside but the page still looks the same. We don't notice that the blackness and whiteness change because the two tones stay the same by comparison to each other. Research by David H. Hubel, a Nobel Prize winner who has studied vision for over thirty–five years, measured the actual amount of light reflected from the black print in broad sunlight and found it was the same as the light reflected off the white of the page in dim light. A brightly lit chunk of coal has a brightness similar to a dimly lit snowball but we know one from the other because we see them compared to other objects in the setting.

A candle flame looks light in a dark setting and dim in a light one. Brightness is only a comparison and not a fact. A pale colour looks paler on the wall and darker as a small chip. What looks grey or light tan in a chip will look white on a wall although I have a hard time convincing people of that. A pale colour looks paler on the walls of a big space than a small one. I sometimes make it darker in a larger space if I want it to look and feel the same as it would in a smaller one.

We know colours only by comparing them. It is a fact that we can see millions of colour nuances and variations if we are comparing one colour to another side by side. We see only a few thousand if we are looking at them separately. You cannot stand on your porch and look across the street and compare your colour to your neighbour's. You have to colour–match yours to a chip and walk that chip over and compare it to know exactly how much darker or lighter it is than yours. Matching to photographs or computer colour is always a rough approximation.

In the past, colour was not only about brightness. It was part of a broader sensory experience. It wasn't just how it looked but how it felt. Tribes of sub–Sahara Africa continued for centuries to divide colour into wet or dry, smooth or rough, and happy or sad. It often seems to me that my clients have difficulty getting started with colour because they tend to fixate on hue and forget that it is still part of a bigger sensory package. We know blue and aqua and shine all seem watery and that autumnal palettes of tan, beige, dirty yellows, burnt oranges, and most browns are dry. It can help if we start with how they want the colours to feel – warm or cool, open or cozy, exciting or calm? Colour psychologists, product designers and packagers, and advertising executives know that we have a large repertoire of very sophisticated links between colour and smell, colour and taste, colour and temperature, colour and age and gender.

Twenty thousand years ago, Palaeolithic man's pigments were limited but they were not inadequate. Earth pigments, carbon, blood, berry juice, and tree resin did the job. Pictures were not meant to be artistic or decorative. Images were painted too deep in the bowels of the rock to be admired or even looked at. They were utilitarian, as functional as the hut built for shelter. Images held power. Their purpose was to exercise some control over the mysteries of the world, to bring protection from evil spirits, success in the hunt or rain needed for crops.

To paint a bison was to give it spirit or life and improve the chance of a good hunt. If it worked and the hunt was successful, the image had done its job and its usefulness was over. It became a "dead" image. Another bison image would be made, often right over top of the last one, and another bison spirit called forth. The images were positioned so far inside caves that it took boys searching for a lost dog almost twenty thousand years later to find them. They were executed as inconveniently far inside the mountain as possible because, like planting a seed, the more deeply embedded they were in Mother Earth, the more firmly their message would take root and exert influence over her.

Primitives looked for meaning and purpose in thunder, sunsets, a fallen tree, a birth and a death, and the patterns in a surface. If they could see human or animal shapes in the colour or shape of a rock, it was a cryptic message sent from mysterious gods. They sometimes enhanced the images by carving or painting more detail into them. With a bit of shaping, a bulbous stone might become a fertility figure. A few strokes with a piece of charcoal could make the bumps on the rock surface into a herd of bison. Gradually they made artefacts "from scratch."

Implements were crude and colours few. Even if they hadn't been, the goal would not be to paint like a Raphael or a Titian. Copying nature would have been a waste of time. If bringing out the spirit in a spear, a mask, or a rock could be achieved with a few strokes or two dots for eyes, then why waste time elaborating?

Colour as an abstract concept may not have been a preoccupation but coloured material was. Pigments held powers and spirit. Red was the most powerful of all. Ochre – red oxide – was the first paint colour. In America, "Red Indians" were natives who painted their skin red. This was to ward off evil, the cold, insects, and illness. In Australia forty thousand years ago cave painters applied it to their caves. A touch of mercury gave the best ochre a slight shimmer but it took a two–month–long annual pilgrimage to get it from a particular mine at the south end of the continent. Until about a hundred years ago, some aboriginal tribes traded ochre like a currency.

Colour started to get interesting in its own right when we started using it as something separate from substance in a more abstract or symbolic way. Nature used colour to organize material – greens for foliage, blues for sky and water, reds for edible fruit, and so on. We too could devise colour coding systems of our own to make the world more organized and understandable. We still use colour coding this way. We use it to remember what level of the lot we're parked on or who won first, second, or third prize.

The first colour codes were applied to the four hemispheres and later the four humours, or temperaments, of man. For some African tribes, the air was white, earth and water were black, and fire was red. White was the south, peace, and harmony. It represented harvest and abundance because it was associated with the time after the rainy season when crops were plentiful. When charitable people died, they were buried in white clothing. Homes were whitewashed to help maintain peace and harmony.

Black was the north, the rainy season, and vegetation. The sky was darker during the rainy season, and gradually the earth absorbed the blackness and produced crops. Rains could be unpredictable. Work had to fit in around them. Success or failure depended on them. Black came to mean pain, uncertainty, and doubt.

The Old Stone Age gave way to the New Stone Age, the Neolithic era, between ten thousand and five thousand years ago, and things became more sophisticated. We went from hunting, gathering, and roaming to settling in groups and farming the land. Makeshift huts gave way to solid structures. We started making complex materials – metal and ceramics – and we clothed ourselves. With clothes we gained a prime opportunity for colour coding. Colour became a language used to signal occupation and social standing. Rank was shown by what colour was placed where and in what quantity. Colour in a garment transferred power to the wearer. In parts of Africa, black and white threads were woven into a checkered buguni band as protection from disease. Men sewed the bands onto the areas of their white clothing where it could do the most good: the spine, the chest, and the shoulders and ribs, front and back. Women sewed them onto their loincloth.

The king wore red since he was the one who could order war or killing. A blacksmith wore red stripes because he manipulated fire, and an elder could wear a red band because he carried the inner fire, the illumination of wisdom.

Colour was a social language and everyone was fluent.

Now, colour is no longer a code we share. All colours are equals. We may prefer some to others but we would never dream of looking at the colour spectrum and not seeing each colour as an equal and essential part of the whole. We would never think that orange played a bit part and purple had a starring role. But to early civilizations red, the colour of blood, birth, and death, of Mother Earth, and light became the colour of power, so important it gradually became a colour category of its own. A new three–colour system consisted of white, red, and black or, more specifically, light, warm, and dark.

A two– or three–colour system might seem too restrictive considering we can see up to seven million hues. But our own relatively new colour system has only six basic categories: purple, blue, green, yellow, orange, and red. Then we subdivide these into variations. In the red group we put hundreds of reds. In the two–colour system, white, red, and yellow went into the white/light group and black, green, and blue into the black/dark group, but within each category even primitive societies were well aware of hundreds of variations.

How we categorize colour has nothing to do with how many we see but how we think about colour and how we talk about it. In 1969 linguists Brent Berlin and Paul Kay studied ninety–eight languages and found that colour terms evolve in predictable and universal ways across all countries and cultures. If there are only two colour categories, they are black and white. If there are three, they are black, white, and red. Four adds either green or yellow. Five adds the missing yellow or green. Then comes blue, then brown, and then, in no fixed order, purple, pink, grey, and orange.

We see millions of colours but we have only about ten abstract colour terms. For example, yellow is an abstract colour word; lemon is not. Our other abstract colour words are black and white, red, blue, yellow, green, purple, grey, pink, and brown. Orange is not a basic term but it is considered a core or basic colour.

To get more mileage out of our paltry repertoire of colour words, we double them up: green–blue or blue–green. The word that comes second is the dominant hue of the two.

This pairing up doesn't get us very far so we expand things by adding the vaguely helpful suffix "ish." "Her hair is reddish brown." "The water has a greenish tint." Beyond that we expand from our few colours to describe the millions of colours we see in the same way primitive man did, by referring to the objects that seem to best represent that colour: grass green, apple green, celadon, khaki. The tricky thing is that these colour descriptions are comprehensible only to the culture in which they originate. If you are not part of that culture, you might be at a loss as to what colour was being described.

Our "sage," "burgundy," or "caramel" would be foreign to the West African M'bay tribe but not because they couldn't see them. They were more aware of subtle hues than we are but their terms would be relevant to their culture. Their "to be like the egg of the fern owl" might be like our "robin's egg blue," but quite different from the blue "to be like the plumage of the bulbul bird." I myself am not as partial to the greens "to be like serpent's poison" or "to be like water in which the *Cochlospermum tinctorium* plant has been soaked" but I love the M'bay colour "that which makes the dogs bark." It is a snappy yellow–green and the colour of new grass shoots. The term came about because in tropical regions, new grass appears at a time called the spring gap. Food supplies from the previous growing season have been depleted and the new crops have not yet ripened. It is a time when man and beast are hungry. The bright green shoots appear when dogs are barking in hunger. My studio is a lovely shade of "that which makes the dogs bark."

The colour descriptions of the past came from direct experience and observation. Today many of our colour terms come from the labels on paint chips. We think we know what the colour terms signify but we are faking it. If I gave you a selection of green colour chips and asked you to match up rosemary, sage, parsley, grass, leaf, lime, and avocado, how accurate would you be? The difficulty in describing colour accurately is that, unlike primitive tribes, we don't really know what we are talking about.

Our colour terms are usually as realistic as the emperor's clothes. Tan is a common example. According to the dictionary, tan is "that which is done to rawhide when it is soaked in tannic acid to turn it into leather." So it is a process and not a colour. If we were familiar with tanning leather, we would better know the colour or colours we are talking about. The M'bay people would not have been so vague.

The dictionary's second definition is perhaps something we do know better. Tan is "that which happens to skin after exposure to the sun's ultra-violet rays." But the range of tones and tints would surely be rather wide. Colour definitions of tan say it is "a kind of beige." What is beige? Beige, depending on your dictionary, is mushroom, taupe, pale yellowish-brown, or fawn. Fawn, according to my computer's synonyms, is tan, beige, taupe, brown, or buff. Buff, I'm told, is beige, camel, off-white, or manila. My computer thinks manila is beige. The Oxford English Dictionary doesn't think manila is a colour at all but a strong brown paper made from hemp and used for wrapping paper and envelopes. I think of those envelopes as too yellow to get us back to tan. The

origin of beige is an obscure French term but today the French word for beige is light brown – *brun très clair* – but *brun* can mean dark and *clair* light, so beige is a sort of nothingness in between, which, I suppose, gets us to the place we call neutral and maybe we should leave it at that, whatever that is.

No wonder for many of us today there is white and, on the other side of the line, the dilemma of colour. Our problem is that not only can we see a million hues, but unlike primitive people, we can actually buy them packaged in a can and removed from nature's context, chemically made colours divorced from life and personal experience. Naming colours is our feeble attempt at reconnecting them to what we know or think we know, like "linen" or "lemon" or "magnolia." But the truth is that names like scarlet, crimson, and vermilion are not things we know well. Colours removed from context are guesswork. Now that we can have as much light as we need and as many colours as we could ever want, we have more colour conundrums than when colours were the stuff of life and "colour" was not even a word.

RED, THE SUPERSTAR

Clare is the precocious only child of friends. She has the reddest hair I have ever seen – not Anne of Green Gables carrot "red" but a beautiful, deep mahogany and she wears pink although she is happy to have other colours as accents, especially red or orange.

One summer, when Clare was six, my daughter Caroline was her nanny, and the little girl was already a force to be reckoned with. She had lots of interesting opinions on a vast array of subjects, including her fondness for red. She was chatting one morning after breakfast, the time of day when she tended to be her most reflective and philosophical and Caroline captured her thoughts on red:

> *My favourite colour is red. I like red because it makes me feel a certain way. I can't quite figure it out . . . but I just like it. My second most favourite colour is pink . . . because it is red's little sister. My third most favourite colour is green because it is the colour of nature and all things were once made of nature, you know. My unfavourite colour is grey. It's ugly and not friendly. I know a girl in my class who only says red is her favourite colour because her name rhymes with red. Guess what her name is? – Ruby. Isn't that silly? She doesn't really have a good reason. I used creativity to pick my favourite colour. Red is the colour of hearts and love. It is the colour of Jell–O and ketchup. It can be the colour of cups and flowers. Boots can be red. Knapsacks can be red. Books can be red.*

Clare wondered why Caroline started to laugh. Caroline pointed out that she was right, "Books can be red but they can also be read." And they both laughed.

Diana Vreeland, the editor of *Harper's Bazaar* and *Vogue* magazines from 1935 to 1971, and an American fashion icon for decades, said, "All my life I have searched for the perfect red. I can never get painters to mix it for me. . . . I want rococo with a spot of Gothic in it and a bit of Buddhist temple [but] they have no idea what I am talking about. About the best red is to copy the colour of a child's cap in any Renaissance portrait."

Red is the second most common favourite colour but is the first for outgoing, animated excitement seekers because red likes to be noticed. Consider this. How do you answer these questions:

What are the three primary colours?

What are the colours of traffic lights?

What are the two most common Christmas colours?

What colour are Smarties?

What are the colours of the rainbow?

Chances are your answers start with "red." In a world that was dense with foliage, red, green's complement, stood out. Red's power to attract attention makes it the most common flag colour. Neolithic people believed red had life–giving powers. Many cultures feel it has protective powers. Russian babushkas wrapped red yarn around their wrists and ankles to ward off agues and fever. They wrapped red threads nine times around a child's neck to protect it from scarlet fever. In the Byzantine and Ottoman empires, a red carpet was the site for settling disputes. In China it is the colour of good luck and happiness so gifts of money are given in little red envelopes. In Pompeii red was a popular wall colour accented with dark green, black, and gold and polished until the marble dust in the paint shone. In medieval times large panels of red damask hung over the barren stone castle walls at entrances and in dining halls. Today red is suited to the same areas.

Red has always been prized among colours and was expensive, up there with lapis lazuli and gold. In Europe red dye was made from kermes, a wingless insect that fed on a small European oak tree. It took seventy thousand bugs to make one ounce of dye. When Cortez and his conquistadors invaded Mexico, they discovered an even brighter red made from cochineal. For hundreds of years it was believed that the speckles of white stuff that natives harvested from prickly–pear cactus and that produced a red dye were grain. In fact it was a wingless female insect that the Aztecs and Mayas collected, fried in ovens or on griddles, further dried in the sun and then pressed. The resulting red substance was mixed with lime juice, metal ores, and other substances to make a dye that was shipped in bulk to Spain where it was sold to other countries for vast profits. It took until the 1800s for its secrets to be revealed and the monopoly broken. Because red dye cost three times as much as blue, it was the clothing colour of choice for those who could afford it. As late as the fourteenth century, medieval dyeing manuals had three recipes for red to every one recipe for blue, but by the eighteenth century, there were more recipes for blue (a reversal that held).

"Scarlet" originally referred not to a colour but to shorn wool of good quality. Red dye was the most expensive dye so it made sense to use the best dye on the best cloth. Consequently, scarlet, which could be dyed black, white, or blue, would more often than not be red. Gradually the scarlet–red link stuck. Cardinals' robes became scarlet to represent Christ's blood but also because red dyed wool was the best cloth that money could buy.

Thirteenth–century French heraldry used a green called sinople, from the Greek word *sinopis*, which meant red! This was so *vert*, green, wouldn't be confused with *vaire*, the striped fur of squirrels. To flip–flop red–green colour words is not quite as odd as it seems. Red and green were considered a close colour pair. Red was green's twin because they were both put in the centre of the light–to–dark colour scale. Pink, on the other hand, would have been an entirely different colour. To reach pink you would have to move way over to the white end of the scale.

Red, the colour of blood, was a sign of life and of death. Red signalled food, weather changes, and sunset and sunrise, the light that bracketed day. Red didn't give answers but alerted us to a question. Is the red sky a sailor's delight or a shepherd's warning? Is the red blood a sign of life or death? Is blazing fire protecting or threatening? Red is still associated with love and its opposite, hate. It is the colour of power and courage.

Red still excites and activates us. According to J.S. Nakshian, writing in the *Journal of General Psychology* (1964), people move more quickly in red rooms. Red increases our pulse rate and our brainwaves and stimulates the metabolism. Unless you are on a diet, it makes an excellent dining room colour. This room is often in the middle of the house where little natural light comes in but red looks beautiful in artificial or candle light.

Red, an advancing colour, brings walls in and makes rooms smaller. Small, dim rooms become warm and cozy, especially if the ceiling is also red. In 1934 American writer and wit Dorothy Parker had the living room of her Bucks County, Pennsylvania, farmhouse painted nine shades of red. My kitchen has six. All good rooms have a little red in them.

Since red is imposing, I wondered if living in an all–red space might test a person's colour limits in a way that my studio green, being nature's wall colour, wouldn't. To find out, I paid a visit to John, an artist who had been living in a loft where the twelve–foot walls were as red as red can be. If it is true that colour is tiring, then John, of all people, should have been feeling fatigued. If there was such a thing as too much colour, he would know.

When I visited John, rather than seeming exhausted by exposure to red, he seemed energized by the colour. He told me his love of red was cultivated during his stay in London, England, as an art student. He spent many a day in the Renaissance galleries of the National Gallery and fell in love with the deep red damask that covered the walls. By the time he moved back to Canada, he knew he could not bear to live in a white space.

This was in the 1980s, and in those days a good red wall paint was hard to find. The reds were too blue – "crimson versus cadmium." His quintessential red could be found only in a scenic paint used for theatre sets that was more transparent than house paint and not as hardy. It took more coats to complete than he likes to remember. He was not tempted to shorten the process by painting just one wall because, in his opinion, this would look "too interior designer–ly." Painting the space had to be like painting a canvas. "Paintings have two basic components," he said, "figure and ground." Art and furniture made up his figure, the foreground subject, and red walls would be their background, the setting. The red space was to be a three–dimensional painting.

He was doing what Matisse did in 1911 in his painting *The Red Studio*. In reality Matisse's studio was not red. It was grey so as not to interfere with or influence the development of his colour–filled palettes. Matisse started his painting realistically with grey walls but something wasn't right. It didn't feel like the studio. He reworked his colour, keeping all the objects in the studio their true colour and changing only the background to make it red. When the objects were surrounded in an ocean of red, the painting worked. The colour had to be bumped up to an energetic red to capture the way the grey studio felt to Matisse.

For John red was the colour he needed in the real studio so he could feel a comfort level more commonly associated with grey. It did not seem too colourful to him.

A few years later another artist, Sarah, moved in with him. The red was immediately comfortable to her. She says it isn't as if you become desensitized to the colour. "If someone comes over and they're wearing something red, I still notice and enjoy it. It is just that, funnily, red becomes your neutral backdrop. If you don't change things, then they become part of a given, part of a pattern that you stop seeing – even red walls." My theory seemed right. There is no such thing as too much colour. Even the most attention–grabbing, high–energy colour of all settles and becomes a comfortable background if it is a colour you like; strong becomes normal.

John sometimes thought about making "the big colour change." He said it would be "a huge renovation without anything structural going on." He would not just shift the tone or shade. Any change would have to be radical, like going from red to green, "maybe a strong peppermint green in high gloss." All that was holding him back was how happy they were with their red and the number of coats it would take to change it.

Some time later I bumped into Sarah at an art opening. She told me they had done it – switched to green – and, yes, they love it equally well. They had several green swatches on one wall for a long time before finally choosing a light chartreuse. They left an inch and a half of the old colour around the top as a sort of homage to the red, an archaeological acknowledgement of what is under the skin of green. Sarah says that their green is another high–key, big–personality kind of colour but it is great to live with. The colour connects the indoors with the outdoors and so makes the space feel more open and bigger.

Did it take long to adjust? No. Could she ever live in a white space? Sure. Sarah said, "Every colour is a colour statement. As long as you do everything in white, then white can be a statement." If they used white, it would be the way most of us would use red – to test their colour limits.

WHITE LIES

THE GREEKS

I see more interior colour mistakes in white than any other colour. This is due in part to the fact that we use so much of it. Our obsession with white goes back a long way and came about because of a big mistake. When the Romans conquered Greece in 146 BC, they loved what they saw and most of it was by then colourless. They were so impressed with the Greeks' achievements that they grabbed as many artefacts as they could get their hands on and they brought Greek artisans back to Rome to make more when the supply ran short. A taste for the past – antiques, traditional art, and architecture – seems to have been as popular two thousand years ago as it is today. To Romans, the achievements of Greek antiquity were the best and the Acropolis was the best of that best. Its Parthenon had magnificent proportions, beautifully carved friezes, and colourless purity. What they didn't realize was that six hundred years of fading had bleached it of the rich colours the Greeks loved and used liberally.

Fading is not something we fuss about on a daily basis. We may keep photographs away from a south–facing window and close the blinds when we go on vacation but the colour of most things seem stable enough. In decorating terminology, "faded colours" refers to a soft palette of muted tones that harmonize well and give an old–world traditional effect.

We are accustomed to the steadfastness of nature's living colours. The trees and flowers don't fade in the sun. Your dog's fur doesn't fade. But colour removed from nature is no longer immortal. The granite rock around the cottage might not lose its speckled pink but the porch fades over a few seasons.

Because I hadn't thought much about how important colour fastness is, I wasn't initially keen when I had an opportunity to learn about fading. It was spring. I was heading off to a Color Marketing Group conference in Hollywood, Florida. My friend Ian, a designer for a manufacturer of playground sets, said he would give me a lift up the coast from the airport to the conference. The only catch was the detour we'd have to make down to Q–Lab Weathering Research Service. He needed to discuss fading because some of his playground pieces had lost their brilliant colour. How tedious, was my first thought. I said I would come and bring a book. Things changed when we walked through the small single–storey office past dozens of busy computer monitors logging the time and weather conditions and headed out back into the bright Florida sunshine. It was like a sci–fi scene. Fields spread before us, acre upon acre, all sprouting tidy rows of racks the size of a table supported by two posts. Each was completely covered in a myriad of specimens of what looked like every material ever made by man, clipped in tightly packed rows. Like heliotropes, the trays all tilted in the direction of the sun.

Somehow it hadn't occurred to me that fading wasn't just the concern of textile makers, antique dealers, or artists whose life's work lasts only as long as their pigments.

Albrecht Dürer (1471–1528) didn't mind assistants helping him paint his paintings, but he wouldn't let anyone get near his colour making. He was his own quality control. At the opposite extreme were colour improvisers like Leonardo da Vinci (1452–1519), Joseph Mallord William Turner (1775–1851), and Mark Rothko (1903–1970). They were prepared to forgo caution and systematic colour preparation in exchange for pulling off a spontaneous aesthetic effect. Fading was the price they paid. Leonardo's *The Last Supper* started to deteriorate almost as soon as it was finished. When modern works begin a quick deterioration, insurance companies call it inherent vice. Sadly, it is not a rare occurrence. Curators and collectors are not happy when works, valued in the millions, by the likes of Mark Rothko, Robert Motherwell, Frank Stella, and Barnett Newman, start to fade and flake before their eyes.

At Q–Labs I found out that cars, carpets, and most of the things around us in daily life wear out before they fade out because product manufacturers take fading very seriously. We were shown around the rows of racks that seemed like a graveyard for mounted mini–bits of flooring, roofing, siding, paint samples. Companies from across the country send Q–Lab samples of materials used in their products, usually four inches by ten inches. Q–Lab's job is to track the effect on each of these specimens of the three big colour killers: heat, light, and moisture. Changes are monitored over a period as brief as a day and as long as thirty years. There were specimens of car parts, wooden flooring, paints and plastics, and even cosmetics.

The tightly packed rows of samples, like little shingles or big fish scales, seemed to say "Touch me, touch me" because they were colourful and because we knew we shouldn't. To even breathe on these things, let alone implant an oily fingerprint, would totally skew results of months and months of precise daily measuring.

Some objects are tested whole – beach balls, sunglasses, vending machines. Immediately behind the office building is a screened-in compound where secret objects, such as unreleased car models, are hidden from view. They sit there in solitary confinement day after day, week after week, under the blazing Florida sun – an endurance test to see if their shine and colour make the grade.

Some objects are mounted under glass in slim display cases. We walked past one containing a row of steering wheels, each at a different stage of weather deterioration. They resembled relics from an archaeological dig. As we wandered, we noticed that some specimens shone brightly in all their colourful glory while others blistered, peeled, cracked, or corroded and became ghosts of their former selves. Some had oxidized to a finish that reminded me of the body of my first and favourite car, a Volvo Canadian 1966, aged twenty when I saw her waiting for a buyer on the corner of a gas station's lot. Time and sun had already baked her curved red body to a chalky matt finish.

It doesn't take more than a short walk through the racks to realize there is something important going on here. A shine that has oxidized on cars that are not old Volvos could seriously affect sales. Fading might be okay for a pair of jeans but not for cars, carpets, and roof shingles.

When Q-Labs discovers that a material has faded too quickly and it does not last the expected life cycle of the product, the manufacturer then has to tinker with the molecular structure of the colour. Colour is not inert. It is not pigment itself but the light waves of energy reflected off pigment. We can't touch it or hold it. It is like the fridge light. It seems to be on all the time, but close the door and it's gone.

The light that makes colour breaks colour. When light reaches the surface of an object, it bangs into the molecules of that surface. The light waves that match the molecular structure of the material get absorbed. The rest bounce back. Colour is what happens to light when parts of its spectrum go missing by being absorbed. Because what we see are the wavelengths of colour that the object rejects, the ruby red slippers in *The Wizard of Oz* are really every colour but red. Grass is every colour but green. An orange is anything but. White reflects back all wavelengths. Black absorbs them.

Absorbed wavelengths excite molecules. It is as if the energy of light and the energy of matter start dancing. Their tango produces heat. The more wavelengths that are absorbed, the more dancing partners there are and so the more heat. Get into a car with a black interior on a sunny day in a pair of shorts and your thighs tell you just where all that absorbed light went and what it turned into!

We are told that white contains all colours and black is the absence of colour. Yes and no. White light does. White pigment does not. White pigment is the snob that rejects all partners and stays as cool as a cucumber, as cold as a corpse.

Colour generates heat but that same heat hurts colour. That is why you wash your coloured clothes in cold water. You don't want heat to get the dye molecules of your favourite T–shirt up on their toes and dancing off into the rinse water.

It is the battle between the colour content in the light and the colour content of the material that can do a colour in. The molecules of every material have a set of chemical bonds specific to its colour. The bonds are like small groupings of atoms holding hands and saying, "We are red" or "We are yellow." The sun comes out. Its rays pour down. Absorbed light pushes at those bonded atoms. When the force exceeds their threshold, the chemical bonds slowly but surely loosen their grip and begin to let go. Eventually they break. Different light has different colour content so it affects atom groups differently. Some chemical bonds aren't affected by artificial light but find ultraviolet hard. Some are the opposite. If a manufacturing company finds its red umbrellas or kiddy climbers fading too quickly, it works on adjusting the makeup of its colouring agent – paint, resin, and so on – reformulating it to get a different chemical bond, one more resistant to their key threat.

Q–Lab builds a computerized log of the weather conditions for every hour of every day and reports back their findings every three months. If time is of the essence, machines inside the Q–Lab building can be set to simulate specific weather patterns in fast–forward mode. Most companies will not wait to see how long it takes to go from full colour to none. They give Q–Lab guidelines. Some might pull the sample when it fades by 20 per cent, because with 20 per cent of the colour gone the product no longer looks right. Unlike ancient Greek ruins, colour loss is not considered an improvement.

For many centuries ancient Greek art and architecture set the standard for beauty to which much of Western art aspired. Because of fading, the once colourfully painted surfaces were colourless and this quality was considered an inherent part of their beauty. This suited Gaius Plinius Secundus, also known as Pliny the Elder (AD 23–AD 79), who disliked colour. He was a Roman who lived almost five centuries after Greek art was at its height. He wrote copious tomes on antiquity and became the most read and quoted authority on the art and architecture of ancient Greece. To this day he is cited as the expert on Greek aesthetics, including their use of colour, even though Ancient Greece would have seemed as close to him as he himself seems to us.

In Pliny's opinion, white represented purity and refinement. Colour was tacky and undisciplined. White looked expensive. Colour looked cheap. White was superior and had snob appeal. (Two thousand years have passed and this still sounds familiar.) He and another Roman theorist, Vitruvius, saw colour as an evil threat. In their opinion, bright colour was a foreign virus coming into Rome from India and Persia. It was part of a decadence that was weakening the empire's strength.

Pliny's theories were based on written descriptions of things he could not see for himself because there were very few original artefacts around or accessible. When he did see an original, the colour was gone. His research combined what he saw, no colour, with what he read, which was not about colour. Colour was a tool, and not a concept; a fact of life and not an intellectual topic. Greeks used and enjoyed colour; it was just not what they talked about. If they did, it was as an optical effect, light, and not an artist's pigment.

Pliny read about the Greek artist Apelles and cited him as a fine example of Greek colour discipline. According to John Gage in *Colour and Culture,* there were no examples of his work extant. Pliny deduced from his readings that the artist restricted his palette to four colours: white, yellow, red, and black. He held this view in the face of contradictory evidence. It is hard to imagine an artist whose fame was based on adroit handling of flesh but who used only those four colours. Also, reproductions of his paintings done in mosaic tile that, unlike paint, did not fade showed lots of bright blue. Pliny reasoned that if Apelles had needed blue, he could have simply lightened, watered down, his black to get a blue effect.

To finish off a painting, Apelles added a dark protective coat of varnish. This reduced the brightness of his colours, a concept Pliny and many after him admired. Most Victorians thought all real art, museum art, had to have the dark colouring of tarnished Old Masters. To this day, many of us find restored Old Masters garish and less comfortable than their murky unrestored neighbours.

So Pliny praised the Greek's restricted use of colour unaware of the rich colours that had originally clothed every surface. For centuries, artists and sculptors read Pliny and so the colour of classical, neo–classical, and neo–neo–classical art and architecture stayed white even when the inconvenient truth – Greeks loved colour – came out.

In the mid–nineteenth century the Greeks' bold colours were unearthed. At the same time, British statesman and scholar and sometime prime minister William Ewart Gladstone (1809–1898) was reading the epic poems of Homer and thinking that Homer's colour terminology seemed wonky. The more epic poetry he read, the more convinced he became that all Greeks were colour–blind. In epic poems, Greek writers, and Homer in particular, were very descriptive but rarely referred to colour. When they did, their use of colour references seemed confused. The sky was never blue. The sea was described in many ways but as "blue" only once. When Homer used the word *glaukos,* it referred to blue, yellow, brown, and grey. What Homer really meant was faded or washed–out colour. Gladstone concluded that "the organ of colour and its impressions were but partially developed among the Greeks of the heroic age." Other scholars agreed. Greeks seemed particularly bad in the yellow–blue section of the spectrum. Colour–blindness had just been discovered, and it seemed like the perfect scientific validation of the theory.

Hard proof, like fragments of Greek pottery, would not have contradicted Gladstone's theories of colour deficiency in yellow and blue. Greek ceramics were mostly terra cotta red and black but that was because the Greeks liked the red and black ceramics from the Orient. They also hadn't managed to achieve glazes that stayed blue or yellow when fired.

Gladstone noticed that when the Greeks mentioned colour, it was not attributed to a "colour–proper" but to "the modes and forms of light and of its opposite, darkness." Gladstone put his finger on the key to Greek colour: they were still using the old dark–to–light system. Homer was not obsessed with light as a vehicle of sight but lighting effects as an enhancement of dramatic action. Homer was not interested in describing hue. Hue was too banal – fixed, permanent, and dead. He assumed you would know that leaves were green and the sky was blue. Green and blue are hardly ever mentioned. Colour did not change but light was all action, constantly shifting and moving. Lighting could increase the drama of a moment. Blue and green were not part of the gleam of weapons, the rising storm, or the dark–light shimmer of the "lustrous" or "wine dark" sea. Unfortunately, it didn't occur to Gladstone that these chromatically vague but conceptually accurate colour terms were intentional and not the sign of a genetic flaw.

John Gage in *Colour and Culture* explains that the Greeks spoke of colour differently. We translate their term *porphuro* as purple but it referred less to colour than to shifting dark–light reflections off waves or the folds of silk. The best silk would have been dyed "Tyrian purple," which was a range of shades, but the most prized was a deep burgundy. Porphuro became linked to "purple."

To Greeks the sky was a white that darkened by increasing amounts of black to reach total darkness, so most blues were really a range of light to dark blacks. A blue sky didn't add much to a story but a dark or changing one could suggest a threat to the sailors boarding their ships. A radiant sky would bode well for their journey. But blue? Who cares?

The Greek word *eruthros* means red. But Homer used *melas,* which means black or dark, when he is describing blood spilled in battle. Blood darkens as it dries. Spilled blood brought death and death was darkness. Lightness and darkness, not colour, animated the scene. Light and not the concrete sameness of colour was the dynamic and effective vehicle for capturing what was noble and ideal.

Homer's heroic, epic writing style used what might be called fancy colour terminology. He was not using the language of the common man. Most Greeks would be happy to call red "red," *eruthros,* and to use the standard method of describing colour – "like a leek," "like honey," "like a violet." They attached a few extra concepts to a colour. C*hloron* meant yellow or green but really it suggested "fresh." (Perhaps it was their version of "that which makes the dogs bark.")

While epic writers were treating colour as lighting effects, philosophers and theorists were too. They developed colour theories based on optical colour. If Gladstone had read some of their colour recipes, he may have concluded that the Greeks were not only colour challenged but taking too many hallucinogens. Plato says that white added to red made pale green but Aristotle says orange with a bit of black made leaf green. They were not referring to pigments but light. They were not messing up their hands with anything as mundane as pigment.

Light was good because, unlike colour, it could be divided tidily into dark and light, which suited the Greeks' penchant for polar opposites: good–bad, male–female, heaven–hell, black and white. But colour was hard to lock down into a system. It kept breaking the rules. The results were varied but most theories of colour were based on a four–colour system. It made the most sense. After all, there were four elements: earth, air, fire, and water. The world had four directions and man had four humours: sanguine, melancholic, choleric, phlegmatic. Pliny had applied the Greek concept of four colours to the artist Apelles because it fit this way of thinking, whether or not it was true.

For almost two thousand years colour theory amounted to whatever Plato and Aristotle said about colour. Plato said vision was the eye dilating and sending out rays of white light that hit objects and illuminated them. Colour was a mixture of light advancing toward and being reflected from an object. Because there was no way to accurately measure colour, it seemed to him vague, unknowable, and less trustworthy than size and shape.

Aristotle searched for a connection between sound and sight. He took a musical octave, a knowable scale, and tried to arrange colours into a similar sequence by expanding it to seven hues, like an octave's seven notes. White, red, and black core colours expanded to crimson, violet, leek green, deep blue, and grey (though this could be considered a type of black) or yellow, which could be considered a type of white. Everything else was a mixture of different proportions of lightness and darkness. He put red near white and violet next to black. Green moved to the middle for the first time. Aristotle said that green was the perfect point between light and dark, the eye dilating and contracting, so it let the eye rest. Green gemstones were ground up and used as eye salves.

Like Plato, his search for order was frustrated because colour could not be broken down into knowable ratios. The eye reads light as a comparison and not a fixed reality. He realized that we never see colours as they are but as they look. Colours are altered by illumination and look different in shadow. They change with the viewing angle or distance. Paying attention to the colour of pigments was not important because optical effects caused by reflections from adjacent surfaces and lighting were what gave colour its appearance. Plato concluded that only God knows colour and any man who thinks he does is a fool.

In Pliny the Elder's defence, even if he'd researched Greek attitudes toward colour until the cows came home, he would have found them more relevant to science than to art and pigment. During the Renaissance, sculptors read Pliny and thought they were copying antiquity when they chose to leave the natural beauty of their materials uncoloured. Michelangelo, for example, loved to use Carrara marble because it was the whitest. But were Michelangelo to have accurately copied Greek antiquity, his *David* would be sporting a very colourful fig leaf. His flesh would be painted a pinkish–beige. His face would have a reddish hue. His hair would be tinted, possibly to the blue that the Greeks used for dark hair or red, as it was described in the Bible. David's lips would be rouged and his eyes inset with semi–precious stones to make the irises glisten. For a finishing touch, as the Greeks would have done,

Michelangelo might have glued a few real hair eyelashes to David's lids.

The colour misconception became so ingrained that it made little difference when the truth was discovered. The ruins of Mycenae and Knossos were excavated fully preserved in all their vibrant and colourful glory but neo–classical architecture, so popular across Europe and North America, continued to be erected in white. The colourful truth came as an unwelcome shock. French sculptor Auguste Rodin (1840–1917), loved the Elgin Marbles, part of the frieze that originally encircled the Parthenon until it was pilfered and brought to England. When Rodin found out that its pure white surfaces were originally brightly coloured, he fell to his knees and prayed that it wasn't true.

Paris continued to be remodelled in the Beaux–Arts style, which was based on Greek and Roman architecture. Students made pilgrimages to Rome to bone up on accurate detail but colour was not infused into the style to update or authenticate the look. The home of American presidents, the White House, was not going to be repainted with red, green, black, gold, blue, and yellow inside and out as the Greeks had actually done. By the end of the nineteenth century, this neo–classical style, so popular in Europe except in medieval times, was all the rage in the United States. Chicago built a massive theme park in the Greco–Roman Beaux–Arts style and called it White City, because it was.

Years later, in 1911, Le Corbusier, the French artist and architect who championed white as the colour of modern architecture, had an epiphany the first time he clasped eyes on the bleached beauty of the Acropolis. He knew it had originally been coloured but this truth didn't diminish his moment. He saw the white surfaces of its centrepiece, the Parthenon, caught in the amber glow of the setting sun and was mesmerized by its colourless beauty. He wrote in his diary that the experience changed him forever. In his memoir *Journey to the East,* he acknowledged that the white surfaces had, as he put it, "once dared to smile with colour." He continued, "Thank God time got the better of it, and from the hill I salute the reconquered monochrome. I write with eyes that have seen the Acropolis, and I will leave with joy. Oh! Light! Marbles! Monochromy!" (The very next year his book *Towards a (New) Architecture* was published. Colour is never once mentioned and classical architecture is deemed irrelevant.)

Pliny and Le Corbusier were not wrong about the beauty of white. White is sublime if the conditions are perfect. White suits the Parthenon because its proportions are harmonious and every detail is adroitly crafted. It is made of marble. Light plays well across its translucent surfaces, and it seems timelessly attractive. Add the bright clarity of Mediterranean sunlight and a panoramic view out over the Aegean Sea. Under such circumstances colour can happily be ditched. However, surrounded by flat drywall in a less than perfect house overlooking less than perfect views or no view at all, maybe colour can do some good. Perhaps contemporary buildings erected quickly and economically with little or no style at all could use some colour enhancement. When we are not dealing with ideals, it is necessary to do as Le Corbusier did and not as Le Corbusier said. He sang white's praises but used increasing amounts of colour. He had an artist's eye for colour and used it well. White walls were a beginning and not an end.

SPEEDO®

BLUE, THE FAVOURITE

Blue was on my mind. I had just been to the Yves Klein show at the Pompidou Centre in Paris. Suddenly I saw his vivid ultramarine blue all over the city. Pay phones in Paris are Yves Klein blue. Christmas tree lights by the Seine were Yves Klein blue. A colour that is on my mind often manages to sneak into my work. I never force the issue. I never intended to push Klein's blue into a project. It just happened.

I came home and almost immediately had the right person and place for Yves Klein blue. I was preparing samples of material for a client presentation and out popped some small glass tiles with an iridescent glow in the colour.

The client meeting went well. We built a palette for his condo in lots of whites and off–whites, a bit of ebony brown, a gold ceiling in the hall and stone tiles in tans and charcoal. The plan was elegant and tame. Then we got to the small, tall, windowless powder room where I suggested an infusion of drama. I pulled out the blue sample. Luckily, he too had seen the show and so, instead of thinking of this bold ultramarine as a sports colour or insanity on my part, he shared my enthusiasm. The blue was approved. I realized how seldom I ever use it. Navy, sometimes, pale blues, yes, especially in bathrooms and kids' bedrooms. But a vivid blue, almost never.

It is odd that blue at its bluest is so seldom used for interiors since, in Western countries, blue is the most common favourite colour. It is associated with good things such as intelligence, logic, efficiency, rationality, trust, and loyalty, which is the reason it is the logo colour of banks, corporations, and conservative political parties around the world. But it is also associated with sadness, loneliness, and melancholia, with death and decay. So why is blue such a favourite?

Perhaps we always want what we cannot have. The less of something there is, the more we want it. And in a world full of colour, blue is the scarcest pigment. Lapis lazuli, also known as ultramarine, *beyond the sea,* is nature's bluest blue. It was so hard to find that it vied for gold as the most expensive pigment of all (for centuries the only known source was Badakshan in northeast Afghanistan). Indigo, the second most popular blue, was made from the leaves of a tropical plant that were soaked and fermented in water, then moulded into cakes that had to be dissolved with urine for use as paint. The dried cakes were so hard that for centuries Europeans thought indigo was a mineral. It was not particularly colour–fast. Smalt, a blue made from ground–up glass, was reasonably priced but was less vivid and also faded. Azurite was affordable for big pieces like frescos but it could not be used for them because it turned green when wet.

In 1704 a German colour–maker named Heinrich Diesbach made Prussian blue, the first synthetic hue, while trying to make red. He inadvertently combined iron sulphate with potash that was tainted with animal oil made from blood. It seemed logical that blood would make a good red but *ferrocyanide* turned out to be the magic ingredient to spawn blue. By 1750 Prussian blue was widely used because it cost about one–tenth the price of ultramarine. By the beginning of the twentieth century, it gave a poor Spanish artist named Picasso, newly arrived in Paris, an affordable blue.

There is very little blue in the world but a great deal of blueness. Astronauts circling space have thought earth looked like a blue pearl. But this is apparent blue and not material blue. Blueness is like a tease. The ocean, the sky, air, and water are a blue of refracted light, and so they are elusive, insubstantial, a mirage. You can look but you cannot touch. In retail stores, blue is often used as the "don't touch" colour that surrounds precious or fragile things. There is so little blue within our grasp that the fovea, our centre of focus, has many fewer cones specializing in blue than it has for red and green. We cannot see blue edges as clearly.

Blue's ephemeral attributes make it the spiritual colour. Ancients thought blue was the gateway to the soul. If red has the effect of a big, warm hug, blue's is more like a deep breath, slowly exhaled. It lets you go, leaves you alone. To feel blue is to feel emptiness, lonely. In the nineteenth century, Afro–American slaves sang songs of sadness, the blues, which became the root of rock and roll.

To a fault, blue respects your space. It gives the sensation of distance and no barriers. Because blue dissolves solidity, pale blue rooms seem more spacious. Pale blue ceilings seem higher.

Blue is relaxing, if not particularly friendly. Most health care facilities use pale aqua blues to calm patients but they usually balance it with warm apricots, especially in maternity wards.

Even though blue flames are the hottest, blue is the cold colour. Clean pastel blues are cold but the darker the blue, the less cold it appears. Denim is not cold, nor is indigo, navy, or periwinkle.

In many languages a single term covered blue and green, often signifying setting, context, background – the big picture hue. It is only in the last eight hundred years that the Japanese stopped using only *ao* to cover both. Now green is *midori* and *ao* means blue. But it also means unripe, fresh, or youthful. What Shakespeare referred to as *salad days* would be *ao*. Green traffic lights are *ao,* meaning "get started." In Russian there are separate words for light blue and deep blue, just as we distinguish between pink and red.

For centuries, deep blue was considered light black, and very light blue was whiter than white. In Egyptian hieroglyphs, blue was often used for men's beards and hair because it was the blackest black. (In comic books, characters with the blackest hair, Superman and Veronica, have indigo highlights.) In India, men's white shirts are sometimes tinted ever so slightly with blue to look whiter than white. In fact, the older the shirts get, the bluer they get because it takes more and more blue to cover the yellowing of age. In the nineteenth century, laundry soap came in the form of blue balls containing a synthetic blue colouring that served the same purpose. It made clothes whiter than white by tinting them blue. My mother remembers her grandmother always swished a small draw–string "blue bag" in the rinse water to whiten the wash. The "blue rinse set" refers to older ladies because some blue–rinse their grey hair. The too–blue effect looks just right to them because aging eyesight sees more yellow in colour.

In many cultures, blue shares black's association with death, evil, and the unknown. Wearing blue jewellery or tying a blue thread or ribbon around the ankle of a newborn warded off evil – like being vaccinated, this was fighting fire with fire. Romans hated blue. It was the colour of barbarians because blue from the woad plant was used by the Celts, invading from the north, to colour their clothes and their flesh. To Romans, blue eyes were a curse, a sign of the devil.

Blue became popular only after medieval artisans started using it as an expensive and brilliantly luminous "black" for the Virgin's robes as a sign of mourning. Soon kings and lords wanted this expensive and saintly colour for themselves. In medieval times, each sin was colour-coded. Green was associated with fertility and later envy. Red was associated with war, love, and passion and later sexual transgression. Blue was guilt-free so even when sumptuary laws forbade the wearing of coloured clothing, blue, being light black, was morally righteous and acceptable for everyone from peasants to kings. It still is. In America, ever since the end of the nineteenth century, when Levi Strauss started making work clothes for men searching for gold in America out of denim, a sturdy cotton duck called *serge de Nîmes,* originally from Nîmes in France, blue has remained the most acceptable sartorial colour choice after black.

At the turn of the century, Marcel Proust, author of *À la recherche du temps perdu* and renowned hypochondriac, spent most of his time in bed in a blue room. The blue walls were twelve feet tall and cork-lined to cut off the sound of the outside world. (Even his window shutters were covered in sound-absorbent felt.) The only light was a pair of candelabra on the mantel, lit for visitors, and a desk light at the side of his bed.

Complexity enhances the beauty of many blues. Without a touch of grey in it, a light blue room can feel like being in an emptied swimming pool or the pelican pool in an aquarium. Bright indigos that are too clean can have the sophistication of a sports arena changing room. In the 1920s,

Basil Ionides (1884–1950), British decorator and author, devised a way to make ultramarine blue sophisticated. In his traditional wood–panelled dining room, he tried to, as he put it, get a vivacity from blue that it usually lacked. First he painted over the eighteenth–century wall panels with a ground coat of pink. Then he stippled another coat of paint – two tones of deep blue suspended in glaze. The blue was set off against vanilla–cream–coloured display niches, a mauve ceiling, crimson candle shades, and rose–coloured curtains.

Light blue is not the most flattering room colour for people with pale skin. I was at an art show at York University's gallery, where the walls were painted in different solid colours. I was chatting to the curator, who had her back to a lovely pale blue wall. After a while I asked if we could change positions. Now black was behind her. In front of the pale blue, she had looked pale and anaemic. Framed in black, she looked strong and bright. When we moved over to where orange filled her background, she looked like she was just back from a tropical holiday. It is a good thing that in a bedroom pale blue can work its relaxing magic and bedding colour can frame the face.

I have recommended black–blue for dining rooms that have wood panelling on the lower walls. These rooms are already dark. It often seems counterintuitive to make a dark room darker, but if it is never going to sparkle, then why not go for drama? Clients are always skeptical but, if brave enough, are delighted at the way it dissolves walls into a mysterious void and focuses the attention on their art and antiques. One client, who thought I was teasing when I suggested she and her husband do this (but her husband was game), says it has completely changed the way she thinks about colour. We need to pay less attention to the colour and more to the effect.

But it was Yves Klein who helped me see blue – blue as it might have been seen when it was as expensive as gold and valued accordingly. At the Paris show, I enjoyed Klein's colour pieces in his version of three primaries: metallic gold, magenta, and blue. But it was the paintings of his transcendental ultramarine, known as IKB (International Klein Blue), that stayed with me. Klein had specially formulated the paint so it would retain the velvet intensity of dry ultramarine pigment and was so thrilled with it that he patented the pigment in 1958.

By covering the walls and ceiling of my client's powder room with tiny pearlescent glass tiles of Yves Klein Blue, I am hoping for an effect that will echo in miniature the magic and simmer of the interior of Greek basilicas and do what blue does best – dissolve the walls and melt the tiny space into a mystical infinity.

EGO
SVM
VIA
VER
ITAS
⁊VI
TA

REALLY GOOD ORANGES

THE MEDIEVAL ERA

The problem with colour is that it is cheap, bountiful, and so easy to get it is almost worthless. We buy the paint; colour comes along for the ride. When value is established, as it usually is, by cost and rarity, who wants colour?

In every other area of my design work, good colour costs money, often lots of money. The better the materials are, the higher the price. My clients agonize over how much has to be spent and whether it is worth going the financial distance to get what they want. As we compare expensive and inexpensive fabrics, they can see and appreciate the subtle colour combinations that money can buy, and they crave it. We notice many British designer palettes seem to draw on colours used by the Bloomsbury artists. Americans and Japanese do interesting textures, and the French are the masters of elaborate traditional patterns; Scandinavians are cleaner, more two–dimensional, and contemporary. All do interesting colour combinations or colourways but the best colour gets expensive.

This conundrum occurs not just with fabrics. The cool brown of natural walnut, the amber tone of fruitwood, or the warmth of cherry can seem infinitely more appealing than less expensive maple or birch stained any colour. No laminate can compete with the translucent colour depth of a lacquer finish that requires fifteen coats to achieve and the price tag that proves it. When I am helping clients choose bathroom fixtures, usually the warm lustre of brushed nickel fixtures looks more desirable than the polished nickel ones, which in turn looks better than chrome, and so on. Gold objects look more beautiful than brass; silver more beautiful than chrome. (Platinum, which should look better than gold, according to the value scale, looks a lot like silver to me.) Surely it is not just the hierarchy of price that makes the most expensive always look better and coveted.

One of the reasons that I love working with paint colour is that I don't have to deal with the tyranny of the price tag. There are higher and lower quality paints. I always recommend the higher because poor coverage and colour stability negate savings. But the price difference between one colour and another is negligible compared to the price difference between a yard of ordinary fabric and an extraordinary one. So with paint colour, I am completely and utterly free. It doesn't matter if my client lives in a basement flat or a vast mansion, the options are the same.

This makes me wonder if everyone would start to appreciate and value paint colour in a whole new way if it were priced the way it was before science and chemistry started pumping it out in limitless quantities. If it were medieval times, things would be different. Whites, neutrals, and earthy colours would be affordable. A can of red would set you back a bar of gold or occasionally more. The blue would come from the other side of the world so you would have to plan ahead and be prepared to wait a few months. It would cost about as much as red so it would be important to know precisely how much you needed. You would hate to run short but would not want to be wasteful. Then when your colours arrived, you would have to hire specialists to prepare them for use, and this could take weeks. Colour would cost so much that perhaps it would be best just to give up the dream of having your own. Instead, to get a look at a good wall or ceiling colour, you would visit a church or a government building where you would probably look at it with an appreciation tinged with envy. It was only when colour was a luxury afforded exclusively by the rich and the powerful that colour was valued as highly as jewels.

When I was at university I studied medieval art because, as an art history major, I had to. It was to be endured rather than enjoyed. My attitude was similar to the one held by Italians during the Renaissance: nothing really exciting came out of the fourteen hundred years between the Roman Empire at its peak and its so–called re–birth. The period between AD 200 and the Renaissance was filler. Italians labelled it with three insults: the Dark Ages, to imply it was a period of obscurity; the Middle Ages, a gap between nobler times; and the Gothic period, meaning the time of barbarians. For me, medieval art was the class between the more interesting subjects like Renaissance Painting and Modern Art and Architecture.

My first assignment was to compare and contrast a segment of the Parthenon's frieze with a medieval alabaster carving. On the last page of what I thought was a pretty well researched and written essay, my medieval art professor had scrawled, "An emotional diatribe. 64 %." I looked up the meaning of diatribe then I looked up the professor.

I learned that I had committed the cardinal sin of art criticism. I had looked at the graceful realism of the Parthenon's figures and decided that the crudely carved, stiff–looking alabaster figures didn't compare favourably. That was putting it mildly. My professor pointed out, in so many words, that I was comparing apples to oranges and complaining that the oranges failed because they weren't good apples even though they might have been fabulous oranges. At first glance, it does look like the Middle Ages made inferior apples. The truth is they were making brilliant oranges.

I came to realize that medieval artisans were obsessed with colour. Colour, not realism, was what gave medieval pieces their sizzle, but colour was the one aspect of their art missing from my textbooks, missing from the black and white lecture slides, and, in many cases, missing from the pieces themselves due to time, weather, and pilfering. Artisans often travelled far to get their colours and struggled hard to turn them into useable pigment. They believed colour held God's spirit and His divine light.

The problem with medieval art, for an uninformed first–year art history major, was that it wasn't realistic. When it comes to what looks real, we are all experts, and our tendency to compare works of art to the real world becomes the first measure by which we rate them. By this standard, medieval art can look like unsuccessful attempts at realism. It becomes easy to think of the Middle Ages the way Renaissance Italians once did: that it was a gap between good art and good art. Surely no one who knew better would intentionally make bodies stiff, space flat, and scale inconsistent. No one who knew better would make images that looked so like every other image that they all started looking the same. Or would they?

Medieval art was not unrealistic due to incompetence. It was unrealistic because of the Church. At a time when "patron" and "designer" were the same word, the Church was becoming the biggest patron of the arts in the Western world. It would also be its most dictatorial boss.

Christianity became the official state religion of the Roman Empire in AD 311, and Emperor Constantine made himself God's earthly representative. Christianity, previously a private gathering in the home of wealthier members, went public. It required buildings, churches, big enough to accommodate growing congregations and impressive enough to glorify both God and the emperor. And they required interior decorating on a mega scale.

Monks had always been the artisans responsible for religious icons and manuscript illumination. They considered their work spiritual meditation, an act worthy in and of itself regardless of the results. But taking on an entire church interior was beyond their powers. Tradesmen were sought, guilds were formed. Each had an area of expertise. A painter of altarpieces would never be asked to paint frescoes. A mosaic specialist would never pick up a paintbrush. An apprenticeship took four to eight years, and "trade secrets" stayed within the guild. Selling them to the competition was punishable by death.

How religious decoration should look was hotly debated at the time. Iconoclasts ("image breakers") thought any images a distraction and wanted them banned from churches, but they were outnumbered by those who argued that religious images were a device for telling biblical stories to the illiterate. However, the Church was very clear about how this was to be done. There was a formula. One altarpiece could, would, and should look like another. The artisan was not meant to be original or dazzle with his skill at carving or painting. Realistic detail would be showing off instead of just telling the story. Images were to be read, not admired. Medieval images, like the words on your page, were to inform in a concise manner.

Textiles were exempt from stringent rules because banners and wall hangings were considered seasonal decoration, not education and not a permanent part of the physical body of the church. Artistic licence left weavers free to weave elaborate patterns of flowers, animals, and hunting scenes. The more brilliant the colours were and the more spectacular the artistry, the better.

Other artisans were treated like manual labourers. A master artisan could be hands–on or act as art director, supervising and handling the business of getting the piece done while several others did the actual work. A master's name on the finished work was less to take artistic credit than to indicate in which workshop the piece had been made. Quality was judged by how successfully colours were prepared and applied, not on a talent for painting. Colour was how a patron such as the Church showed off. At a time when richly coloured garments, textiles, or walls were luxuries afforded only by the wealthiest, colour had huge status. Colour's presence had a powerful, unearthly effect equal to what we might feel if we were sitting in a quiet church and a requiem by Mozart, Verdi, or Mahler burst forth and enveloped us in its sound.

To an early Christian, images were not just telling biblical stories. They radiated the divine spirit through glowing colours. Colour was the exterior indicator of material's inner makeup and so, the more brilliant the colour, the greater the spiritual power. Coloured materials were God's handiwork. Being in the presence of a beautifully coloured religious work was being closer to God.

The best colours were luminous and stable and cost a fortune. Gems were sometimes added, embedded into the mantel of the Virgin or bishop like chunks of 3–D transparent colour, the closest thing to light. They were uncut so as not to waste any of their precious substance. If the budget for pigments and gems was lavish, the artisan was not even to think about bumping up his fees accordingly. Contracts were drawn up specifying how much of which pigments would be supplied or paid for by the patron and how they were to be distributed in the piece. Inspectors were hired to make sure there was no cheating, no cheaper substitutions used in place of the contracted materials.

To get good colours, artisans were forced to travel great distances to pigment importers in urban centres. Travel budgets were written into many contracts. Before going, the artisan had to calculate precisely how much of each colour was needed because he could not afford to purchase too little or too much. A spill, a mistake, or a miscalculation would have been disastrous.

Once acquired, colour material was still far from useable. Pigment preparation was the first thing guild members had to master. Cennino Cennini (1370–1440), who wrote about artists' methods, was not trying to be funny when he said that if you ground your vermilion every day for twenty years it would still be improving. Some pigments gained brilliance with grinding, while some lost it. Lapis lazuli had to be sieved, washed, and filtered in a long and drawn–out manner. If it was ground fine enough to adhere to a surface with egg white, it was too fine to retain its beautiful colour. If it was left coarse enough to be vivid, then it had to be applied with special glue from the boiled scrapings of animal skins used to make vellum.

When his materials were finally ready, the medieval artisan faced another challenge. Mixing was forbidden. Reverence for colour or, more accurately, for God's coloured materials, made it an evil act of alchemy to put one material into another. This was messing with God's creation. Artisans, textile dyers, doctors, and pharmacists were viewed with almost as much suspicion as alchemists because their work required them to tinker with matter.

Anyone with a paint box knows that if you mix two colours together, the resulting hue is not as bright. Mixing matter and reducing God's divine light was sacrilegious. Some mixing was considered worse than others. For example, mixing like with like – vegetable pigment with vegetable pigment – was bad but not as bad as mixing animal with vegetable. Putting vegetable or animal with mineral matter was the worst mixing of all because it mixed living material with dead.

Dyeing was considered a particularly shady business and a dirty one. Dyers' premises and their water–polluting processes were kept beyond the outskirts of town. In Paris dyers had to be "at least two bow shots" from the closest suburb. Dyers located in close proximity to one another squabbled between themselves because if the dyers of one colour were working upstream, those of another colour had to wait until the river water ran clear before they could get on with their work.

Guilds were very strict. A dyer would be licensed to dye a certain colour or a few specific colours and a specific cloth. Dyers of blue and cotton, for example, could not have red dye or wool on their premises. A dyer of green was allowed to get it from blue and yellow but only by dyeing the indigo first, then re–dyeing the cloth in a new dye bath of yellow. A dyer of red might get special guild permission to dye yellow because yellow and red were colours that required a mordant, the ingredient added to colour to make it colour–fast. If the mordant that worked was the same for two colours, it implied some similarity in their makeup so their mixing was a lesser evil. Also red and yellow were both considered light colours. Blue was a dark colour and one that didn't need a mordant and so could not be mixed with red. The rules regarding colour–work were so restrictive that a dyer allowed to dye fabric could not dye yarn, only weavers could. Weavers could make their own colours but they had to get special guild permission for each dye. Experimenting with new dye materials avoided some of the hassles of stepping on a dyer's colour turf.

It is hard for me to imagine a time when mixing colour was considered an act of corruption. During the season I spent as a fabric dyer in theatre, I was surrounded by dozens of buckets each holding a different dye colour. For my first assignment, I was given a twenty–six–yard piece of Japanese silk for Gertrud's nightgown in the bedroom scene with Hamlet and I was asked to match it to a tiny sample of platinum grey ribbon. Concocting the colour was like making a scientifically accurate soup. In a pot of water set on a hot plate, I would build the colour recipes with a pinch of this and a touch of that, measuring and recording each addition. I made sure the powdered dye had completely dissolved before I put a small swatch of fabric onto the end of a clothes peg and swirled it in the pot. The duration of the dyeing time would be duly noted under the formula. I rinsed and ironed the swatch, compared it to the target colour and, if it were not exact, make another dye addition or possibly start all over again. It was a great way to train my eye to see tiny variations in colour and how things like surface sheen and texture affected the way a colour looked.

My swatch charts looked like tonal rainbows, and I stuck them up on the wall, partly for future reference but mostly because I just enjoyed having them around. I still like to have colours in gentle gradations around when I am trying to work out combinations. And I have developed a fondness for using several variations of a single colour, like five greens to make a green tiled backsplash or the five reds on my kitchen cabinets. It gives a sense of greenness or redness that is somehow more alive than only one would be. It would not have been very satisfying to be in a medieval dye establishment with a single bucket of blue and told to get on with it!

Not having a full repertoire of colours was not important. Handling colour, any colour, was like dealing with a magical or divine power. (The difference between magical and spiritual was not as clear–cut as the Church might have liked. They were like two sides of the same coin.) And so, according to Michel Pastourau in *Blue: The History of a Colour,* medieval colour recipes were more interested in using mystical proportions and sequences than recording precise technical information. More important than achieving a specific shade was maximizing the value of the mystic powers of a colour through significant numbers and ratios, like magic spells, that were put on everything from daily tasks to colour mixing. Mathematics was like a code that, if cracked, would explain the mysteries of the world. Certain numbers or proportions held more power than others. Three, for example, was potent. It related to birth, death and regeneration: Christ was resurrected on the third day. A child is in the womb for nine months. So, whereas I would measure out every ounce of dye and time my dye baths down to the second, a medieval recipe for a dye might state that it should be mixed for three days or nine days or nine months; three was what was essential!

The process was not to be rushed. Nature must be allowed to run its course. Speeding things up was tampering with God's creation. Every bowl, vessel, or vat that was used for mixing colour had to be chosen with great care. Material, shape, and size all affected the dark and dangerous process of making colour.

Copying nature with its millions of colour nuances would have been impossible because painters could not mix their colours but fortunately that was not their intention. Colour was to be laid out in a harmonious arrangement that could be admired as a beautiful pattern, like a quilt or an abstract painting.

Organizing colour so all the pieces add up to a balanced whole is the way I like to think about colour in any physical space. It is not about individual rooms and halls but how one

part opens up to another and how colours unfold and relate – the glimpse through an open door, a colour that reveals itself only when a corner is turned, the balance of the strong highlights with the quieter tones that don't compete for attention. The cumulative relationship is fully experienced only through seeing the whole.

As with every other aspect of their art, when laying out colour rules had to be followed. The most expensive colour had to go to the most important character and so on down the line. Symmetry was one of the cornerstones of beauty so *isochromatism,* symmetrical colour placement, was another challenge to be met. If red was on the right side of the piece, the artisan would want some on the left to balance it while still maintaining the colour–importance hierarchy. And, of course, no two characters in the same colour could be side by side because they would turn into one big indistinguishable blob. The figures themselves had to be placed and sized according to their importance, starting with Christ or the Virgin large and in the centre and, moving outward, saints, angels, and bishops getting progressively smaller. With limited colours, laying out a medieval piece was about as easy as doing superior–level Sudoku.

An artisan had no vivid orange pigments. Greens faded. Purples were wishy–washy or too red to be considered anything other than red. Good reds and blues were as expensive as gold. Gold was the perfect "colour." It glowed. It didn't tarnish or fade. It was pricey but always on hand because gold coins were the currency of the time. They could be pounded into thin sheets of gold leaf whenever an artisan needed to fill the background of icons and altarpieces with the colour of Heaven. Red, second to gold, was sometimes used as an undercoat for gold, producing a warm gold – the most divine of all hues.

Black was the opposite of light and, since generating God's light was the purpose of religious art, black was out. It couldn't even be used to give shadowing effects to the other colours because that would be reducing their light. To create three–dimensionality, artisans applied their colour full strength, and, without black to provide depth, white was used to bring the surface forward. This practice faded yellow pigments to near invisibility and gave deeper colours a pastel cast common in medieval art.

But in their day, these medieval works would have seemed magnificent. Anyone viewing them would have marvelled at the colours themselves as though they were crown jewels. Just as we know the difference between quartz and diamond, medieval viewers knew an expensive vermilion, made from the mineral cinnabar and usually mined and shipped from China, and an inexpensive one, crimson lake made from vegetable dyes that faded. Just as we value gold over brass and brass over metallic paint, they valued an expensive blue like lapis lazuli, a scarce mineral from what is now Afghanistan, over a cheaper one like azurite. If, in the image of Saint Francis, he gives his cloak, painted in lapis lazuli, away to a poor man, leaving himself in a tunic painted in azurite, it emphasized the depth of his generosity.

Today gold and gems, the most brilliant part of the medieval colour palette, are usually gone, pilfered and recycled. Many of the colours have faded to grey or white. Some colours have darkened. But because we don't give different pigments different value, we don't appreciate the colour that has survived. Colour communication is lost on us. Realism, the signature of the Renaissance, made it easy to ignore colour as a thing of beauty in and of itself. From then until the birth of abstract art in the twentieth century, we became more inclined to look at what is being said, the narrative, and not what is saying it, the colour and placement. Even if we are not colour–blind we are colour–deaf.

In my Medieval Art class, black and white slides of Byzantine basilicas like Hagia Sophia, in what is now Istanbul, gave us no sense of the mind–bending virtual–reality experience that awaited all those who entered.

What was achieved was not less artistic. It was just different. In fact, medieval artisans might well have wondered why on earth anyone would *want* to adopt the Renaissance ways that followed. Why create smaller images that looked good only when you were standing directly in front of them if you had the chance to make ones that were so vast they took over the entire space? Why not make the entire church interior into one mind-blowing trip? If the idea was to evoke a spiritual world rather than an earthly one, why put Christ in an ordinary landscape full of banal objects when you could float him in an atmosphere of gold that glowed like the light of Heaven? Why squeeze him into the confines of a picture frame when he could cover the ceiling high above the congregation, bigger than a billboard? Medieval art was unrealistic because its intentions were divine contemplation, not earthly preoccupation. Rather than be caught up in admiring specific details, you were meant to feel like you were no longer on terra firma but had achieved spiritual lift-off.

Most church services took place at night. The interior was lit with thousands of candles and lanterns, the flickering light making the mosaic-covered walls and ceiling look like a shimmering mass of molten gold. Christian images filled the walls from floor to ceiling. The walls seemed to melt seamlessly into floors of striated marble, in patterns looking like the waves of the sea. No surface seemed solid and static. Lighting and colour, the two aspects of interior design that are so often handled crudely in homes, offices, and churches today, were used masterfully back then.

To add shimmer, mosaic cubes, or tesserae, were set into plaster and then raked to slightly different angles. A few silver tesserae were scattered through the gold to add sparkle. Some of the gold cubes were flipped so the metal leaf sat near the surface, and some sat at the back to add bounce to the light. To make the gold as rich as possible, red glass was used as the bed for some of the gold metal in the tesserae. Sometimes gold sat on top of red, and cubes were laid unevenly so red edges showed. Others were flipped so the red glass glazed the gold foil. A red tint was added to the grout.

> I have a sense of the way the gold mosaic tiles added a light and shimmer that animated even the dimmest and darkest space because I set up a microcosm of it in my own powder room. It is a windowless space about the size of a public toilet cubicle tucked away behind cherrywood panelling. But open the door and turn on the light and it is a dazzling box of radiant gold light thanks to the small glass mosaic tiles with a gold–coloured back and a pearlescent finish, grouted in yellow that wraps two walls and melts out over part of the floor. The shimmering slightly uneven surface seems to double the dimensions and triple the voltage.

Medieval church interiors were set up to lead the viewer through a journey of discovery. Light shimmered, making images come alive. This illusion of movement helped the artisan convey a life force, an effect later lost when single–point perspective entered religious art. A medieval congregation was not watching but moving through a space where each detail and every surface was geared to creating the sensation of entering a mini–version of Heavenly Jerusalem.

By the twelfth century, flying buttresses were taking the burden of gravity away from the walls of Gothic cathedrals. Now it was possible to open them up to the light. Huge windows of stained glass made Byzantine–era mosaic look old–fashioned. Artisans painted frescoes now that light could reach the walls. As it came through the transparent images in the coloured glass, they seemed to move and shimmer, making the "Bible of the Poor" come to life.

Abbot Suger (1081–1151) takes credit for inventing the use of large stained-glass windows. He used them extensively in the Cathedral of St. Denis, just north of Paris, which took from 1137 to 1140 to build. Suger wanted the best of everything for his church because nothing was too good for God. If having the best church also made him look good, so much the better.

He inlaid sections of the walls with onyx and precious stones. He draped the interior with purple silks. He ordered huge windows and picked the colour. White and blue were the most expensive glass colours to make. There was a reasonably priced blue glass made of cobalt but the most expensive was made from recycling blue glass of earlier times. Ancient vessels, Roman scent bottles, Byzantine tesserae were all ground up and recycled into medieval stained-glass windows. Suger chose the dramatic gloom of blue over the clarity of white.

He reasoned that glassmakers were makers of artificial gemstones. Sapphire was considered the gem of gems because it held the power to protect, to dispose people to prayer, and to cure several diseases. Blue glass would bring these properties into the church.

Also, blue was still considered light black rather than a colour in its own right. Abbot Suger agreed with the Dionysian notion that black was not evil but rather the darkness beyond visible light, too divine to be seen. Divine light became brighter and became visible as it reached earth because it got mixed with earthly white light. Light, therefore, emerged from superior darkness. Blue could be bright black, the colour of darkness in light. Blue, he decided, was a more fitting choice than white for his expensive windows.

By the thirteenth century light wasn't God's spiritual essence emanating from matter. Light was an earthly physical phenomena connected with optics. Any connection to the divine was symbolic. Throughout the Gothic period a shift had begun. Artisans began to care less about what a colour was – God's perfect matter – and more about what it could do – artist's pigment. Reverence toward coloured materials waned as respect for artistic skill increased. With skill, extraordinary effects could be achieved with the most ordinary materials. A painter could use inexpensive pigments to create the illusion of light and gold. If his skill was recognized as being a gift of God, then he could begin to use it to improve upon God's handiwork. In the Renaissance there would be no holding him back. He was free to make a silk purse out of a sow's ear.

And so colour that in medieval times had been as precious as gold and admired as if it were the crown jewels was taken down off its pedestal. Colour was becoming the servant to the master. It was taking a big step toward where we are today. Now we can stand in a paint store, able to have whatever colour we could possibly want, and wonder if we really want any colour at all.

ORANGE: WHAT'S NOT TO LIKE?

My San Francisco client was not happy with her white living room. The sun could be shining full blast outside but it never lit up the room. Everything felt grey and drab. We looked at the white walls and the white slipcovered sofas and she said she wanted the room to be lighter. White seemed to me to be about as light as you can get. Where does one go from there? Then I realized what she wanted was not lighter but brighter. She wanted the room to glow. She wanted the sense of sunlight. I proposed a strong yellow–orange on the walls and a hint of yellow in the ceiling.

Orange, like black, is a useful and beautiful but undervalued colour. During a colour workshop I was giving in a large paint store several years ago, I asked how many in the group liked orange. Of the two dozen or more people, only one, a burly paint contractor, put up his hand. In colour parlance "orange," like "beige," is a bad word. Beige is more happily known these days as tan, taupe, putty, or linen. Orange has to be made palatable by terms such as pumpkin, apricot, melon, or terra cotta. If it must be "orange," it should at least be "burnt." It is odd that orange is so ill–favoured when you consider how many of the things we love come with abundant amounts of orange: fall leaves, the setting sun, the pine interior of a summer cottage, the crackled patina of an Old Master oil painting, candlelight.

It is a comfort colour and the most welcoming of all hues. It has the warmth of red without its overbearing aspect. It has the positive energy of yellow without the high key. In rooms like my client's in San Francisco that have little or no natural light, where red might seem heavy and yellow shrill, orange can be the ideal solution. Orange blends well with wood, often lifting forward wood's brighter tones. In houses where stained wood panelling and trim make the place seem dark, adding white to the walls only leaves the wood looking heavier and the space duller. Orange, in even its more muted varieties, adds a lustre. Orange is surprisingly comfortable with almost any other colour, which is why the orange–based tones of many kinds of wood never seem to clash with anything. The trick is to put dirty oranges with a muted colour palette and clean or saturated oranges with a clean one. Not everyone needs to embrace orange 360 degrees and do a whole room. Sometimes the stronger a colour, the less of it is needed. I did a one–quart colour block of full–strength orange

on one side of my uninspiring and narrow Victorian hall. It gave it the zap that transformed it from being a functional passageway, a dead zone halfway between the front hall and the back room, into an energized space that is as welcoming as a fire burning in the hearth.

British artist and aesthete Aubrey Beardsley (1872–1898), known for his decadent illustrations, painted the drawing room–studio in his Pimlico, London, home orange and the woodwork indigo enamel. On the walls he hung Japanese erotica and a pair of huge gold ormolu Empire candlesticks. His intention was that the room only be seen at night, which is when he thought the orange looked its best.

Orange pigment has a short history. Natural orange pigments – minium, orpiment (yellow arsenic sulphide), and later, realgar – were used as little as possible. They were toxic and reactive. They did not agree with thc painter or his other pigments and had to be kept away from all the colours with lead or copper bases. It was not until the end of the eighteenth century that synthetic orange became available. Because it resembled the orange of iron oxide, it was called Mars orange after the Roman god of iron and it was just in time for the Impressionists. As blue's complement, it was essential in their sunny, blue–skied plein–air paintings. Orange enjoyed a popularity boost in the early twentieth century because of a growing taste for bold exotic colours. It began with exhibitions of paintings by the Fauves and Post–Impressionists. Picasso and others were finding bold colours in African artefacts. And in 1910 Diaghilev and his Ballets Russe toured Europe performing the shockingly modern *The Firebird Suite* by Igor Stravinsky and following it up in 1913 with *The Rite of Spring,* a work so sexual, tribal, and musically strange that in Paris a riot broke out. The boldly coloured costumes

designed by Leon Bakst were better received than the music, and orange was part of the package. Orange felt like a warm and vibrant antidote to the soft, muted, and often grey–greens of the art nouveau and Arts and Crafts styles. Later it cut through the drabness of the war years. Tangerine and tango, a red–orange, captured the energy of the Jazz Age. In 1950s America burnt orange was part of the relaxed "autumn" palette that brought the outside inside. It suited the interior walls of the new split–level homes that used exterior materials, flagstone, brick, slate, and a lot of teak–coloured wood. It was a signature colour for the sixties. Bright, clean orange suited the powerful youth market and its psychedelic tastes. By the seventies, it was being paired unpleasantly with brown, white, and turquoise and looked particularly bad shown with brown in floral carpets. Fast–food joints adopted orange because it enhances appetite and is friendly. Most people's immediate negative response to orange comes from its association with the worst of 1970s fast–food restaurants, highway diners, and pizza chains. It became associated with cheap and cheerful things.

For those young enough to think of orange as a retro colour, it has lost its bad reputation and become the colour they want. Orange is the signature colour of Citroën's C3 Pluriel and a new generation of sporty cars. Gloss orange has made its way into high–end Italian kitchen cabinetry. Orange is the name and branding colour for a successful U.K. mobile phone service provider who sued another company, easyMobile.com, in 2005 for having the audacity to use any of "their" colour in easyMobile advertising.

After the negative response to the orange question in my colour workshop, I inculcated the group with images of beautiful orange objects – Tuscan landscapes, Impressionist paintings, terra cotta pots, Mexican plaster walls, and luxurious cut velvets. Then I repeated the question. This time there wasn't a hand that wasn't raised in favour of orange.

When the room in San Francisco was painted orange, it lit up like a lantern and looked good with all my client's white furniture. Orange radiates a warm glow. Dim places do not benefit from white. Without enough light, white looks grey and the effect is lifeless. Yellow–based colours bring in the sunshine. Orange adds its warmth.

LEONARDO'S SHADOWS

THE RENAISSANCE

I wonder if we would all be artists if we were content to paint and colour the way we feel and not concern ourselves with how real the results look. It was in the Renaissance that beautiful colour took second place to realistic images, and anonymous artisans were replaced by creative superstars – the artists.

I was taking a colour course in San Diego, and one day I walked into the classroom and noticed a stack of brand-new, unopened boxes of coloured pastels next to large sheets of pristine newsprint on the table at the back of the room. My heart did a little "Oh, this will be a fun day" leap just like it used to do in grade school on Friday afternoon when we had art. I don't think there was one person who came into the room who didn't pause, look at the boxes of colour, and make some little involuntary expression of delight.

The day did not disappoint. We were exploring synaesthesia, the way one sense triggers a response in another. A sound, a smell, or a taste can be linked to a particular colour. For some people, names and numbers or smells are specific colours, and tastes have shapes. We listened to different kinds of music and were to colour whatever came into our heads. As we listened to African music sung by Oumou Sangaré, bold geometric patterns in strong, clear colours burst across my newsprint. Then came Spanish piano music which sounded more like sunlight on water and a Turneresque seascape emerged.

Later we delved into colour psychology. We used colour to draw a representation of our personality. As the day progressed and the sheets were taped up on the walls, the sterile room was transformed. It became as full of creativity as my grade school art room.

I loved reconnecting with coloured crayons and big sheets of cheap paper. I loved feeling pushed to be free and spontaneous. There was no hesitant pondering, no meticulous drafting, no indecisive scratching away at the page. I didn't have to worry about making a mistake that would ruin everything. Why? Because we were not making art. We were using colour to express ourselves, to capture something internal rather than making pictures of things in the real world. It was exciting and liberating. It is sad to think we stop painting when realism becomes more important than self–expression.

Children don't care how real their paintings look. They paint the way medieval artisans painted. They paint from inside their experiences without worrying about realistic details. Objects get bigger or smaller according to their importance. Perspective is non–existent or idiosyncratic. Colours are chosen freely. The system expresses an inner reality. From inside, it is perfectly logical for the most important thing in the picture to be the biggest. That is how it feels. From inside the medieval Christian experience, it made sense to have Christ so large he covered the domed ceiling of the basilica. From inside a child's experience, it makes sense to make himself or herself bigger than a horse or a bus or a house. Self is the huge presence from which everything "out there" is viewed. A child, like a medieval artist, paints a totally accurate and expressive inner realism. The difference is that a child's is personal rather than spiritual.

I like to think that I use interior colour this way too – from the inside out, as feelings given external expression and an experience of place that resonates with those using it.

As we grow up, we are taught to be less self–absorbed and less emotionally spontaneous. We learn to be more aware of others, more restrained and rational. But with objectivity comes self–consciousness. We start to worry more about external realities than internal ones. When it becomes important to make our art look realistic, the impossibility of achieving it kills our creative urges forever or makes them a full–time job. Our admiration for those who succeed where we have failed is part of the appeal of and fascination with Renaissance art. Their apples look like apples. To achieve this meant reinventing colour. It would cease to be pigment and as valuable as jewels and would start becoming paint.

The Renaissance began around the beginning of AD 1400, although you could make the case that it began about a hundred years earlier when Florentine painter Giotto di Bondone (1267–1337) started to break the rules and rigid formulae the Church had imposed on artisans. He began doing what others had feared to do – to *innovate*. It is easy to look at *The Betrayal of Christ,* one of Giotto's series of paintings from 1305 for the Arena Chapel in Padua, and not be amazed and dazzled by his genius. It was radically different, shockingly new.

By clearing the path for creative innovation, Giotto made it possible for artisans to become artists. In this painting, he put all his highlights on one side, making it look as if his image was lit with natural lighting. He did the unheard of and moved Christ out of the centre of the picture. He not only moved him off–side, he reduced him to human scale and put him in a crowd. Not only is Christ one–of–the–guys, he is almost completely hidden behind Judas. Then Giotto, for the first time in history, turned Christ's face to the side. All of this was staged so he could have Judas and Christ face–to–face, eye–to–eye, sharing the dramatic moment. Choreographing the scene to add the new dimension of emotion made it more difficult for viewers to sort out who was who. Colour solved the problem. Each important figure would have a signature colour. Judas may have his back to us but we know him because he is always the guy in the yellow robe. The sequence of images told the story as dramatically then as a film does now.

Rather than being ostracized by the Church for not being subservient to its preordained artistic codes, Giotto became its star. After Giotto, artisans were allowed to use their talents – a gift from God. Realism was one of the ways artists attracted attention and got commissions. However, in order to achieve realistic effects, they needed to control colour and manipulate it in ways that had never been tried before.

Before the Renaissance there were coloured materials – vermilion, lapus lazuli, and malachite. There was no red, blue, or green. There was no notion of colour as an abstract quality independent of those materials. Because colour materials were never mixed to make new colours, the number of colours was limited to the number of materials available, and that was about a dozen. For a medieval artisan, to paint abstract images of the Kingdom of God with so few hues was a challenge. For Renaissance painters, following Giotto's lead became impossible.

In the real world, colours don't bump against each other in the clearly defined chunks that were acceptable to the medieval painter. They change and blend and melt into each other. That requires hundreds of nuances, like the variations and gradations we take for granted when we look at a rack of paint chips in any paint store. The Renaissance goal was to paint the colours seen, *optical colour,* not the colour known, *local colour.* The colour of your shirt might be red and you could probably match the colour to a paint chip accurately enough. But if you were asked to do a painting of your shirt and all you had was that one red, you would not be able to make it look realistic. It would look flat, like a cartoon. With one colour you can match the cloth's colour but not paint your shirt. To paint how the shirt looks and not just what it is made of requires painting light and how light falls on the shirt. A single colour is inadequate.

The medieval artisan had his reds – his vermilion, his madder, or his lake, a transparent dye from fruit and berries. But he had very limited means to alter its *value,* its lightness or darkness, to make a red shirt look three-dimensional. He could add some white lead to his red for highlights. He could adjust how he ground the pigment to make it a bit brighter or darker. He was not allowed to mix or add black. Adding highlights but not shadows brought objects forward but did not give them depth. The shirt would look less flat but not totally real. It also left the shirt a little on the pink side.

By the Renaissance this was not good enough. To capture the three dimensions required in realistic painting artists needed to paint light. That required darkness as well as light, shadows not just highlights. Real objects under realistic lighting conditions would turn his scene into a real moment frozen in time – a virtual reality. This talent for mimicking reality became the quality most prized and admired and the measure of artistic success.

Pigments became a utilitarian means to an artistic end. With their status lowered, colours could be used and abused in any way possible. One colour was as good as another as long as it did the job.

Red had always been the supreme colour but with the new attitude toward pigments, blue became its rival. Gold fell out of favour because it was a nuisance. Gold bounced light off the surface of the painting, ruining the realistic lighting effect artists were trying so hard to paint. And so, in 1435, when theorist, amateur artist, and architect Leone Battista Alberti (1404–1472) wrote the Renaissance guide to good painting technique, *Della Pittura,* he cautioned artists to avoid gold and to use artistic skill instead to make cheaper pigments look like gold. The results would be more realistic and much more impressive.

Today we don't treat metals as colours but as materials. When Renaissance artists started mixing to get their colours, metals were banished. Vermilion and crimson were suddenly both red, an abstract concept set apart from what made it. Gold was painted with cheap pigments and the real thing that had, in medieval times, spanned the backgrounds of everything from small altarpieces to the massive vaulted ceilings of many a basilica now had shrunk down to a small accent. Gilt was placed on the edge of a halo or the hem of a robe to represent the presence of the Divine Spirit. Because its shine did not match the lighting set–up in the painting, it was effective for suggesting light from another sphere, God's light. In *Birth of Venus* (1485) Sandro Botticelli (1445–1510) painted real gold highlights into Venus's hair so she would look like an allegorical symbol and less like a naked girl coming up from the water on a shell.

Shiny was out and shadows were in. Black was added to the colour repertoire. Before the Renaissance, pure colour was the darkest colour, the base upon which highlights were added. Now pure colour was the middle ground between highlight and shadow. Highlights pulled shapes forward and dark tones drew them back. The third dimension was complete. Artists were warned not to overdo the highlights and shadows or there would be too little pure, perfect colour left. Alberti cautioned artists to use black and white pigments as sparingly as if they were "the pearls Cleopatra dissolved in vinegar." Allowing artists to darken colour meant they could balance up tones that had always been uneven. For the first time even yellow could be deepened to balance with a red or blue. With so many nuances of colour now available, your red shirt could be painted realistically.

The odd thing about realism is how many different versions of "real" there can be. No matter how many artists were to paint your shirt, no two versions would look the same. Creating three–dimensional realism on a two–dimensional surface is an act of translation. Renaissance painters were explorers and experimenters, their decisions a matter of individual taste and style. Style is always as personal as a signature and colour was one of its key components. Suddenly you could tell whether it was Leonardo da Vinci or Michelangelo who painted your shirt.

We all have our own colour sensibility, and helping others express theirs is what makes my work endlessly interesting. I am asked if my taste "colours" my choices for others. I like to think that I turn my own taste off or down. I am very flexible in choosing colours. Bold hues to whites, it's all colour to me. What makes my colour sense different from another designer's is not what colours I use but how I use them.

Sandra, a client from the United States, often visits family and friends in Canada. On one visit Sandra saw the big old house that her friend Sharon had moved into. On another she saw it painted in its new colours. Another time she went to a different city and another friend. She walked into Ruth's house, saw new colours that were totally different from Sharon's, and asked, "Was Janice here?" And Ruth said, "How did you know?" The colours were different but there was something in the strategy of how they were used that resonated. So when Sandra asked if I could recommend someone closer to California who did colour the way I did, I had to say no. Designers, architects, and colour consultants are all experienced with colour but everyone does it a little differently. Architects tend to avoid it or intellectualize it more than I do. Other designers have signature palettes, and many love lots of neutrals with interesting accents. Just like the work of one Renaissance painter compared to another, there is no right and wrong, but individual ways of seeing and expressing. Because my colour sensibilities were honed studying art and architecture, painting, dyeing and designing for theatre, my approach will differ from those trained in design schools. And that is why I found myself on a plane heading toward Sandra's house in California.

Style is the result of innovation, and innovation in the Renaissance was due to competition. From Giotto onward, city officials and clergy took great pride in the talents of their artists and vied to secure the best for commissions in their cities or cathedrals. In a spirit of one–up–manship, competing artists tried to be different to get the attention that would land the job.

Single–point perspective was an innovation discovered by Filippo Brunelleschi (1377–1446) around 1425. It gave art the mathematical grounding it needed to be counted as a liberal art, "up there" with philosophy, science, poetry, and rhetoric. Leonardo would now argue that an artist was no more a manual labourer than a poet who had to pull his pen across paper to write his verse.

Leonardo da Vinci (1452–1519) was a musician, surveyor, and engineer who did painting on the side (although for a few hundred years his paintings were ignored and his drawings praised). If anyone could meld geometry, science, and painting to establish painting as a liberal art, he was the one. Shadows would be his colour innovation.

As Leonardo scrutinized nature, he came face to face with colour optics. We know grass is a specific green but it looks different depending on distance and lighting. The artist had to forget about the colour grass is in order to paint it the colour it looks, optical colour, which changes from moment to moment because of lighting, reflections, and "accidents of nature." Like Impressionist painters of the nineteenth century, Leonardo saw colour truth in transient atmospheric effects. The difference was they focused on light and Leonardo, on shadow.

Leonardo wrote a great deal about shadows, the midpoint between darkness and light and which he thought held greater power than light.

Bright light created strong contrasts that confused and hurt the eye. In dim light, the eye dilated, opening up to colour's subtle nuances. The diffuse light of dull weather or the soft light just before sunset was the ideal time to paint portraits or else awnings should be hung above to act as a diffuser. Black velvet, like flats at the side of a theatre set, would further absorb any bouncing light. The goal was to reduce contrasts, to soften colour and blur its edges.

Colour emerging from dark shadow became Leonardo's tool for controlling the eye of the viewer and drawing it toward what was important. To focus attention on Christ or the Virgin Mary, the medieval artisan depended on scale and placement in a symmetrically arranged composition. Realism required a different strategy. Leonardo used darkness. His study of optics revealed the eye always gravitates toward what is lightest (which is why I loathe white ceilings in coloured rooms). Shadows became the foil against which his figures shone. Most artists primed the surface on which they were about to paint with white gesso so as not to reduce the colour in their pigments. Leonardo always started with a dark ground and modelled his colours up. The more important the figure was, the lighter, although never so much so that it separated itself from the background. There are no sharp edges, no interruption between one surface and the next. Leonardo's colours are so void of high contrast that his paintings verge on becoming monochromatic.

Like Leonardo, I find darkness an essential way to manipulate what the eye sees. You want people to notice something? Make it light. You want them to ignore it? Put it into shadow. In the savannahs, background colours were rarely brighter than the things we were supposed to notice. Colour flow requires reducing sharp contrasts to create more fluid tonal harmonies. Contrary to the desires or presumptions of many a client, there is quiet beauty in shadows and darkness. In theatre design, it was second nature to use light or bright colour to attract the eye and shadow tones to avoid it. The performers were lighter than the set, which was lighter than the stage. The more important the character, the brighter or lighter the costume. The edges of the sets were always sprayed down so that they blended into the black of the wings, avoiding an abrupt end. Removing the edge with a shadow tone helped the set emerge out of darkness and not look as if it were a temporary installation.

When homes have lovely trim and beautiful cornices and handsome stair spindles, I am happy to recommend light or white tones. When things are not worth looking at, they get camouflaged with the wall colour. But sometimes the bulk of an entire room needs to be de–emphasized by putting it into shadow.

I went to Maralyn's large country house. It was an open plan, centred on a great room that had a very high, peaked ceiling and an end wall of windows overlooking a forest. Like her house, Maralyn, with long black hair and black glasses, was dramatic. Like Leonardo, she began building her palette with a dark base. Her flooring and kitchen cabinetry were dark charcoal. I encouraged her not to stop there. Bland and bleached was not her style, and white or light walls would make her great room seem undressed, empty, like a huge packing box. Putting the walls into shadow with a mid–tone grey would achieve a Leonardo effect, a deep tonal background to let lighter things be focal points: large off–white furniture, a spectacular carpet, and a big chandelier. With the room in shadow, the view through the windows would become the art and the focal feature. Rather than define the dimensions of the room, shadow colour would be more like the effect of the stone walls in a Gothic cathedral that lead the eye to windows or the altar. In Maralyn's house, colour needed the *sfumato* vagueness of a shadow colour.

When I was just starting my post–theatre career as a stylist for photographers, I found out first–hand just how brilliantly Leonardo balanced his light–dark values and controlled what the eye takes in. I was asked by photographer Nigel Dickson to costume a prominent advertising agency executive, Gary Prouk, as the Mona Lisa. It was a spoof for the cover of a trade magazine. This was in the days of photography before the expression "we'll fix it in post" meant you could get away with murder and digital technology would make everything perfect. Nigel had to get as close to perfection as he could directly on film. That was an art in itself and one at which Nigel was particularly adroit. Nonetheless, making what was real look like Leonardo's interpretation of real proved to be truly impossible.

Doing the Mona Lisa's wardrobe was not the easiest job to be starting out on. I bought fine silk chiffon for Lisa's veil. I dyed it and over–dyed it several times to get the colour as close as I could to his deep raw umber. But even the finest veil was too opaque for the effect Leonardo had created across Mona Lisa's forehead. Leonardo suggested the presence of the veil with only one fine line. He did not want to shorten the shape of the face with the brown veil fabric. After a bit of trial and error, Nigel and I decided Leonardo's realism was not real at all. To mimic his effect, we pulled the veil back and off the face then suggested it was still there by drawing a line across Gary's brow with an eyeliner pencil.

Leonardo manipulated the sheen on the clothes to highlight what we should notice – her face, hands, and unrealistically high cleavage – and not notice what wasn't important, her body mass. How was I to get sheen on the folds of Gary's brown satin and velvet clothing only where the highlights were desired and not everywhere that they were in real life? Leonardo's realism was not geared to things as they are but as they seem.

Thankfully, Leonardo not only edited highlights but fashion details. Mona Lisa has no fashionable hair–do, no jewellery, not even a wedding ring. This is not because Bartolomeo di Zanobi del Giocondo, a noble citizen of Florence, was a cheapskate but because Leonardo was painting a universal woman rather than just his patron's third wife. In the same way, timeless interior design is often edited to the core essentials and not swamped in style–specific details.

Once Gary was dressed and styled, the next trick was to make him melt into the setting, to have him emerge gently from the shadows with edges as soft as velvet. No matter how dark the clothing or how subtle its detailing, he sat there, large as life. There was nothing *sfumato* about this broad. To get the signature smokiness that makes a Leonardo look like a Leonardo, Nigel had to throw an 81EF filter on the lens that added what he calls a Rembrandt–esque tobacco stain over the image, mimicking Leonardo's dulled tonal unity by knocking the whites or light tones back, then he polarized the image to make the bright tones more saturated and velvet looking. This reduced contrasts so colours had no edges. "Very Leonardo," we thought. For me it was like taking away the contrasting white trim and ceiling in rooms so colours and tones can flow uninterrupted in an atmospheric space, all part of a unified whole, nothing popping out and showing off.

But Nigel had to go a step further to blend Gary with his setting. He printed up the image. Then, using information he'd read on the subject of art forgeries, he covered the print with a fine varnish and baked the whole thing in the oven until it became further discoloured and crackled. Then and only then did it look dark and muted as we have come to think an Old Master should look.

Leonardo had discovered how to build his compositions, not with an arrangement of light colours and dark colours, but in a light to dark range within each colour. Even yellow could vary from being a dark to a light colour and hold its own with red, blue, and green. We take this for granted now but it was totally unprecedented at the time. The subtle gradations allowed his figures to be integrated with their surrounding and not sit out in front. The even tonal balance of his colours was what Nigel had to fake and bake so laboriously into his photograph.

What made Leonardo's controlled colour possible was the newly fashionable oil paint. Now we avoid oil paint because, besides being smelly and a pain to clean out of brushes, it is slow drying. This was precisely why Leonardo loved it. Flemish artist Jan van Eyck (1390–1441) is credited with pioneering oil painting. It was not actually new but he used it with such skill that others came to appreciate its potential for the first time. Previously, oil paint was like the Renaissance equivalent of house paint – fine for mundane things like painting on metal, stone, or door trim but not ideal for art. Some artists didn't like its long drying time. In earlier times when colour was laid on, unmixed, side by side, the faster the colours dried the better. Quick–drying egg tempera was the preferred artist's paint. Slow–drying oil started to make sense only when, in pursuit of realism, colours were not hard–edged but blurred, blended, and mixed.

The secret to van Eyck's real–looking colour was suspending pigments in an oil glaze and applying them in thin layers over a white primed surface. As one translucent layer of coloured glaze covered another, beautiful new colours emerged. The glaze refracted the light and made the colours vivid the way water intensifies colour. Colour suspended in oil shone like jewels.

I rarely get to use glazes in my design work now but in my theatre days they were a staple. Almost every painted surface – walls, floors, rocks, benches, pillars, and posts – had several glaze coats in various colours over a base colour. Even a grey wall would have raw umber glazed areas, to add depth and dimension, and fine speckled coats of pink, green, and blue to allow surfaces to engage with the mood–changing stage lights. Because of glazed colour nothing looked flat or fake.

Oil paint solved the riddle of how to get a range of mixed colour without losing intensity. No colour made by stirring two pigments together physically before applying them to the surface would look as bright as these optically mixed hues. Layering red over blue, van Eyck made a beautiful optical purple. Brush strokes could be blended in and made invisible. Shapes and contour merged seamlessly.

Many artists, including van Eyck, did the first stages of a painting – priming the surface and drafting out a composition – in egg tempera because speed was an asset. Egg tempera also continued to be favoured for skin tones. Oil, which stayed wet for days or even weeks, was used for the main composition where the ability to continuously blend and adjust colour was desirable.

Pigments that worked brilliantly in egg tempera did not work well in oil and vice versa. Oil turned vibrant lapis lazuli black. Vermilion lost its glow. On the other hand, lakes painted from the juice of berries that were too transparent and faded as tempera colours worked beautifully under oil's protective glaze. Even pigments that had chemically reacted against each other were safe because oil encapsulated the pigments.

Oil paint became the new trend after several of van Eycks' paintings were exported to Italy and Flemish oil painters started getting the commissions. Rather than be outdone by the upstart Flemish, Italian artists, especially in Florence, began to use oils and copy van Eyck's technique. Slow–drying oil paints suited Leonardo's method. He could work and rework his colours to his heart's desire. When oil dried, he could continue to add more layers. That was the good news. The bad news was that it meant he was even less likely to finish anything. His mind was so active, his interests so broad and the challenge of matching his art to his vision so arduous that he often abandoned a piece in mid–struggle. Or he tweaked paintings for years, never sure when a piece was finished. He worked on the *Mona Lisa* for over three years. As her fame grew and others started to copy her, Leonardo continued to tweak. He never did feel she was ready to deliver up to his patron. He took the painting with him wherever he went and it was with him in France when he died.

Venetian artists took to oil paint for entirely different reasons. With oil they could forget about meticulous preparation and paint as spontaneously as many a contemporary artist. If they made a mistake, they could just paint over it. Tizano Vecelli Titian (1485–1576) and his peers loaded up their brushes and laid paint on in thick strokes called *impasto*. Titian would go boldly into a painting, turn it to the wall for a period of time, then have another go, often using his fingers as well as his brush. Sometimes he painted his background then dropped his figures into the setting like characters on a stage set and painted over anything that didn't work. Titian was not drawing contours and colouring them in. He was composing with colour itself.

Sadly many people today treat colour as if they were Florentines and not with the freedom of a Titian, even though, as in Venice, colour is always at hand. Venetians could use it more freely because they had the luxury of being able to make a mistake, since they lived in one of the colour capitals of the world. Venice was a centre for trading and commerce. Pigments landed and were manufactured into usable colour. Venetian artists got first dibs. New colours were like fashion, something that caught the eye and got attention. New colours helped get the commissions. In *Bacchus and Ariadne* (1520–1522) Titian used every pigment known to man, including the newest one, a vivid orange of arsenic sulphide called realgar.

When Michelangelo came back from a visit to Titian's studio, he was very critical of this bold colour and spontaneous ways. Florentines were still more preoccupied with what the ancients had done. They read and agreed with Pliny: colour was vulgar and decadent. Line gave art its unity, harmony,

and balance. Line was rational and linked art to mathematics and science. Colour was wild and unruly. Colourists were a dime a dozen. A good draftsman was the rarity. *Disegno* versus *colore* was a debate that continued for another two hundred years.

Colour was important to Venetian artists not just because it was available but because they lived in a city that was full of luminous colours. Unlike Leonardo, Venetian painters tended to make the sky, the atmosphere, the landscape itself just as colourful and important as the foreground. Centuries later Turner, Whistler, and Monet would make their way to Venice to paint its atmospheric light, which by then was beginning to be caused by air pollution and not morning mists.

The size of paintings grew in Venice because it was a ship-building city with lots of sail canvas to be had. Venetians started painting on canvas instead of the usual wood panel because in the humid setting, canvas didn't warp and crack. Also paintings could be as large as desired and simply rolled up for transporting around the narrow streets of the canal town.

Leonardo's main contemporary rival was Michelangelo Buonarroti (1475–1564), who was twenty-three years younger than Leonardo and outlived him by forty-five. Michelangelo was commissioned to do the most ambitious painting project ever – the ceiling of the Sistine Chapel – even though he thought of himself as a sculptor not a painter and thought the job a kind of punishment for bad attitude. He had just spent six months in the marble quarries of Carrara selecting the perfect stone for sculpting a tomb for Pope Julius II. Whether due to cost over-runs on St. Peter's

Basilica or superstition, the tomb project was cancelled. Michelangelo was furious and got the Sistine ceiling as a consolation prize.

After the contract was drawn up and the price agreed upon, Michelangelo decided the proposal – a *trompe l'oeil* ceiling with twelve apostles around the perimeter – was not ambitious enough for the demands of the space. Pope Julius agreed and told him to do whatever he wanted.

Michelangelo hired no assistants. Academies were replacing guilds as centres for learning but with ready–made colour increasingly available, some artists preferred to do everything themselves. Celebrity artists usually had apprentices but Michelangelo spent four years climbing up a four–storey–high scaffold to work alone, lying on his back and painting in poor light.

The ceiling became a showpiece for his skill with the human form but his manly women and pasty–fleshed figures look as if they are made of marble, studies for the sculptural pieces that he would rather have been doing.

Michelangelo's colours seem oddly old–fashioned: no shadows, only highlights. Rather than blending, they are clear and bright and laid into his sharply defined forms. The foundation of Leonardo's tonal unity was *sfumato*. Michelangelo's was *unione,* hard–edged and bright. To keep colour light he didn't mix pigments, but to expand this restricted colour repertoire, he used a device Giotto and medieval artists had favoured called *cangiantismo,* in which a light colour substitutes for white as the highlight on darker hues, colour pairing that adds variety. A pale pink or mauve might highlight a blue; yellow, a red or green. The effect was like a shot fabric woven with two colours, a silk for example that looks red in one direction but blue where the light hits the folds. Michelangelo pushed *cangiantismo* to a new limit and came up with all sorts of shocking colour combinations that no one had ever seen before.

He wanted his colours to be as bright as possible to compensate for the gloom of the vaulted space. A dark palette like Leonardo's would be oppressive, not a celebration of Michelangelo's religious optimism. As artists had done for centuries before the Renaissance, Michelangelo felt he was using colour itself to illuminate dark space with God's glorious light. Many of his contemporaries felt his colours were licentious and inappropriate. He didn't use these colours everywhere. He chose to put the brightest brights on the prophets. Unlike the robust poses of the allegorical figures, these earthly characters had to be shown in stationary positions. Vivid colour gives them life. It is the external sign of their inner spiritual energy and dynamism.

Over the years layers of dirt gave the ceiling an almost Leonardo-like dimness. When it was cleaned, the bright colours shocked again. This time artificial lighting was part of the problem. It was needed when the ceiling was covered in dirt but no one thought to dim it when the original bright colours were restored.

Because I often suggest the *sfumato* strategy of dark wall colours and light accents in dark spaces, adding extra lighting becomes important; the reverse, a dark to light colour change is resolved with dimmers. Colour and light are a pairing that has to be finessed, not treated separately.

In the meantime what started to preoccupy artists was not how many colours were available. Mixing had made the number infinite. In *Adoration of the Magi* (1475) Botticelli made over twenty red and pink tones using only four pigments. The question became how few. The concept of primary colours was emerging. What were the essential colours from which all others could be made?

And what happened to Realism? It peaked in the Renaissance with Raffaello Santi (1483–1520). Raphael was easier to get along with than the moody, temperamental Michelangelo and not so distracted by other career opportunities as Leonardo. While the solitary and brooding Michelangelo was up on his scaffolding doing the Sistine ceiling, Raphael and his students and assistants were down the hall, painting huge frescos in a suite of Vatican rooms. As he watched Michelangelo's progress, his own work began to look similar. Michelangelo complained that everything he, Michelangelo, knew, he learned from studying the ancients; everything Raphael knew, he learned from copying him.

Raphael mastered colour in both the *unione* manner of Michelangelo and Leonardo's *sfumato* technique and used whichever suited the job, both if need be. His *Sistine Madonna* (1513–1514) would win a beauty contest over Leonardo's Mona Lisa or Michelangelo's manly dames any day. Two putti looking over the bottom edge of the *Sistine Madonna* are so appealing they continue to be used on one of the most popular greeting cards of all time, the sublime reduced to kitsch. But when we think of the great artists of the Renaissance, we rarely put Raphael's name ahead of Leonardo and Michelangelo. Raphael's mastery was too perfect. His paintings seem to lack the struggle that pulls us in and doesn't let us go.

Once apples looked just like apples, the goal of artists would change. If a real-looking object was good, then an ideal one would be better. Mannerism, the style that followed in the baroque period, saw artists trying to invent a more perfect perfect. What they achieved ranged from idiosyncratic to bizarre. Colour would go in and out of favour. Science, in the meantime, would start to crack colour's codes and secrets. It would take a scientific mind like Sir Isaac Newton's to discover the truth about colour. And the truth would connect it right back to light.

BLACK, THE COLOUR OF CONFIDENCE

Katherine, a writer, needed no convincing when it came to injecting a hit of black into her rooms. She understood black as the dark that makes things bright. And so we chose black chalkboard paint for the main wall of her front hall. Guests love writing messages over it every time she hosts a party or a book launch. The ceiling of a small pale yellow bathroom is now black. The upstairs den is a blue–black that shows off the ochre spines of her husband's large collection of Penguin paperbacks. The view through a series of long slim windows looks like back–lit images glowing through the darkness.

To Katherine, black has an elegance missing from browns, which are heavier and more specifically masculine. "It is the same as liking black and white photography or black and white type on the printed page," she says. "Black is sharp, spunky. There is clarity to it. It picks up on the other blacks like the ones in the pattern of the carpet. It makes the house readable. White is so pale and ghostly. White is what makes *me* nervous."

I love black. I am not depressed, on drugs, or trying to recapture some aspect of a lost adolescence. I just like and appreciate it. In clothing I am trying to curb the black habit slightly but black walls, a terrifying idea for most people over the age of nineteen, are clean, crisp, and gorgeous. Black accent walls are to the home what Chanel's black toe caps and collars were to her beige outfits – the punctuation that defines and sharpens. In a world of ubiquitous white, black is essential. And for all the people in the world who find their white rooms boring but don't want colour, black can bring balance, an anchor, without colour.

In many African cultures black was a good thing. Painted on the male body, it was thought to add strength and beauty and a camouflage that hid them from evil. Kohl around the eyes was originally worn to ward off evil by intensifying one's gaze. It had the side benefit of making one more attractive to the opposite sex, so to this day, some of us would never be seen dead in public without it.

Since the fifteenth century, in Western cultures, black has been the clothing colour of choice or necessity. After the plague decimated the population of Europe, the Church decreed black clothing should be worn to show humility and a moral righteousness that might appease an avenging God. The textile industry realized that if the upper classes and not just peasants were going to have to wear black, then they needed to develop some good ones – rich, dark, and colour–fast. Once they succeeded, black often became the colour of choice.

Portrait painters like Titian, Van Dyck, and Goya mastered the art of painting beautiful blacks – the velvets, silks, and taffetas that set off their sitter's features. Margaret of Navarre (1492–1549), sister of the French King Francis I and wife of King Henry II of Navarre, always slept naked and always on black sheets because she liked the way they set off her pale skin.

In sixteenth-century Europe, strict laws imposed black clothing for long periods of mourning. In Victorian England, widow's weeds were worn for a year and a day. After World War I, when there were so many to mourn, the rules about black broke down. Some who lost next of kin refused to wear it and others who hadn't did.

When synthetic colour was invented and bright colour could finally be afforded by all, colour lost its sartorial status. It immediately looked cheap, gaudy, and unfashionable. Businessmen, servants, clerics, and the upper classes chose black. Black and grey suits became the ubiquitous male attire, and by the 1920s women were adopting that wardrobe staple, the little black dress. Black has lingered as the colour of clothing for serious events and occasions. Those who break the code of dark clothing today, as in medieval times, are those who are not in the social mainstream – artists, musicians, actors, and rebels. Old habits die hard, and although laws imposing black are long gone, anyone not wearing black at a formal funeral looks inappropriately dressed. The more colourful or light the clothing, the more disrespectful the attire. Conversely, I recently wore black to a wedding. All the young bride's friends arrived in a plethora of bold and brilliant colours and patterns, and I thought how wonderful and fitting they looked, how full of life and freshness. I decided there can be too much wearing of black in this life.

For most of the twentieth century, black was the colour of function and quality. Henry Ford said of his cars, "You can have any colour so long as

it is black." Black was the built–to–last product colour of telephones, typewriters, and shoes. Colour was for fashion items and indicated a shorter life cycle. By the end of the century, Apple started making computers in colour. Ditching "office" black and boring beige in favour of four fun transparent colours signalled that these were not mysterious and complicated machines nor a lifetime investment but as user–friendly as toys and, due to ever–changing technology, as quickly outgrown. Now that Apple's user–friendliness is a given, the signature colour is white and not just any white. This is white with a translucent depth that signals, like a silver car, an elegant machine that is easy to manoeuvre, light on its feet.

Black is the strong and silent type, a potent presence with weight and monumentality. When choosing wall colours it can seem hard to separate black from its links to death and gloom and to see it as elegant and confident. Black is not white's alter ego, the bad to white's good. Black is a hard worker, a problem solver and, for the brave souls who try it, a thing of surprising beauty.

Psychologists say teens want black to distinguish their space from their parents'. Black sets their zone apart and is a statement of independence. For teenagers black is not the cave, it is the shelter. Contrary to parental opinion, black can feel like a security blanket, private and safe. It lets teenagers decompress from the stimulation of their day. Because it reduces visual stimulation and light's energy level, it is relaxing. It also heightens the other senses. Surrounded by black, we can hear better, think better, feel more. Don't we close our eyes to experience a kiss? If they want a black room, go out and get them the paint.

Artists from Leonardo da Vinci to Turner said light could not be painted without using dark colours. We always look at the brightest things. Have you ever tried to look at the midnight sky and not the stars? Black makes the walls recede and focuses attention on things in the foreground. White reveals; black conceals.

Josef Albers, who taught colour at the Bauhaus school of architecture and design in Weimar, Germany, in the early twentieth century, found that colours popped if they were put against white. They glowed against black. Swiss–born French architect Le Corbusier often specified black or charcoal window frames because the eye can float across dark mullions without the view being interrupted.

With a few exceptions, clients are usually reluctant to use black but those who give it a try become instant converts. I have yet to get the call to say it was a bad idea. An artist from Montreal said she liked the semi–gloss brown–black colour block in her upstairs art wall so much that she hated to hang art on it. Another used black on the walls around her white cabinets and called with great excitement to say, "Oh, my God! It looks fabulous. The black upgrades everything. I can't decide if it looks New York or Paris but it sure looks good. I never would have thought!" Another called to say she loved the black in her powder room so much she used the leftover paint in a little hallway and it doubled the size and quadrupled its appeal.

One client, Roy, put it better than I could when he described the effect of something as simple and as terrifying as having his white kitchen ceiling painted black: "The entire top of the room recedes and is opened up, so perhaps that's why people don't notice it immediately. Their eyes are tricked. But once we point it out, their jaws kind of drop. I'm guessing most have never seen a black kitchen ceiling let alone painting any ceiling in a house. It strikes such a great balance between opening up the space by obliterating the ceiling, yet warming it up considerably."

Or as Katherine so aptly put it, "Black is a statement of confidence. You just have to be confident enough to make it."

COLOUR'S DARK AGE

BAROQUE AND BEYOND

I met C.J. Volk at a Color Marketing Group conference and soon learned how mixing one colour with another can make not only more colours but better colours. C.J. is a slim animated woman with pixie–like features, short wispy auburn hair, and funky black glasses. Within minutes of our first colour conversation, we were kindred spirits finishing each other's sentences. She too is a colour designer so we gushed with a mutual enthusiasm about colour and the amazing things that happen to people who let good colours into their lives. That led us to discuss what it is that makes a colour good. Like me, C.J. had become intrigued with the full–spectrum colour that was being put forward by Donald Kaufman. He is a New York–based colour designer who chooses colours for galleries such as the Metropolitan Museum of Art and who designed colour for the late architect Philip Johnson. (In the bedroom of Johnson's New York apartment, Kaufman used fourteen colours!)

According to Kaufman, the best colours have within them a little bit of every colour. Like a dash of salt that brings out the flavour of the soup, adding a bit of any colour's complementary colour brings out its beauty and enhances its luminosity. Adding a bit of green to red makes a superior red because green contains yellow and blue. A pinch of red makes a better green. Complexity, Kaufman noticed, made even the most artificially produced colour look more natural.

In the natural world no colour is made from a single hue. The bark of a tree is not grey but greys. The green of a leaf varies because of the way light plays with its translucency. This is why nature's colours blend easily. Complex paint colours do the same.

What worked on the canvas, Kaufman realized, worked just as effectively on walls. Full–spectrum colour was not a new idea but he was one of the first to package and promote the concept in a line of paint. The Donald Kaufman Color Collection has thirty colours and each one, even his whites, is full–spectrum. Interior spaces painted with these colours became more atmospheric, more like being in nature. Complex or full–spectrum colours engage with every kind and colour of light–morning sun, amber sunset, cool winter daylight – because of the presence of every colour. Walls acquire depth and seem to breathe. They are alive and, in built environments, anything that puts life into a space is a good thing.

At our conference C.J. told me that she did mixing experiments to test Kaufman's theory. As we sat around the conference table, she gave me a little demonstration. She picked up two tiles, one stone and the other glass with a pearlescent finish. We tried to coordinate standard off–white paint chips with these natural materials. They looked too yellow or too green or too grey. Then we put a complex off–white next to each. The same one matched both! It was as if the colour was a chameleon that shifted its hue ever so slightly to fit in with what was around. Any neighbouring colour finds itself represented in the complex colour and pulls itself forward.

Colour always acts like a magnet, drawing itself out from other colours. That is why changing the wall colour in a room changes the look of the art and the upholstery. The wall colour becomes the prominent colour. It starts emerging from wherever it was hiding in the room. This is an asset because this shift can make the familiar seem new and fresh to our eyes. By putting the colour we like on the wall we get more of it from all our things.

C.J.'s experiments proved that complex colours or full–spectrum colours are better colours – luminous, alive, and easier to colour–match. Convinced of their importance, she approached every commercial paint manufacturer in America but none was interested in producing a line of full–spectrum paint. And so C.J. started Citron Paint Company and began manufacturing her own.

To make colour, most paint companies often use a base white and two to four pigments – usually including black or raw umber. C.J. says that what makes her colours "yummy" is the use of up to fifteen tints and "never black!" Black takes away light. It makes colours muddy and less luminous.

I looked at her colour card of about ninety–six colours, all inspired by what she sees around her – the yellow–green of the palo verde tree outside her Tucson, Arizona, home or pumpkin pie. Customers like the names and the stories behind them and will say, "Oh, I've got Double Latte and Puppy Fur in my bedroom." The latest colour, Tarnished Silver, was almost two years in the making. "I kept tweaking it till it was just right. I will spend any amount of time to get each colour perfect."

A few months later, I was standing in the National Gallery in London looking at a self–portrait that Rembrandt did at the age of sixty–three in the last year of his life and I thought about C.J. and Kaufman and the whole complex colour business. Rembrandt's colours were compressed in range to an almost monochromatic set of complex browns. Brown can seem like such a heavy, cumbersome colour, boring as mud and as elegant as dirt. But Rembrandt's brown is not just brown. It is a complex mixture so full of colour that it transcends itself and becomes a velvet hue, with the depth and richness of black but more warm–blooded.

Complex colours, like C.J.'s or Rembrandt's, are the ones you never find on the almighty colour wheel. The colour wheel contains the spectrum, the colours of the rainbow. It has no light–dark dimension. Look as you may, you will never find pink or burgundy. Nor are there any complex colours – no brown, grey, or muddy colours. If all colour decisions were geared to the colours of the colour wheel, the choice would be simple. It would be a matter of choosing one of six colours – red, orange, yellow, green, blue, or violet – or the variations in between. Most people know what they like when it comes to this dimension of colour, which is referred to as hue, a synonym for colour.

But colour is messier and more interesting than the wheel. Colour is not two–dimensional but three. Colour is not a flat circle but a globe. Hues, or the colours of the spectrum, are all at the equator. We know white and black are not on the colour wheel. White is at one pole and black is at the other. We map degrees of lightness and darkness, called value, along the lines of longitude. Colours that are above the equator on the way to white are tones and those below, on their way to black, are shades. (To be honest, everyone seems to refer to colour, or hue, as tone or shade. In theory, they don't describe pure colour – the reddest red or the bluest blue – but rather their variations.) Pink is a tone between red at the equator and the white pole. Burgundy is a shade below red on its way to the black pole.

But the most interesting, challenging, and confusing part of colour is in the middle of the globe. At the equator's surface, hue is 100 per cent colour and called saturated. You couldn't squeeze any more pure colour into these colours if you tried. In the design world we call them clean colours. As colour goes toward the core from pure colour at the equator, it picks up more and more complex grey until, near the core, colour becomes neutral. In my experience the most frequent colour mistakes are not to do with hue but with value and saturation. The colours can be right. The challenge is not making them too dark or light or too clean. Clean colours are strong colours and to knock them back we tend to add white. White is not the colour softener. It is the brightener. Adding a touch of a colour's complement, a shot of complexity, is what pulls them into line. Complex grey, the colour that has a bit of every colour in it, like Kaufman's paint, is what turns paint into luminous hues. Like C.J.'s complex hues, they are easy to coordinate and great to live with.

Complex colour entered art in the two hundred years between the Renaissance, when jewel–like colour was suspended in oil, and the nineteenth century, when chemistry brought an explosion of bright, new, synthetic colours into the world. It was a time when colour was adroitly handled by the likes of Rembrandt, Velasquez, Vermeer, and Rubens and Dutch or Flemish artists who used it so well you think you can almost smell their flowers and squeeze their fruit. Then there were those I think of as the painters of gloom whose lugubrious works from the mannerist, baroque, and rococo periods fill endless miles of rooms in any major art gallery.

For centuries serious art had to be dark art, and the notion persists. I have many a client living with dark art and "antiques" that seem awkward in their space but are revered simply because they are old and serious and therefore of value. In many cases the dark colours we see now weren't always the intention of seventeenth- and eighteenth-century artists. Time is not colour's friend. Unless artists knew their pigments and took great care with them, brilliantly coloured works faded and cracked and varnished top coats darkened or yellowed, turning everything beneath into a dull, tonal soup.

By the nineteenth century this look suited a growing middle class who thought Old Masters *should* look old. Many an art restorer had no qualms about "fixing" a painting with a good dose of dark shellac to be sure it looked old and valuable. By late in the century, Impressionist painters would occasionally be asked by potential patrons to tone down a particular work with a glaze so they looked better when hung in their collection.

In the 1960s when the discoloured top layer of varnish was removed from Titian's *Bacchus and Ariadne* at the National Gallery in London, the public and curators alike were shocked. The colours seemed so bright and so vulgar. The blue sky was the most shocking of all, and the response was overwhelmingly negative. Brightening a paint colour on a canvas can apparently be as shocking as changing it on a wall. They both require a gestation period to feel familiar and comfortable. Ever since then, it is not unusual for paintings to be worked on in stages so viewers get acclimatized to the colour intensity of their old but vivid masters.

Starting back in 1347 dark and drab hues became appropriate clothing colour for all but the rich and powerful in Europe. The population had been decimated by the bubonic plague. In Paris it was halved. Florence's population was reduced by almost four-fifths. Two-thirds of Venetians died. The total number of those who died in the SARS pandemic in

2002–2003 was the same number that died every two days in Avignon, a typically affected small town. The scourge was so extensive and horrible that survivors thought God was punishing or perhaps exterminating the human race. To appease His wrath, the pope forbade gambling, drinking, and cursing and tried to curb consumption by imposing sumptuary laws that legislated what every man, woman, and child could own. Limits were set on possessions of every kind from size of house to the number of animals (even breed of dog).What clothing, in what fabrics and colour, became a matter for the law to decide.

Clothing had always been an indicator of status. Under sumptuary laws, monarchs and aristocrats were entitled to wear colour but the common man was not. Even if he had been, the price would have been prohibitive. A yard of expensive scarlet (usually wool dyed with kermes and later cochineal) was equal to two months' wages. The best a peasant could acquire was a duller, madder–dyed red cloth.

Before sumptuary laws took effect, a woman's entire dowry was sometimes sewn into the jewels on her frock. Women and youths were considered particularly susceptible to a desire for new and novel colours and accessories, but many a man lost his fortune in an effort to dress beyond his means. Such frivolous extravagances and sinful ostentation were to be curtailed and the purchasing of more virtuous, practical things encouraged. In times of turmoil, buying a horse was more useful than an extra set of clothes.

Philip the Good, Duke of Burgundy (1396–1467) began wearing black by choice in 1419 when his father, John the Fearless, was murdered. (White was the colour of mourning for queens from medieval times until the fifteenth century, lasting even longer in Spain.) Philip was head of a domain held together by loose alliances and allegiances and because the sovereignty he craved would never be his, pomp and ceremony were his tools for garnering admiration and loyalty. He continued to wear black after the period of mourning because he realized he stood out in the crowd if all the noblemen of Bruges were flaunting colour (quite the reverse of where we are at today).

The Spanish also loved black clothing. It made a beautiful backdrop for all manner of decorative trimmings and jewels and was therefore particularly popular in the wardrobes of the wealthy. King Charles VI, who took over the Spanish throne from the childless Charles II, perpetuated its popularity, and the trend lasted over two hundred years.

By the sixteenth century, sumptuary laws made black *de rigueur* for anyone with good Christian virtues. Blue was also morally acceptable because it was still considered light black. Among the lower classes, bold colour was for misfits and outcasts – a public warning system. Colour was compulsory for anyone with a mental or physical deficiency since flaws were considered a sign of sin. Non–Christians were required to wear a badge of a particular colour, often yellow, set at a predetermined place on their clothing – the sleeve, shoulder, or chest. Anyone practising dubious professions – musicians, crooks, prostitutes, and doctors – all had to wear colour. The specifics varied with time and place.

When I was working on productions of Shakespearean plays at Stratford, it was often the costumes for these "colourful characters" that presented a designer with the best opportunities to let loose and have some fun. It was essential, however, to learn the rules. For example, prostitutes wore a red dress, scarf, or hat depending on the town. In London or Bristol, they had to wear stripes. In Venice, they wore a yellow scarf; in Milan, a white cloak; and in Seville, green and yellow sleeves.

By the seventeenth century in Northern Europe, colour was removed from art and church interiors. Colour, previously so revered for containing God's spirit, become an evil thing. It did not suit the rising Protestantism and the Reformation. Martin Luther (1483–1546) and others believed that Catholicism had become decadent, extravagant, and corrupt. Popes seemed more interested in living the good life than the pious one. Colour in a church interior was like makeup on a face, superfluous decoration and, like art and any other elaborate trappings, decadent. Protestants felt sombre tones that would not excite the senses were more appropriate. And because the best colour was no colour at all, they began scraping, scratching, and scrubbing colour away from church interiors. If that didn't work, then plaster and whitewash would do the job. Washing away colour was washing away sin. (My neighbourhood church's cold white interior is a hangover from the Reformation that began in Europe at the beginning of the sixteenth century.)

For artists of the Protestant north, the Reformation's anti–colour, anti–frills attitude meant they had to look elsewhere for work. Rome remained an artistic hub, so many northern artists journeyed south and were as likely as Italians to pick up the pope's commissions. Another source of work came from a rapidly expanding middle class of merchants and businessmen, especially in the Netherlands. Domestic interiors became more important because a tax on servants meant that "the woman of the house" was responsible for its upkeep. The home became her domain and making it look good was a point of pride. In the Netherlands, interior walls were left white and decorated with mirrors, maps, and, much to artists' relief, paintings, lots and lots of paintings. The middle class wanted pictures of flowers – especially the luxury item, tulips – landscapes, their homes, their gardens, and portraits of themselves. Jan Vermeer (1632–1675), a painter not averse to beautiful colour, was one of the first artists to make women at home his subject, but Dutch taste was, for the most part, sober and conservative. Rather than being free to develop their own style, artists had to buy into this conservatism because many were, for the first time, painting on spec, hoping to find a buyer after the fact. Some artists had to supplement their income with day jobs as customs inspectors or inn keepers to make ends meet.

In Italy, artistic freedom was suddenly curtailed by a Catholic Church desperate to counter the spread of Protestantism south. The Council of Trent was set up in 1545 to define the rules of artistic acceptability. To make sure that art was effective as religious propaganda, the content of every piece had to be crystal clear. Angels had to be painted with wings, saints with halos. If the identity of a painting's subjects was not obvious, a label had to be added. (Michelangelo's Sistine Chapel ceiling started looking too licentious. It narrowly escaped erasure, and instead bits of drapery were painted over the private parts of his naked figures.)

Paolo Veronese (1528–1588) used ingenuity to defend the creative licence he took in his painting *The Last Supper*. When asked by the Inquisitors why he populated it with figures that were not mentioned in the Bible he answered, "To fill up space." When that didn't wash and he was ordered to get rid of them, he came up with a better idea. *The Last Supper* was renamed *Feast in the Home of Levi*, making it a rule–free secular piece.

The Catholic Church was not against colour. It contributed to the all–important dramatic effect they wanted from art. Colour was part of the splendour that could captivate the eye and stir the soul into an ecstatic spiritual state but if drama could be had without colour, then colour could go.

The stage was set for a young and artistic thug who arrived in Rome from Northern Italy in 1590 and developed a style that would doom colour. Both Protestants with their distaste for colour and Catholics with their love of drama approved of the high–contrast light and shadow style of Michelangelo Merisi, a.k.a. Caravaggio (1571–1610). He didn't invent *chiaroscuro* but his technique and timing were perfect. If Leonardo had seen the beauty and brilliance in shadow, Caravaggio went deeper into darkness itself. He reduced three–dimensional settings to a stage or a black room with light coming from a single angle above the picture's frame. The work gained the intensity of close–up. Caravaggio used high contrast to neutralize colour like an over–exposed photograph. Colour to Caravaggio was "the poison of tone."

Although Caravaggio's style was copied and his technique emulated, his own paintings were loathed by most of his contemporaries. It was not how he painted that bothered people, it was what he painted. Like most artists, he used prostitutes and peasants as models for his religious characters but his looked common and real. His saints looked too much like ordinary people with dirty fingernails. The results were vulgar rather than uplifting.

Caravaggio's low–life ways and belligerent nature did not improve his career opportunities. He was always on the run from the police. (He apparently killed a man over a disputed game score.) He was always angry about being unappreciated. Only a few loyal patrons, like Cardinal Francesco Maria del Monte in Rome, kept him going.

In spite of the distaste for Caravaggio's person and his paintings, his style spawned a school of chiaroscuro painters called *Tenebrists,* from *tenebrusto,* meaning dark and gloomy. For the next two hundred years, the ranks of gloomy painters grew and colour went into shadow, dimmed by a thick layer of bitumen varnish. Lesser artists copied the chiaroscuro style partly because it obviated the need for elaborate three–dimensional settings and all the colour challenges that went with them. A taste developed for "good art" to be drab art. As artist and connoisseur George Beaumont put it, "A good picture, like a good fiddle, should be brown."

It is not that brown, lowly as it is in the chromatic hierarchy, is a bad thing. Tenebrists de La Tour (1593–1652) in France and Rembrandt van Rijn (1606–1669) in Holland were among those who used it most and used it best. Sir Joshua Reynolds made small studies of Old Masters to see how tones were balanced. He estimated that in Rembrandt's *Night Watch,* the dark-to-light ratio of the painting was eight to one. Rembrandt applied his dark pigments so thickly that it was said that one of his paintings could be picked up off the floor "by its nose."

Earth pigments suited to dulled colour palettes were cheap and plentiful and didn't require a lot of work to use. For the shadowy depths, raw umber and burnt umber (not from the town of Umbria but from the Latin for shadow) were widely used. For the warm highlights to offset the deep shadows, there were several popular yellows. From the town of Sienna came raw sienna, an ochre hue, and burnt sienna, the same pigment roasted to an amber colour. The new bright yellow was Naples yellow. A deeper Indian yellow was hugely popular by the eighteenth century and a banned substance in the nineteenth. Indian yellow, also known as *puri,* was imported by Dutch traders in the form of hard, dirty-looking malodorous balls about three inches in diameter. No one was sure how it was made or of what until the mystery was solved in 1883. Indian yellow came from one small village near Bihar province, and was made from the dried urine of cows fed only on mango leaves. This diet left the cows dehydrated and in constant ill health. Once the truth was known, the practice was banned.

Another of the era's masters, Anthony van Dyck (1599–1641), used so much brown that one of his pigments, Cassel earth, an organic material made from peat or lignite, was later called van Dyck brown. A child prodigy, van Dyck studied under Rubens, then went to England to paint portraits. His style with its deep brown hues was so copied that it established the look of portraiture in Britain and France for the next hundred years.

To give his shadows greater depth, van Dyck used brown glazes. Some were tinted with blister, a tarry pigment from the soot of burnt beechwood or birchbark. He also used bitumen, a brown sludge–like substance left over from the distillation of crude oil. Although van Dyck and Rembrandt used bitumen well, many of the British artists who copied van Dyck did not. If used thickly, it is like a syrup that does not dry properly. Reynolds, an experimenter, used it liberally, and all the pigments he layered on top slowly wrinkled, and crinkled and cracked. A small Reynolds painting, *A Girl with a Baby* (1782) at the Dulwich Picture Gallery, just outside of London, has so deteriorated and so much pigment has flaked off that the image now looks vague, almost Impressionistic. Nearby Rembrandt's *Girl at a Window* (1645), a century and a half older, looks as though time has had no effect on the adroitly used hues.

In his early years, Rembrandt used up to twelve pigments in his paintings, including very expensive and vivid traditional ones like azurite, vermilion, and malachite green but over time he used them less and earth pigments more. In his painting *The Night Watch* (1642), he used eight pigments in just one layer. Later almost all of his pigments were earths. Was necessity the mother of his creation and the cause of this shift? Were these all he could afford? He had been the most sought after and successful Dutch painter of his time but his success and affluence declined steadily after 1640. Some think *The Night Watch*, a portrait of the military company of Captain Franz Banning, led to his difficulties. The brilliance of the painting was probably lost on those in Banning's company who paid for the commission but were depicted in profile, in shadow, or in both. When Rembrandt died almost thirty years later, he had lost his beloved wife, Saskia, his home, and his substantial art collection, and he was penniless with only his bed and paintbox to his name. He had been using less and less colour until his works were almost sepia and amber monochromes. I like to think it was not because he was poor and his eyesight failing but because, like someone whose eyes have adjusted to the dark, he could see more and more colour in less and less.

By 1650, Rembrandt's palette may have been reduced but not its complexity. Philip Ball in *Bright Earth,* a wonderfully in–depth book on the history of pigments, describes the dark wall in the background of *Portrait of Jacob Trip* as a dark brown under a layer made with red, orange, and yellow earths mixed up with bone black and a bit of lead white topped with a glaze of blue smalt, red ochre, and yellow lake. Where the shadow is deeper, another glaze of black, red lake, and red ochre is added. The result is a wall barely distinguishable from black. Rembrandt's complex colours had become, in Ball's words, "concoctions of truly Baroque proportions."

If ever I try to convince a client that brown is beautiful for their walls, I have to come up with euphemistic similes – "like a sepia print," "like the rich, dark chocolate," but "like a Rembrandt" tends to work best.

Sometimes brown's appearance was not anticipated. In the chromatic soup that made up a seventeenth– or eighteenth–century artist's complex hue, it took only one pigment turning brown over time to dull all the others. (Sometimes this was built into the process. Even two centuries later, van Gogh would use colours that were brighter than desired because he predicted they would dim with time. Little did he know how much duller some of his vivid sunflowers would become.) Greens often went brown. The natural world is abundant in greens but stingy with the green pigments. During the seventeenth and eighteenth centuries, artists had not a single bright green pigment. They mixed green from blue and yellow and sometimes black, but the results were never vivid. New yellows mixed with blue in order to make green turned many a painting to brown over time. It might be a very different experience to walk through gallery rooms full of landscape paintings of the sixteenth and seventeenth centuries and see them in their original colour intensities.

But at the time, because not all of their pigment colours were available in equal brilliance, artists mixed down strong hues to level the chromatic playing field. To mimic how colours look in nature, artists often eliminated strong colour and contrasts creating a flatter tonal range, orchestrating colour in a lower key. French landscape and seascape painter Claude Lorrain (1600–1682) was very keen to get nature's colour right. He would get up before the sun rose, get his pigments ready to mix, then rush out in the brief reddened light to observe and match colours. Then he rushed back to the studio to paint. This might have resulted in his doing brighter paintings than anyone else, except he knew he couldn't match literally. He had to adjust his colours, transpose them down to this lower key. He said that to look accurate, they must no longer look like themselves. Lorrain deleted what he called their "hardness." Here again an artist chose complexity, the slight dirtying of a colour with little bits of other colours, to create a muted hue that looks real.

Seventeenth-century artists painted colours not the way we see them up close but the way we remember them, softened by aerial perspective, muted as they recede into the distance and meld into generalized hues. We are biologically conditioned to play down background so that it doesn't distract us from focusing on specifics that are critical to notice, like predators and food. If you try to imagine any natural setting, no colours jump out and steal the focus. The colours are even. But if you picture objects up close – a bowl of ripe tomatoes or a blade of grass – they pop up in full and vivid colour. Close-ups retain their vivid colour in our perceptual memory. Flemish paintings depict flowers, birds, and fruit in all their colour brilliance, while landscapes and the backgrounds for portraits and still lifes were subdued.

In the sixteen and seventeen hundreds, colour brightness was not important. "Breaking" or "corrupting" colour was not an evil to be avoided, it was a common technical practice. Recipes for an artist's colour often recommended a mixture of up to five pigments. Previously, artists had organized colours along a scale from light colours to dark colours. By mixing, every colour could have its own dark to light scale. Colour designers call these tonal variations on a single colour *let downs.* We take them for granted when we look at displays of paint chips, but in the 1600s this was a new invention. It meant that most colours were now mixtures.

By necessity greens had been mixed but now even blues often had more than one pigment in them. Van Gogh thought he counted twenty–eight different colours in the black of one of Franz Hals's portraits. Some of Tintoretto's dark shadow colours are made with such a complex concoction of pigments that researchers believe they are the result of scraping up all the colours left on his palette to use them up. The wooden palette itself had shifted its role from being a transportation device to get pigment from the mixing table to a place within reach of the canvas, to being the surface upon which pigments were mixed.

> **We cannot import nature's brilliant colours directly into our home. We can't put green on the walls and blue on the ceiling, and mud brown on the floor and feel that all our colour decisions are over. We need the effect of aerial perspective, the muting down that puts expansive things like walls into the background. Like the difference between the colour of a blade of grass and a field of it, we need to do as these artists did, and translate colours into a lower key so they go from foreground into background when we go from a little chip to a large wall.**

For a few hundred years, artists' colour practices carried on unchanged, little knowing that, in 1666, Sir Isaac Newton (1643–1727), then a teenager with time on his hands, was doing experiments in his bedroom and discovering colour was not just pigment but light.

Newton, who was at Cambridge University in 1665, was sent home to the town of Woolsthorpe because the plague forced the university to close its doors. To pass the time he set about discovering things like binomial theorem, differential and integral calculus, the unification of celestial mechanics, the theory of gravity, and, as it turns out, the theory of colour in optics.

He also discovered that colour was not just pigment after he drilled a hole in his window shutter. He placed a prism where it could catch the beam of light coming through the hole throwing the colour spectrum, like a rainbow, onto his wall. This was nothing new. In those days everyone knew that prisms were amazing things that could take white (clear) light and magically put colour into it. Light went in colourless and came out like a rainbow.

Newton then took another prism, turned it upside down, and put it where it would catch the coloured light. This time the light going in was coloured and what came out was white. Most of us would have assumed that the amazing prism was at work again. It not only made colour appear, it made it disappear.

Newton was not so easily convinced. Would the same thing happen if the prism were dealing with only one colour? He got out a board, put a narrow slit in it, and placed it between the first prism and the second, adjusting it until the slit let only one colour – let's say yellow – through. Yellow hit the second prism. It went in coloured and it came out – coloured! The prism wasn't changing the white light into coloured light. It was bending light, fanning white light's contents out into the spectrum or bending the spectrum back into white light.

Glass is denser than air so when white light hit it, it was like a speeding car going from tarmac to gravel. The sudden drag pulled it off course. Light waves travelling at the same speed have different frequencies; the faster the frequency, the sharper the swerve upon impact. Blue, like the fastest car, swerves most sharply and ends up at the far end of the spectrum. Red swerves least and ends up at the other extreme. The other colours line up in order of frequency in between. (Frequency and not aesthetics is what keeps the colours of the spectrum locked in their strict order.) Newton had discovered that the prism was not magic. It didn't have the power to put colour into light. Colour was there already.

Newton also noticed that although red, the longest wavelength, was as physically different from violet, the shortest, as it was possible to be, they still looked alike. In 1710, he bent the spectrum's rainbow until its opposite ends touched. With this act, so simple and so brilliant, he formed a circle of uninterrupted colour. Colour would no longer be organized as a straight line from dark to light. Colour switched from a tonal scale to a spectral one. Black and white were banished, and colour's hierarchy that had favoured red and blue was dissolved into a democracy of equals. Colour was no longer matter – vermilion and lapis lazuli – it was an abstract optical phenomenon. Red, orange, yellow, green, blue, and violet were born.

Although the wheel of colour could be subdivided to infinity, Newton first divided the spectrum into eleven basic colours. Later he decided there were five. In 1706, he revised this to seven by adding orange and indigo. (I can see orange but indigo, which was a trendy colour in Newton's day, is a bit of a stretch.) Newton did this because both music and colour were kinds of vibrations so he wanted colour to fit the tidy rules of music. Colour was given the same number as there are notes in an octave.

But science and art had gone their separate ways by this time so Newton's discoveries had no ripple effect. Artists would not meet up with Newton's ideas for a hundred years but, now that they could make an infinite number of colours by mixing, they were confronting the issue not of how *many* colours they needed, but how *few*. What were the most essential, core, or primary colours?

Meanwhile in France by the end of the seventeenth century, colours in clothing were emerging from black's long shadow under the influence of Louis XIV, The Sun King. The French now outshone the Spanish as the official trend–setters of Europe. In Holland conservative taste preferred the old and sombre ways but the French could not resist the new fashion. Hues began appearing with names like "laughing monkey," "kiss–me–my–love," "wasted time," and "mortal sin." (They may sound amusing and hard to picture but what colour will future generations attribute to current paint colour names such as "Aged to Perfection," "Beautiful Promise," or "Heart's Desire," which are chestnut brown, pale blue, and vintage red?) French followers of fashion carried around little black velvet "beauty spots" for sticking onto their face. Black, as well as green, became popular lipstick colours. And grey and blue, which had previously been worn only by peasants, became popular when French royals realized that they did not look faded and weak if made up in silk or taffeta. They shone and looked like silver. Deep indigo blues, associated with the Virgin Mary, were always a favourite. The king had "patent" coats made for seventy–five of his "favourites" in blue with gold trim. They were used like a security pass. With these on, courtiers could follow him anywhere without special permission.

By the end of the eighteenth century, artists' colours started to brighten too and, as is always the case, the response was negative. To the modern eye, the palettes of eighteen–century painters Reynolds and Gainsborough seem very subdued. To their contemporaries, they were far too bright. By the early nineteenth century when British artist John Constable (1776–1837) was painting his large and, to my eye, subdued landscapes, his contemporaries found his colours garish. One critic referred to one of his landscapes dismissively as "that green thing." Little did anyone know that there loomed on the horizon a colour revolution that would unleash an infinite array of colours brighter than anyone could imagine. Intense hues were about to proliferate like weeds as soon as chemists realized that inventing a new colour was as profitable as winning a lottery. Science was about to cut colour's umbilical cord to nature. Where nature was stingy, science would be generous. Science would also begin to break down colour optics and discover its secret ways. In the meantime, compared to what Constable's peers were doing, his colours may have looked as bright as if one had taken off a pair of sunglasses. Compared to what was to follow, it was as if the sunglasses had just been put back on.

GREY, COLOUR'S GROUND ZERO

It was a fellow lover of red who taught me the value of grey. It was December, and I was nearing the deadline on my monthly design column for a national newspaper when Beverly called to say I should write about her apartment. In a previous piece I had commented that I loved red. Everything in her apartment was, she said, red. Perfect timing. I could acknowledge the holiday season but without focusing on seasonal decorating and bric–a–brac. I asked Beverly a few questions and concluded it was a go.

I booked my photographer and off we went. There was only one problem. When we arrived I noticed, much to my chagrin, that everything was not red. Oh, she had lots of lover–of–red things – red sofas, bathroom fixtures, telephones, kitchen backsplash – but the apartment was grey, pale grey! How was it she had said it was red? Then I realized that the grey was completely invisible to Beverly. Grey was the blank slate against which she could see and enjoy all her reds. Red was her foreground. Grey faded into the background. White walls do not do this. They are bright and assertive, and anyone who thinks that white is not a colour is wrong. White is loud. Grey is a very useful "not there" hue that neutralizes walls so we can focus on more important things.

Grey, often considered a dull or dirty white or faded black, is associated with pessimism, with ashes and sackcloth and giving up the sins of the flesh. Grey is viewed as functional and not fun. The brain, the seat of wisdom, may be our grey matter but things unclear or vague are grey areas.

In the history of colour, grey gets short shrift. In the seventeenth century, colour–hating Calvinists popularized *grisaille* (from the French word *gris*, for grey), a style of painting with black and white pigments. Grisaille had been used since medieval times because it was cheaper than using colour but also it was an effective faux painting technique for making flat surfaces look sculpted. Images on the exterior of altarpieces were done in grisaille so that they looked like they were made of stone. The contrast between the outside and the spectacularly coloured interior made the colours all the more awe–inspiring.

Grisaille stained–glass windows looked like intricate, lacy patterns or faux metalwork. In the Renaissance, painters used grisaille to lay out their compositions and plan their dark–light areas to avoid making costly colour mistakes.

The Dutch developed a penchant for all forms of colourless art – paintings in black and white, etchings, and pencil drawings, which, for the first time, were bought as finished pieces and not just roughs for future paintings. They used grisaille to cover walls and ceilings with fake 3–D sculptural effects. Jacob de Wit (1695–1754) was so adroit at painting these – his angels or putti seemed to burst out from the wall – that the grisaille technique itself was often called *witjes,* "whites," a pun on his name and the colour of these fake sculptures. By the eighteenth century, grisaille was popular across Europe for adding dimensionality to the walls and ceilings of neo–classical decorating schemes.

Grey is usually associated with things dull and drab. When the great man of letters James Boswell (1740–1795) wrote in his daily diaries that he was having a bad writing day because he was feeling dull, he was probably feeling grey, the emptiness of the blues without the bite of pain or the poetic potential of longing.

Grey is connected to depression because it is often a kind of absence, a lack. Grey days are dull because of the absence of the vitalizing sun. Too many grey days in succession can get dull and depressing but I don't envy those living in places where every day is a sunny day. Without the variety offered by a soft grey day, how can we appreciate sunshine?

When I went to see Jasper Johns (b. 1930): Gray, an exhibition of the artist's all–grey paintings done since the mid–1950s, at the Metropolitan Museum of Art in New York, I couldn't bear to stay for very long. Johns, like Japanese watercolourists, felt that colours talked to the eye; black, white, and grey talked to the mind. But for me, seeing only grey paintings in room after room was like being ill. It felt wrong. Getting back out to rooms full of colour was a relief.

Grey was the colour of World War II battleships, although Louis Mountbatten, the 1st Earl Mountbatten of Burma, had his flotilla painted Mountbatten pink, grey with a touch of red because he thought the lavender tint made for better camouflage. This was true only at sunrise and sunset so by 1944 it was no longer used.

A friend told me that when he was a boy in England in the 1950s grey was the "serviceable" shirt colour preferred by mothers who lacked washing machines, over the white ones worn by the sons of mothers who had them.

> Grey was the official colour of Confederate uniforms of the South in the American Civil War of the 1860s. But instead of being the consistent grey we might imagine, they were any colour of grey or brown, often dyed with a tree bark solution. They were not opposed to wearing a blue Union overcoat, preferably faded to light blue, if they could "acquire" one.

In politics, as in home decor, grey may not be good in the spotlight but it is a great background colour. *Éminence grise* is someone who discreetly wields power from behind the scenes. The original éminence grise was the French monk François Leclerc du Tremblay (1577–1638), a.k.a. Père Joseph, the confidant of and political agent for Cardinal Richelieu. The monk in grey was conveniently rendered as invisible as Beverly's walls by the cardinal robed in red.

With grey, as with most things in life, its flaw is also its feature, its weakness is its strength. Unlike white, a colour that can look good on its own, grey works only in the company of colours. Grey is the foil, not the solo act. Grey urban landscapes, institutional walls, corporate settings, miles of urban halls and rooms of grey paintings are debilitating because the grey is unrelieved by colour.

Unlike white, grey treats all colour with respect. White makes them strong and strident. Grey makes them beautiful. Grey is a hard worker, the silent partner, content to be background. However, there are good greys and there are bad greys. The bad ones are mixtures of black and white. The result is cold and dead, colourless. Good greys are the wonderful sludge greys you get when you mix colours together. This achromatic soup is, ironically, the most complete colour package possible, the most *complex.*

Nature loves complex greys, the colour of rocks, trees, and old wood. This grey is nature's white – an unbleached, unprocessed, colour-friendly neutral. Even the fluffiest white cloud is more blue and grey than white. In nature, what seems grey from our perspective is full of colour to an insect walking across the surface. A tree trunk would be like a pointillist painting in brown, tan, heather mauves, and verdigris, all adding up to our grey.

It always makes my blood boil when I am up in woodsy cottage country and I see that a cottager has dared to impose white on the deep greens, blues, and greys of the landscape. I don't care if it is the door of the boat house, the porch pickets, or the cottage itself, white in nature's lush settings looks as foreign and intrusive as a billboard. Cottages should blend with nature by dressing in the appropriate hues, the grey of bark. Save white for the beaches and terraces of urbanized tropical settings where silver sand and white buildings are the context.

Grey is colour's Mr. Fix–It. Those pretty little paint swatches that translate into wall colours that are too strong, too colourful, too clean – the green that looks like toothpaste or a yellow that makes you reach for your sunglasses – can be turned into a thing of beauty, not by adding white, but by adding complex grey to make them softer. Harsh colours are often too saturated and too full of one colour. Complex grey makes colours calm and easy to coordinate with other colours. Grey puts nature back into colour.

THE NINETEE

TH CENTURY

THE INVENTION OF COLOUR

THE NINETEENTH CENTURY

Before the nineteenth century, an artist was lucky to have two dozen pigments. A house painter would have fewer. By the end of the century, there were hundreds of colours. Today we have thousands. Are there too many colours?

If we had only a few dozen to choose from, picking from them would be easy. Too much choice is why my clients call for help. When I arrive, I'm carrying a kit that contains an inventory of almost two thousand off–the–rack hues. This might seem like too much of a good thing, like hundreds of ways to go wrong. But for me there can never be too many colours. In fact, within the colour repertoire of any paint company, I always feel there are missing notes. It is like playing a piano with a few keys not working. For example, a British company has about 120 colours, all of them good (which is not the case with big paint companies) but it is not enough to cover all contingencies. Yet I need their whites because of the way the light plays off their natural pigments. I must have their pale aqua because of its spa–like breath–of–blueness that isn't cold or their light blue because, unlike most light blues, it is not too blue or too childlike. It has a greyed, mature serenity. Another company has good whites but is missing some soft straw yellows. Another has those yellows but misses a few reds, like the dark purple maroon leather of old book covers or the red of Japanese maples. But even more of a problem than the missing hues is the missing tones. The colours jump from dark to light too quickly, leaving out mid–tone transitions that would so often be perfect. The best range of yellow–greens and tinted blacks comes from still another company. And so it goes. All are good; none is perfect.

Because I work with thousands of paint chips all the time I've become as familiar with them as a card shark with his favourite deck. The right colours seem to leap from the pack. There can never be too many – if anything there aren't enough.

I am not the only one who thinks having lots of colours is still not enough. Chandra Sanders, a Texas resident, filed a lawsuit against Apple because the 2007 twenty–inch aluminum iMacs are capable of displaying only 264,144 colours and not the millions it says in its advertisements. Only the larger models can display 16.7 million. (I want to know who's counting?)

At the beginning of the nineteenth century things still moved slowly in the world of colour. Nothing much had changed for a few centuries. In art academies, classes in drawing and composition were taught extensively. Pupils still studied and sketched statues from antiquity to learn about form. Colour was not taught at all. Aspiring artists were self–taught. They copied Old Masters or got into the studio of a professional painter for some mentoring.

House painters, like artists, were still grinding pigments on site from a limited range of ingredients, many of which were unstable. The oil in wall paint yellowed and the colours, often made with things like ground animal hooves and dried blood, didn't last. Milk paint chalked off or could be removed completely with water and vinegar. Walls were repainted every few years. Colour itself was a challenge. Colour matching was a thing of the future. Colour theory was still pretty much whatever Aristotle and Plato had said, cobbled together with Newton's findings into a rather confusing muddle. In the nineteenth century for the first time ever, science was learning what colour is and chemists were learning how to make it in such abundance that it would never again be a rare and precious thing.

What is colour? We have been on our colour journey for a long time so we should be able to answer that question by now. Write down your response and look at it again when you have finished the book.

By the end of the century, everyone could have colour and so fewer and fewer would want it. That a colour revolution was running parallel to the Industrial Revolution was made obvious when the two were united in what many at the time considered an offensive eyesore and now is the symbol of Paris. Eighteen thousand iron girders weighing ten thousand tons were put together under the skilful supervision of engineer Alexandre Gustave Eiffel (1832–1923) and installed like a huge iron quadruped on the Left Bank of the Seine to launch the 1889 International Exhibition of Paris. And as if that weren't shocking enough, the Eiffel Tower was then coated with sixty tons of orange–red paint. Author

Guy de Maupassant said he ate lunch in the tower's restaurant every day because it was the one place in all of Paris where he didn't have to look at the thing.

Around 1800 it was not a scientist but a poet and playwright, Johann Wolfgang von Goethe (1749–1832), who challenged Sir Isaac Newton's work on colour. Newton had discovered that colour was not just pigment but light at a time when scientific discoveries were considered beyond the layman's understanding. Newton was a superstar to scientists but his theories held no direct relevance for artists. Goethe bridged the gap.

Goethe knew there was something wrong with Newton's ideas. Newton said that mixing coloured light together as the prism did makes "white" light but it was clear and that mixing all material colours together made white. But anyone who has ever had a paintbox knows doing so makes muddy grey. Newton and Goethe both understood that light and pigment were parts of one phenomenon, colour, but neither could understand the difference between coloured light and coloured materials. Newton called light "apparent" colour and pigment "material" colour but he considered both to be matter of different kinds. Neither understood that coloured light has a different set of primary or *primitive* colours. Pigment primaries are red, yellow, and blue. Light's are red (long wavelength), green (medium wavelength), and blue (long wavelength). Newton kept changing his mind about how many primaries light had until he landed on seven. Goethe had some odd–ball notion that blue and yellow were the foundation of colour and if these two were *augmented,* they made red. (Hmmmm, remember, he was not a scientist.)

Fifty years later German physicist Hermann Ludwig Ferdinand von Helmholtz (1821–1894) worked out that light and pigment had very different colour systems. Mixing coloured light is an *additive* process; mixing pigment is *subtractive.* Adding two colours of light doesn't reduce light but changes its colour to the average of the two wavelengths. Red (640 nanometres) and green (530 nanometres) mix to yellow (585 nanometres). The amount of light is not reduced so it is *additive*. Mixing pigments together reduces light because it produces a colour that absorbs all the wavelengths of light absorbed by each. When mixed, red and green pigments make mud grey, or the chromatic equivalent of no colour, because together they absorb the wavelengths of all colours. Because the amount of light wavelengths reflected is therefore decreased, light is subtracted and the system is called *subtractive*.

Goethe organized the colour in six hues rather than Newton's seven. His symmetrical colour wheel could now be divided down the middle into polar opposites: *plus* colours – red, orange, and yellow – and *minus* colours – green, blue, and violet. The former he classified as warm, masculine, vibrant, active, positive, and light. The other group were cool, feminine, weak, sad, and the colours of shadows and darkness. Decades before colour psychology came into being, Goethe was attributing psychological and physiological traits like emotion and temperature to colour.

Warm–cool was a new way of thinking about colour. Even though it is a psychological attribute, it has a physiological effect. Research has shown that the temperature of a red room is experienced as three degrees warmer than the same room painted light blue.

Goethe's belief that colour was subjective was at odds with Newton's notion that colour "is a deed done by light of certain wavelengths hitting the eye." In *Theory of Colour* Goethe tries to prove that colour is a subjective experience, the individual response triggered by that light. A hundred years later, science proved them both right – and both wrong. Colour wasn't *either–or*. It was *first–second*. Our colour experience begins as Newton speculated. Light of certain wavelengths hits the eye. But it does not become colour until, like Goethe said, that light stimulation activates the brain. The brain gives meaning to light's information and part of that meaning is colour. Colour begins in Newton's passive realm, which is physics. Then it enters Goethe's active realm, biology.

Goethe advocated relying on the eye rather than theory to understand colour's behaviour. He paid attention to afterimages or *simultaneous contrast*. Charles Darwin's father, Robert Waring Darwin, studied this a few decades later but Goethe figured it out by ogling a woman in a tavern. If we stare at one colour for any length of time, our eyes get tired, and if we look away we see a ghost or afterimage of what we were looking at but in its complementary colour. Goethe was staring at a woman in a red bodice leaning against a white wall. When she moved away, he saw the teal–coloured afterimage of the red bodice on the wall where she had been standing. (One might wonder what he had been drinking to keep his eyes on the wall and not the woman.) This afterimage is why today teal green is worn in operating rooms. It camouflages the afterimage of what surgeons have been looking at when they look up from the operating table.

Afterimages led Goethe to thinking about complementary colours. If we stare at one colour and end up seeing its opposite colour, then there are specific colour pairings in our colour vision. These pairs he called *competing colours* but we call them complementary. Looking at his colour wheel, the three primary colours, red, yellow, and blue, separated by three mixed or secondary colours, orange, green, and purple, put his competing colours diagonally across from each other. (Everyone ignores the fact that, on the colour wheel, green is opposite red and taken as its complementary but in our afterimage it is really a teal, green's neighbour. Colour will just never play along with the rules.) These diametrically opposed pairs contain all colour because together they contain all three primaries. Green is red's complement and is made up of the other two primaries, yellow and blue. Orange is blue's complement and is made of red and yellow.

Black and white were exiled from the colour wheel. How did they fit into the system? Goethe argued that they didn't. Shadows were not dark neutrals but full of colour, the complementary colour of the object. If the colour of light hitting an object was warm, yellow or orange, then the shadow would be violet or blue. In the course of the nineteenth century, Impressionist artists learned about coloured shadows and complementaries through the paintings of two Goethe converts, Joseph Mallord William Turner (1775–1851) and Eugene Delacroix (1798–1851).

By 1856, chemists and not nature became the big colour–makers. Chemistry had previously been viewed as an impractical waste of time. Now it was becoming the best way to make millions. In *Mauve: How One Man Invented a Colour That Changed the World,* Simon Garfield covers in great detail how William Henry Perkins (1838–1907), an eighteen–year–old doing scientific experiments in his parents' backyard shed, started the colour revolution.

Perkins was a student at London's Royal College of Chemistry when his teacher, August Wilhelm von Hofmann, suggested that he try to make synthetic quinine as a school assignment. Quinine was the only known cure for malaria and in many parts of the world, including England, malaria (also called ague) was running rampant. The drug was available but far too expensive for common use.

Perkins set about trying to make synthetic quinine out of coal tar, a plentiful by–product of the coal industry. Instead of solving the riddle of synthetic quinine, Perkins's experiments only made a dark and seemingly useless sludge. Being a curious teenager and a bit of an amateur artist, rather than pitching it, he started messing about with it. It had a nice purple tint. He picked up a piece of silk and swished it in the liquid. It took on a very attractive mauve hue. This would not have been of much interest to more senior and serious chemists. Chemistry had no connection with frivolous things like colour. But you cannot be an artist and not marvel at the beauty of a remarkable colour no matter where or how you find it. This mauve was too beautiful for Perkins to ignore.

Perkins sent his sample of mauve silk to a dyer, Robert Pullar, in Scotland. The dyer loved the colour and said that the ladies would love it too, *if* it could be made stable and affordable. It was neither.

Even though he had no experience in the dye trade, no capital to invest, nowhere to make the dye, no way to make it colour-fast on most fabrics, and no guarantee that fabric dyers would use it, Perkins was not deterred.

Perkins convinced his father to put all his money into his dye manufacturing scheme. He talked his brother into giving up a career as an architect to help out. Meanwhile, he started looking for a place to build a factory and spent eighteen-hour days designing the implements needed to make his dye. He commuted to Scotland to offer tech support to the dyers. The breakthrough came when he discovered that tannin was the mordant needed to make his colour adhere to most fabrics, including cotton, a big seller at the time.

According to Garfield, two timely events secured Perkins's colour fortunes and launched the colour's success. In England, Queen Victoria wore mauve to her daughter's wedding. In France, Emperor Napoleon II encouraged his attractive wife, Empress Eugenie, to wear heavy silks made in Lyon as a way of promoting French textiles. And the colour she, the most influential fashion maven in the world, wanted was mauve, the colour that matched her eyes.

The profitability of colour was not harmed by the fashion for large skirts. In 1859, they reached their largest circumference ever. Hundreds of yards of dyed materials were needed for skirts, underskirts, and all the trimmings draped over large steel birdcages. (While Perkins was inventing mauve, Sheffield was producing the wire for half a million crinolines a week.) When the crinoline was replaced by a smaller horsehair bustle, skirts still required lots of fabric because overskirts, swagged panels, ruffles, trains, and visible petticoats kept fabric quantities up. In

1863, four years after Prince Albert's death, his widow, Queen Victoria, eased her way from black to mauve for the colour of her mourning clothes. By 1860, the mauve trend took off and the twenty-two-year-old William Henry Perkins made his fortune.

Royalty and the rich and famous are the traditional leaders of style but in the nineteenth century their influence was more widespread than ever. Advances in printing methods made popular coloured lithographs, fashion plates, and ladies' magazines possible. And improved transportation systems disseminated them. Fashion and decor ideas crossed countries and continents.

After Perkins's success, every chemist hoped to invent the colour that would be the next big trend. Chemists in different countries raced to take out patents ahead of competitors. While patent offices were trying to decide who made a colour first and whether some colours were too similar to warrant individual patents, another chemist might try to beat out both contenders and sneak his colour into the front of the queue. Even Professor von Hofman got on board. He discovered that aniline, a colourless oily liquid, was the basic chemical from which any colour could be built. By 1868 mauve was on the way out as the passion for a new colour called *fushine* and a deep pink called *magenta* grew.

Artists were as delighted as middle-class fashionistas by the new colour possibilities. For the first time ever, science was giving them a strong orange, a clean violet, and vivid greens – nice to have if you were a landscape artist. From time to time, an artist might complain that an artificial colour, ultramarine blue, for example, did not have quite that magic something that the real thing had but it was hard not to like when it was so much cheaper. Wealthy patrons willing to pay an artist's colour tab were largely a thing of the past so if the aniline blue was between two hundred and two thousand times cheaper than the real thing, the choice was not hard to make.

As artists gained new colours, they lost control of their pigments. So–called *colour men,* often chemists by trade, sold artists pre–made colours. Some colour men doctored the colours with fillers and extenders, often at the expense of longevity. Pre–Raphaelite artist Holman Hunt was not alone when he complained that he lost eight months of his life repainting a work in which one of his colours had gone off. Artists like van Gogh occasionally ground their own pigment but more often they couldn't resist the hundreds of never–seen–before, ready–to–use hues.

Not just the paint but the packaging made life easier. Oil paint could be bought off the shelf in newly invented and very convenient zinc tubes. The still extant company Windsor (chemist) and Newton (artist) invented small "cakes" of water–soluble colour. Watercolours could be organized into easily portable trays set in metal boxes with a slot for brushes. The days of wrapping up pricey bits of carefully processed pigment in little pouches made of pigs' bladder tied with twine were over. No more need to prick the skin, squeeze out a bit of pigment, and hope the paint would congeal enough to seal up the pouch. It was so easy to throw a paintbox together and go outside that landscape painting became a popular hobby, a creative getaway from big, crowded, industrialized cities. Due to urban sprawl and pollution, natural settings became newly appreciated and romanticized. Nature was no longer a wilderness but a spiritual place and an artist's ideal subject. Even Queen Victoria was among the artists and amateurs who flocked to the fields.

At this time entomologists were trying to classify all flora and fauna. Colour was part of their categorizing, so they had to devise methods and terminologies to help record it accurately. Geologist Abraham Gottlieb Werner (1755–1817) prepared elaborate colour charts to be used by naturalists on field trips to assist them in describing a colour. A Scottish miniaturist, Patrick Syme, edited Werner's charts into a book that was used by Charles Darwin (1809–1882) when he journeyed out aboard the *Beagle* from 1831 to 1836. It helped him peg the colours of everything from cuttlefish tentacles to butterfly wings.

Painters were not the only ones capturing the beauty of nature. In 1826, a Frenchman by the name of Joseph Nicéphore Niépce (1765–1833) took one of the first photographs. It took eight hours to develop the photograph, making a camera more suitable for shooting stationary objects – trees, rocks, and buildings – than people but the new technology had some artists worried. Pictures did not have to be made by hand, they could be taken by a camera. Reality could be reproduced in all its detail; everything, that is, except its colour.

Picture–taking technology kept improving, making it easier and faster. By 1888, George Eastman had invented camera film to replace fragile and cumbersome glass plates. By 1900, his company, Eastman Kodak, whose motto was "You push the button, we do the rest," was making cameras cheap enough (a dollar), and compact and simple enough that anyone could take pictures. To attract young people, he called them Box Brownies after storybook elves and brownies created by Canadian author and illustrator, Palmer Cox (1840–1924). Within the first year 100,000 were sold. The six–shot roll for fifteen cents could be sent back to be developed. It would take another forty–one years to add colour.

But recording reality and the minutiae of daily life had never been the sole goal of artists. In fact, photography liberated them from it. Artists were now free to concentrate on the evocative nuances and emotion beneath the surface. They could also turn their eye to the present, the here and now, and capture the moment, in situ, with greater speed and freedom than ever before and in bolder colour. By the end of the century, for the first time since the medieval era, artists like Gauguin and Matisse valued colour as much for its power to make harmoniously arranged patterns or evoke feelings as for accurate mimicking of reality.

In the nineteenth century colour became available to a growing middle class which had begun to take great pride in their homes. They got new ideas by travelling (the Grand Tour of Europe was popular) and reading magazines. They could afford to buy consumer goods like paint and wallpaper and mass–produced furnishing and they started the first major decorating boom. Improved transportation systems delivered goods and tradesmen to even remote communities in Europe and abroad. British military men, out of work after the Napoleonic Wars, became the builders and craftsmen of North America. In the West, a proliferation of British publications provided how–to's for every aspect of domestic and public life, which meant British taste showed up in the design of everything from civic buildings to houses to the garden privy.

American landscape designer Andrew Jackson Downing (Central Park in New York City was his idea) studied British tastes in domestic architecture and wrote the *Encyclopaedia of Cottage, Farm and Villa Architecture and Furniture.* This bible of tasteful style and colour was published in 1833 and was reprinted constantly until the end of the century. Downing advocated rejecting the neo–classical era's taste for whites and pastels in favour of a more natural palette: the colours of stone, earth, bark, wood. He objected to green on buildings because it was the colour of soft, pliable leaves and not the colour of structural materials. It was inappropriate for an exterior colour. On this he was overruled. Dark green was the favourite colour for shutters because, when *closed,* they still gave the look of a window reflecting greenery. (I would say that today those greens can look old–fashioned or out–of–fashion and Downing's muted structural colours seem timelessly appropriate.)

As more synthetic pigments were developed, Downing's muddy shades gave way to richer tertiary colours. In an effort to encourage consumers to use the newly developed hues, paint companies started printing and distributing colour cards. The elaborately detailed exteriors of three-storey frame houses of the period demanded a lot of paint. Little swatches never have been enough to elicit colour confidence, so paint companies also printed out coloured lithographs of houses showing elaborate colour schemes using as many as eight colours – one for each storey, another for window sashes, others for trim. This may not have been as helpful as being able to put a picture of your house into a computer program to play with how it looks in different colours, but it certainly helped map out new possibilities.

Today, San Francisco's Painted Ladies, large frame houses from the same period, still show how all the decorative elements, verandas and turrets and pilasters and pediments, invite chromatic variety. So do the homes in Tampa, Florida's Hyde Park neighbourhood. When I drove around it in a car full of exterior colour designers, we all marvelled at the variety of colour, the sophistication of the combinations, and the restrained use of white. James Martin, from Denver, Colorado, whose company, The Color People, does exteriors across the continent, kept commenting on the way creamy trim colours tinted to blend with the main house colours were soooooo beautiful. He loved the way the off-whites and creams hold shadows better than white and show off the form of the moulding or architectural trim components. Columns, for instance, look and feel round in cream but are just one-dimensional in white.

According to Martin the key to color in a room or on the exterior of a house is in balancing the contrast. The trim color

> should modulate body color not fight it. "I hate white because it is hard, sharp, and cold. Using a softer off–white not only blends better with the body color but it allows the two colors to team up to create a mood instead of just one color, bam, and another color, bam."

Baseboards were often painted black to hide dirt and trim was a deeper colour than the walls. (We really should do this more often. White trim plays into our obsession with keeping rooms light on their feet, but white trim often looks stark. Deepening the tone is calmly elegant, darkening it is handsome.)

From 1714 to 1830 during the Georgian period (covering the reigns of George I, II, III, and IV) colour schemes went from dark colour – burgundy, sage green, or blue–grey – to paler pinks, greys, greens, and Wedgwood blue. Often a room and everything in it – walls, trims, windows, and doors – was done in one colour. The ceiling and floor were all that was different. I have seen an apricot red dining room done this way and it looks so stunningly beautiful that I am now brave enough to suggest it myself when it seems appropriate and I think I can pry a client from the grip of white trim.

By mid–century, the Gothic Revival in architecture was making rich and deep colours and dark wood finishes fashionable again because they were associated with the medieval period. William Morris, one of the leaders of the Arts and Crafts movement, designed and produced wallpapers with elaborate floral patterns reminiscent of medieval textiles. By the end of the century, wallpaper had become such a craze that it was not unusual to paper every room except the kitchen and every surface except the floors. Unlike colour schemes today, it was usually the deepest colour from the wallpaper that was used for the trim, mouldings, cornices, and doors.

Victorians loved faux finishes. Inexpensive wood was painted to look like more expensive panelling or marble. Walls were stencilled and stippled. The only no–no was white.

New mass–produced colours were not without their problems. An emerald green, Scheele's green, a copper arsenate, was poisonous. This was not a huge problem when artists were using it in small amounts. On walls it was a different story. Because it was cheap to make, it was used for house paint or for the very fashionable flocked wallpapers. When it got damp or the surface was brushed against, the green pigments decomposed and released a highly poisonous arsenic gas (arsenic trihydride). In England, the green walls were responsible for children dying in their newly decorated bedrooms. In the 1860s, its use was banned. Historical records indicate that Napoleon died from stomach cancer but the green walls of his residence when he was exiled in Elba may have contributed to his demise. Popular lore has it that in 1900 when Oscar Wilde lay dying in his green room at a cheap Paris hotel, now the chic "L'Hotel," his last words were "Either that wallpaper goes or I do." The paper is still green.

MAUVE, THE ELUSIVE HUE

"Janice, what does it tell you about me that I am craving pale mauve?" asked Sarah. I answered slightly facetiously, "You are complex or what is going on in your life is. You are artistic. Probably a bit of an oddball or an outsider. Why do you ask?"

Sarah said she was itching to part with some of her wall–to–wall creamy neutrals. She wanted a mauve living room. The challenge was to make it subtle. I wasn't surprised that she was having difficulty. As a collector of art and a journalist on the subject, she was savvy enough to know that hitting the right note was tricky. For me the hardest hue to get perfect after white is mauve. This is why I love the challenge of trying.

Mauve is light purple, the royal colour. The most famous purple was called Tyrian purple because it was made in Tyre, the city on the Mediterranean that was the Phoenician centre for dyeing as early as 1500 BC. For centuries, Phoenicians kept their recipe for this richly coloured and incredibly durable dye a secret.

The colour-making process for purple was long, tedious, and so complex that when the colour fell out of favour and the secret technique had faded from memory by the ninth century AD, it took until the early twentieth century to figure it out again. Vast quantities of the small *Murex* mollusc had to be caught. Each little shell had to be opened up and a tiny bit of clear liquid extracted from a gland near the head. This precious liquid was colourless. It had to be exposed to sunlight and carefully monitored as it changed from yellow to green to mauve and finally the reddish colour Phoenicians turned into dye. (Purple back then was a colour we might classify as red.) Because 250,000 molluscs were needed to make one ounce of the dye, it was as valuable as gold. The most precious cloth was double-dyed, once in a bright tint from the *Murex* molluscs and again in a darker tint from the *Purpura* molluscs. Silk dyed Tyrian purple shimmered with a dark-light lustre that was considered the most perfect colour of all because it captured the full range of dark to light values. Purple was so prized in Imperial Rome that only the emperor wore it. Dignitaries and war heroes might earn a band of it. Wearing purple without permission was an act of treason punishable by death. Purple has never lost its association with things regal, luxurious, and noble.

In the mid-nineteenth century, William Perkins discovered how to make synthetic light purple and gave it the old French name for mallow or rose-of-Sharon, mauve. I am not a mauve person but the colour fascinates me. At the International Association of Color Consultants (IACC) course in San Diego, I had a chance to see how mauve felt. We were analyzing the psychological effect of different colours. Each was projected on a film screen for several minutes. When the overhead lights came back on, we wrote down our response. Mauve went up on the screen and my first response was – oh, what a beautiful colour. It was as ethereal as blue but somehow more complicated. Was it warm or cool? Was it young or old? Happy or sad? It was confusing. It started to seem indecisive, almost schizophrenic. By the end of the time I spent looking at it, it had become incredibly unsettling.

When the group started comparing notes, everyone experienced this ambivalence toward the colour. Each person then went beyond indecision and took a side. It would seem we are either for or against mauve but we never keep waffling.

It is no wonder mauves have always been favoured by poets and romantics. Some attribute to mauve an otherworldly, spiritual aura. It is associated with introversion, decadence, but also awareness at a higher level.

Sarah told me she associated mauve with egress, escape. She observed that mauve is always on the horizon, always elusive. When you try to approach it, it keeps moving farther away. And when you go toward it, it disappears. The spot where the mauve was has become brown or blue or anything but mauve. Mauve has moved on. I have discovered that between the Canadian fall and the winter is a time when the landscape seems all grey and tan but if you really pay attention, mauves appear in the leafless shrubs and the dried grasses. Blink and they can disappear. Mauve, or violet, is the bridge between visible and invisible. It is the last colour we see at the shortwave end of the spectrum, the marker between visible blue and invisible ultraviolet.

Mauve makes its most spectacular appearances in the fleeting transitions between light and darkness. I was on a shuttle bus crossing an airline terminal very early one morning when I would normally have been asleep. The banal landscape was barren and colourless – grey tarmac, the concrete and glass buildings, equipment and planes. But as the sun crested over the horizon, it cast a mauve wash over the setting. Every surface was infused with the most exquisite colour imaginable. (Monet thought that if you had to pick one colour for the air, the atmosphere, the ether, it was mauve. This would surely have been the one he was imagining.) I watched through fatigued eyes as my headphones oozed some ambient electronica into my brain. Airports are always an out–of–time and –place limbo but the mauve wash and my soundscape made it hallucinogenically beautiful.

Unfortunately, it disappeared as quickly as it arrived. Within moments, the carriage was a pumpkin; the bus returned from nirvana back to the airport. By the time we reached the terminal, had I mentioned what I had seen to anyone else on the bus, they probably would have wondered what I was talking about.

For many months I had more than two dozen mauve colour chips stuck up on the whiteboard near my desk. I was trying to find a mauve that, as in nature, would be so subtle you wouldn't know it was there unless you were paying attention. I wanted to use this soft hue as a tinted white on the trim and balcony railings of houses being built in the Bahamas. I wanted it to be so subtle you would think it was grey–white, a porcelain colour except at certain times of day. It would be so much more interesting than white but, if I didn't get it dead right, it would be dead wrong.

I would glance over and watch what happened to the colours posted there as the light in my studio changed and moved. I especially liked looking at what happens to these mauves in the late afternoon when the lowering sun hits them full force.

Claude Monet, like all Impressionist painters, embraced synthetic colours. They were new, easy, and affordable but he believed that there was no ready–made, out–of–the–tube mauve that was subtle enough. He made up his own with complex pigment mixtures because they looked more ethereal and atmospheric.

As I studied my mauves, I discovered an interesting thing. The breath–of–mauve paint chips that looked colourless at first, with time grew more colourful, gradually becoming too colourful. I put up new samples with less and less mauve in them. Finally I hit the target and found the subtle hue that sits on the cusp between colour and no colour, the mauve at the edge of a shadow.

Anyone who asks for a mauve room is rarely asking if a mauve room would be a good idea. If they want one, they *want* one. It is more a passionate decision than a decorating concept and it is unwise to dissuade them. When a client *needs* mauve, my challenge is to hit the target bang on. If mauve is too clean, it will seem too juvenile, playful or silly. If it is too dusty, it will seem old and dreary. Get it right and it has a sophisticated beauty and refinement I associate with the sort of room Marie Antoinette would have loved – a porcelain fragility and sublime elegance. When I pull out the paint chips, I am not surprised when the client says the colour I am showing isn't mauve but grey. I have to help them bring mauve into focus. I show them a true grey and hold the mauve against it. Out comes the reclusive hue. Gradually it can look too mauve even to my client. We shift to increasingly subtler versions. No other colour behaves quite this way.

At a colour conference a while ago my up–and–coming "trend" colour was what I called *Shadow*. It was one of those not–mauves tested on my board. When my workshop group wanted to put it in with the other mauves and purples as a colour, I insisted they move it over into the neutral grouping. My mauve had finally taken the tiny shift that pushed it over from colour into achromatism – there but not there, at least not unless you were really looking for it.

WHAT COLOUR HAS TO DO WITH DINNER

COLOUR VISION

No one understood colour vision until the mid-nineteenth century. No one even knew it existed until the end of the eighteenth when British chemist John Dalton (1766–1844), known for the Atomic Theory of Matter, discovered his own. He bought his mother a pair of stockings. When he asked her how she liked her birthday present, the blue stockings, her response was: "Blue?" The condition came to be called *Daltonism*.

My first colour-blind client's response to colours came as a nasty surprise. He looked at the colours I was recommending. He asked me to tell him what colour each colour was. This was difficult. How do you describe green to someone who can't see green? I tried relating colours to objects. "It is a cream that is almost banana colour." Or "It's the same brown–red as the pattern in the centre of your carpet." But my apples were his oranges. I was like a person who speaks Greek talking to some-one who speaks Swahili and thinking they would understand better if I just said everything a few more times and at a louder volume. To compare a colour chip to his carpet did not help us see things the same way. None the less, he paused and he pondered. Then he shook his head. "No." Excuse me? is what my expression said. "No, I don't think that one will work. And this one, I'm not sure. I would have to think about it."

His wife was sitting beside him and did not rush to my assistance by telling him how great the colours looked if only he had the faculties with which to see them. He had the visual problem, yet he was telling me what worked and what didn't! Hey, Daddy–o, I am the one who studied colour, pays constant attention to colour, works all the time with colour, and is gearing the entire colour selection to your darn furniture and art collection! It was beyond frustrating. I wonder if I would have found it a challenge and not such an effrontery if he had asked me to select colour by *value,* lightness, and darkness and not hue. That was something we had in common. Better yet, why not just trust me? Why should his wife and children and all his guests be subjected to *his* version of what worked? In my theatre designing days, I might have said, "Okay. Have it your way but take my name off the programme."

Along came my second colour–blind client and, lo and behold, his response was the same! He asked to see some yellows. "That's not yellow," he said, as I pulled out a soft butter yellow called Hay. "That's beige. I want yellow." I tried another deeper yellow. "That's not yellow. It has too much green in it," he informed me, as if he were dealing with a colour–challenged moron. I pulled out a bright primary–school yellow, what I would call a migraine yellow. "There," he said. "Now that's yellow." This time I found the situation less frustrating. I now knew that a colour–blind person's colours are as real to them as yours and mine are to us. When it came to colour–blind clients, my challenge was to meet their colour needs without sending their spouses or friends running for chromatic cover.

About 8 per cent of Caucasian men and 4 per cent of black males are classified as colour–blind. Women are less prone to colour–blindness (only one in one hundred are colour–blind) because most colour–blindness is in red–green genes, which are situated on the X chromosome. Men have one X chromosome while women have two, doubling their chances of getting it right. Occasionally the yellow–blue gene is the problem. It would be more accurate to call colour–blind people colour–different.

We take it for granted that the world is full of colour and what we see is what is real. If our pets or clients don't see what we see, they are colour incorrect or colour–blind. If colour abilities were reversed and virtually everyone confused reds and greens or yellows and blues, then we would think that this was normal and anything else was a colour flaw. Daniel Dennett in *Consciousness Explained* points out that if we saw red and green as "gred" then we would have no way of understanding what a person seeing red and green independently was on about. Not even if they said: sage, moss, khaki, banana, the colour of your carpet. In fact, does anyone know what anyone else is really seeing? And if we are told that what we see as orange is dozens of colours to certain birds, might we not want to see what we are missing? More is always better, isn't it?

Or conversely do we need colour at all? Today so many colours are arbitrarily applied to so many objects – cars, walls, clothes – it holds no meaning. Maybe colour vision itself is merely a nice extra. Living without it might be like when I watched black and white television as a kid. I didn't think I was missing anything vital. Our first colour television was exciting but colour seemed like just a wonderful bonus. In the modern world, colour can seem wonderful but non–essential. It wasn't so in our past.

Our ability to see colour evolved entirely out of need. We do not see all the colours there are, not by a long shot. We see only the ones that were useful. There was nothing frivolous or decorative about it. To see what wasn't useful would be like a car manufacturer putting a spectroscope, a colour detector, on the dashboard of a car. It would measure and calibrate the colours we were driving toward. But this would be stupid. It would take up precious dashboard room and distract us from what is essential to the act of driving. Nature is even more stringent than car designers and manufacturers.

If, to survive, we ate live critters rather than fruit hanging quiet and still in foliage, we would all have become colour–blind dichromates dividing colour into warm and cool, long– and short–wave lengths, and detecting objects by movement, shape, and tonal contrasts. But looking for fruit in a dappled and leafy landscape meant we had to spot it at a distance and amid a lot of visual complexity. Movement detection was useless for the task. Light–dark contrasts were too ubiquitous to use as a way to sort the fruit from the leaves. And shape was camouflaged unless we were standing up close to a fruit–laden tree. We needed to develop a more complex colour vision so we could use colour to make fruit jump out from its context. The colours we evolved to see were the colours of what we wanted to eat.

It is hard to think of nature's beautiful colours as merely functional. When our children were little, we took them on a family holiday to Italy. One sunny day, we visited the ruins of an ancient aqueduct in an open field. Tiny daisies and not the aqueduct captured our daughter's attention. As she gathered her bouquet, she tried to pick only the daisies with pink tips on their petals. To her these were the prettiest. Surely such pretty colour had been put on earth for the delight of mankind by a benevolent God. For hundreds of years, this had been the thinking. From time to time over the centuries, an observant monk might suggest that perhaps colour served a more practical and, dare he say, reproductive purpose.

For such observations, the monk would have been severely reprimanded.

The concept was put forward again in the seventeenth century by Swedish naturalist Carl Linnaeus (1707–1778). He was the son of a clergyman but was always more inclined to botany than the Bible. Because he was a keen observer of nature and an inferior student of theology, his teachers suggested he study medicine. Plants were, at that time, the source of medicinal remedies and so he did. He became obsessed with organizing every kind of plant into categories according to their physical and reproductive characteristics. Colour was part of his categorizing. This was the first comprehensive classification system. His copious writings and charismatic teaching helped convince theologians, among others, that there was more to colour than meets the eye.

In the next century Christian Konrad Sprengel (1750–1816), a rector and teacher at a secondary school in Germany, picked up the ball. He determined that flowers were reproductive organs and that their colours had nothing to do with our delight and everything to do with the birds and the bees. There was not a single colour, he noted, that did not in some way contribute to plant reproduction. In 1793, he laid out the observations of a lifetime in *The Secret of Nature Revealed in the Structure and Fertilization of Flowers*. He explained that the lovely ring of yellow around the corollary opening of a blue forget–me–not was a strategic device. The coloured pattern acted as a signpost directing pollinating insects to nectar. Colour's usefulness was, he thought, "one of the most admirable and wondrous institutions of Nature." Others disagreed. The scientific proof to back up Sprengel's theories would not be available for decades, and his reward for a lifetime of study and observation was prompt and mandatory early retirement – his magnum opus was shelved. Another half–century went by before Charles Darwin popularized the concept and the dust was brushed off Sprengel's ideas.

So how could the pink tips on my daughter's daisies be functional? Why were most daisies white and only some pink tipped? We noticed that as a daisy died, it pulled its petals up over itself and the underside of the petals were entirely pink. The daisy head became a small pink ball.

Insects do not see colour the way we do. Bees, for example, are colour–blind at the red end of the spectrum. Pink flowers would be hard for them to see. Older pink flowers would become inconspicuous, letting young white pollen–filled blooms catch the attention of pollinators. The daisies that looked white and less interesting to us would look much more colourful to a bee. What Caroline and I, and poor old Sprengel, couldn't see was the amazing ultraviolet patterns on the white petals, patterns as obvious to the bees as lights on a runway to a pilot, directing bees straight to the pollen.

By the mid–nineteenth century, Charles Darwin had convinced the world that plant or animal colours had a specific survival advantage. Colours in nature are used for contrast or camouflage, for hiding, warning, mating, or eating. Little by little, plant and animal life co–evolve to suit each other. And in this life there are things that it is advantageous to see and eyes that need to be equipped to do the seeing.

Colour is a mutually beneficial relationship that evolves between the thing seen and the thing seeing. Colour is not as consistent as shape, texture, or mass. Light stimulus received from the outside world is processed by the animal's nervous system. Because every species has a different internal processing system, each animal translates information from the outside world differently, including colour.

It is incorrect to think that what we see is reality and what other animals (or colour–blind clients) see is wrong or less accurate. Species select what is relevant to them, and one of the most relevant colour drivers, as it turns out, is dinner: what you eat and what eats you.

By our standards most animals are colour–blind. Your dog doesn't know what colour his ball is and relies on movement and scent to retrieve it. Your cat hasn't a clue about the colour of the sofa she curls up on. And what we call full–colour vision is only our notion of full colour. We are colour–challenged compared to a pigeon. With the exception of birds, insects, fish, and some primates, most animals have monochromatic vision.

Dichromats, like your dog or cat, can see the difference between blues and greens but everything else is differentiated by lightness and darkness. Dichromats see well even in very dark lighting conditions.

Our colour is based on a three–colour processing system like colour printing or colour photography. We share our trichromatic vision with old world monkeys and apes. Birds descended from the dinosaurs and have more complex colour vision with a broader spectrum and are able to distinguish more colours within it. They would think we were all colour–blind. Squirrels, fish, and insects see colour but their colours are not the same as ours.

Bees see in a different range, one that stops before red but extends beyond blue into their specialty, ultraviolet. Green, yellow, and orange are a single colour. An owl's nocturnal vision extends in the opposite direction. They can't see ultraviolet or blues but they do see beyond red into infrared. We can't *see* infrared but we feel it as heat. Seeing infrared helps the owl track prey, such as a mouse running along the ground, as it flies through the night.

Surface–dwelling fish, turtles, and insects all have good colour vision, which includes ultraviolet so they can spot certain plants. Fish that live close to the surface of water have better colour vision than those down in the depths where there is little light. If they tend to swim up and down, they have both systems and shift back and forth like we do, but quicker.

Birds take the colour–vision prize. They are tetrachromats and see with four–, sometimes five–colour vision. We cannot begin to know what that looks like. Where we have one cone for reds and oranges, pigeons have three. Orange is one of their specialties. It is not that they see orange better than we do but that they see other colour categories within orange. Just as a bee sees our green, yellow, and orange as a single colour, we see a bird's many colours as one. Orange is enough for us.

Pigeons' eyes have two foveae, one focuses out front for slow-moving and close things like looking for worms, and another for peripheral vision used in flight to see fast-moving and distant things. They switch back and forth for optimum function like we would change gears in a car.

The reason monkeys, humans, and birds see such a profusion of colours compared to other mammals is because we eat fruit. Eating fruit, vegetables, and nuts requires a much more sophisticated set of colour skills than eating meat or grass. Birds' colour vision is best because they have been eating fruit the longest. We became fructivores only about 30 million years ago when tropical trees started producing big orange and yellow fruit. The fruit was too large for birds but arboreal monkeys started to gorge on it. This suited the trees. Monkeys distributed the seeds by spitting them out whole or, even better, defecating them in one piece along with a nice bit of fertilizer.

Fructivores use colour analysis, not just to seek fruit, but to determine how ripe it is or how long it will take to become ripe. They need to be skilled at calculating the day, week, or month so they can be the first ones there to do the picking. Every year it irritates me to discover that the birds are more experienced at this than I am. I watch clusters of cherries grow and ripen on our cherry tree. Then, because the birds seem to know ripeness to the minute, they eat them all. I think myself lucky if they miss one (my husband suggests that it isn't superior colour vision that gives them the competitive advantage but that I am not spending enough time in cherry trees).

We might wonder how red got to be such an important colour. It looks glorious when the fall leaves change, but in tropical climates where we evolved no one was out picking apples. As it happens, there is a time between growing seasons called the gap, a time when old crops are finished and the new ones are not ready. In Africa or South America before any fruit ripens, there are tender new leaves that are easy to digest and their colour is red. By the time the fruit is ripe, these leaves turn green and are too tough and fibrous to digest. Greenness indicated the leaves were past their best–before date, so recognizing the red leaves became important to survival. Fruit follows this green code in reverse. Green means tough, so unripe fruit stays camouflaged until it is soft, sweet, and juicy.

Carnivores are nocturnal. Finding meat at night doesn't require colour. Movement is the key, and tigers are six times better at seeing it than we are. They can spot the tiniest movement at a very long distance with very little light. To bring home the bacon, a carnivore tracks movement, sound, and smell. Shape, size, and texture are more informative than colour because all meat is red. Meat that isn't red isn't fresh. Smell, not colour, will let you know. Even we trichromats hold the baloney up to our noses to find out if it has been in the fridge too long.

Herbivores don't need colour vision either because they eat grass and grass gets tall and then gets stiff. It doesn't get ripe.

Plants and animals use colour camouflage for protection or colour contrast to attract attention. It might seem like a few green stripes or spots would be a good camouflage for an animal that stalks its prey in the tall grass, but there are no green herbivores or carnivores. When both prey and predator are colour–blind, it is pattern and texture that provide camouflage. The orange, black, and white striped tiger feels totally invisible as it creeps across the green jungle floor toward the "inconspicuous" zebra.

Colour is not just a food detector. Plumage colour is a quick way for birds to identify their own species. Medieval soldiers adopted the use of bold colours on their heraldry to avoid killing their own.

Colour also signals sexual maturity, sexual ripeness. A mature animal uses colour as a big draw when attracting and

impressing the opposite sex. The more colourful the body parts, the more likely they are to beat out rivals. The male peacock fans open his tail of iridescent feathers. We often try to compensate for our lack of colour by painting or dyeing our bodies. We clothe it or touch it up with cosmetics and apply tattoos imitating more colourful creatures. But even the brightest scarlet applied to nails and lips seems feeble when compared to the bright red calluses on the female baboon's rump. And what do we have that can compare with the male mandrill's red, blue, and violet genitalia or the old world monkey's blue scrotum surrounded by yellow fur?

Birds that look dull, like sparrows, might appear in glorious, ultraviolet technicolor to their sparrow suitors. They use some of the ultraviolet colouring in their plumage the way we use a blush, to signal attraction.

To us, the females of many bird species are un–*attractive*. And that is the point if you happen to lay eggs and stay in the same spot for a long time "like a sitting duck." If your predators don't see ultraviolet, then it makes sense to be covered in a stunningly attractive pattern only appreciated by UV–sighted creatures like your mate and keep a low profile to anything else. Those dull feathers that blend into dead leaves and twigs hold a beauty we will never know. Conversely, if a predator happened to be closing in on your hiding place, having a mate with dazzling colours attractive to predators makes sense.

Some animals change colour to blend in with different settings. An octopus or a squid can change colour to suit the setting by pushing coloured pigment out of little flattened sacs controlled by tiny muscles in the walls of their skin. Each cell has its own muscle. In the blink of an eye, colour flows into little clear cell pockets. Chameleons change more slowly. They sense the colour of the surroundings and send that message out so that colour pigment moves into their cells. A rabbit only changes colour seasonally.

Some animals don't need to change colour because their colour is a built–in camouflage. Penguins look very visible when they waddle about on white snow with their tuxedo colouring, but that is because to escape predators, they don't run, they swim. They stay close to water. If a land predator comes along, they jump in. Their black back matches the water when a predator looks down. Their white fronts look like ice floes to underwater predators looking up.

Colours can trick or scare predators. When threatened, many moths and butterflies fan out a set of forewings marked with a colourful pattern that can be mistaken for a huge pair of eyes. The fooled predator believes the creature they belonged to would be too big to fit into its mouth. In case this strategy doesn't work, the backup plan is a second "set of eyes" on the rear wings that can be flapped open and closed as if the eyes of a larger creature were blinking. While the attacker is confused, the moth or butterfly takes the opportunity to escape.

Colour vision is a customized colour arrangement specifically geared to what a species eats or what eats them. Roses are not red and violets are not blue for all. The only place that our unique colours exist is in our head. Out there is light, electromagnetic energy of different frequencies. Surfaces of objects are absorbing and reflecting them. Eyes are receptors that take the useful parts of the signal, the small range of wavelengths is edited and translated by our brains into our unique experience of colour.

This is not a new idea. Darwin wrote that colour was a neurological response to external stimulation. Galileo, in 1623, said that colour was in the brain and not the object, and if you took away all living creatures, colour in the world would be annihilated (there's a cheerful thought).

Sceptics might argue that because we can measure the wavelength of the light reflected off an object, and that measurement tells us what colour is reflected, then colour is a fact that exists out there. We can absolutely say that 450 nanometres is 450 nanometres no matter who or what is looking at it. It is 450 nm even if no one is looking at it. And 450 nm makes blue. Yes. But to think it is blue to all creatures is very anthropocentric. That same wavelength becomes different according to the visual set–up of the eye and brain and central nervous system of what is looking at it and the algorithm it applies to the information. To us, a dog's information package which has little colour but many more smells and sounds, would be information clutter that would interfere with our ability to cope. Different species extract different information, including colour. And so do individuals. And all those wavelengths of around 580 nanometres that I saw as gorgeous yellows were just so many boring beiges or greens to my colour–blind client.

We are all colour experts with nature's colour coding. It is new colours, arbitrary colours, paint colours that are difficult. It is hard to go to a paint store to pick a colour that matches something that we didn't bring with us. The bedspread perhaps? Our memory bank might know apples and oranges but it does not have a bedspread category. We haven't experienced the bedspread over time and in varied circumstances. Our colour calculations are not exact because, like the song in the *Sound of Music* says, "How can you catch a moonbeam in a jar?" How can you catch a zillion light waves from a given scene and fix them by colour and position? Our calculations are accurate enough to handle survival in nature but were never meant for matching your bedspread without the bedspread in hand. And how do we think we can translate a one–inch tomato red paint chip into a tomato red room if we don't have a stored memory bank of tomato red rooms? That wasn't the sort of calibration needed for survival in our evolutionary past. We should not be hard on ourselves or feel foolish when a colour catches us by surprise.

Colour choice is complicated by the fact that our eyes are trained according to nature's rules and hues but so many colours now are synthetic, unhooked from nature physically and functionally. Our brain still assumes every colour is logical, helpful, and communicative but look up from the page. How many colours around you hold meaning? Why is your pencil yellow, your mug blue, your chair green, or your stereo black and your ceiling white? It has been said that from the minute we give a baby a string of big coloured beads or a multicoloured toy, we are starting to take the real meaning out of colour. Arbitrary colour frustrates our ingrained responses. It lies to us. It talks but doesn't make a point. Like those who heard the boy who called wolf, we start to ignore it.

In our past it may not have been essential that we know rubies are red and emeralds are green. Colour vision came with a few non–essential bonuses. Now it seems that most colour is non–essential frill. We can enjoy the beauty of the sunset without caring what it is telling us about time and weather conditions. It is difficult to fathom how each of the millions of nuances of hue we see was at one time a necessity, geared to our survival. All those colours and not one just for decoration. Thank goodness we eat fruit.

PINK, NOT JUST FOR GIRLS

An architect sent me to his client to "sort out her interior." He had designed some exterior detailing but he stayed away from the inside, where every room was pink and so were most of her things. I asked her if she was happy with the colour. She was a general practitioner who lived on her own and she said she found it soothing to come home to at the end of a long day. I asked if she felt the need of a change. She said she didn't. Instead of trying to shift her from pink to please the architect, I concentrated on editing out some of the frilly bric–a–brac that was making it cloying and suggested she add more intensity to the pink in areas like her dressing room.

Shortly afterwards I was in another pink house and my client felt the same way. Rather than going with less pink, she got excited by the idea of more pinks and stronger pinks. Her husband, she assured me, would be fine with it. Pink was more interesting than white as the background for her large floral paintings and the myriad of bold upholstery patterns and textures she enjoyed.

Pink is not light red, just as grey is not really light black. Colours that have their own names have their own effect. Red excites our appetite but pink makes us crave sugar. Red arouses but pink calms.

Pink was originally yellow. "Pink" referred to a process rather than a colour. It meant the binding of an organic colourant, usually from berries, to an inorganic powder – usually chalk, alum, or baked ground eggshell – to make it into a useable pigment. Until the end of the eighteenth century, pinks were green, brown, or pink but the most popular pinks were yellow.

In the eighteenth century, Limoges, the French china company, came out with a new glaze colour in dusty rose and called it Pompadour Pink in honour of Madame Pompadour, mistress of Louis XV. She was one of the first female arbiters of taste and one of their best customers. (In winter she had the gardens of Versailles planted with porcelain flowers.) Besides influencing the king's running of the country, she influenced the look of its interiors, and from then on pink was pink. Well, not always.

In England pink was also red, the red wool used to make fox hunting jackets. Pink refers to the cloth and "pinks" are the jackets.

I used this convoluted history as the rationale for calling my company Pink and making my logo a red dot. We make automatic associations to things frilly and feminine when we hear the word pink – not my style. We assume pink means pink, a light version of red. In fact, "pink" does not have to mean a colour at all. It is also a rather quaint expression meaning "something good" as in "I am feeling in the pink" or "She is in the pink of health." So if my work is about getting people to be more open–minded about colour, and if, in the English language, there are only a few colour terms, most of which are "taken," too loaded with symbolic meaning and associations, then PINK, which doesn't have to mean pink, seemed like a peachy idea.

In the nineteenth century, pink fell out of fashion as an interior colour. Heavier colours and lots of greens ruled the day. In the 1930s, a passion for pink resurfaced when fashion designer Elsa Schiaparelli came out with evening gowns in her signature colour, a deep bluish pink verging on magenta still known as Shocking Pink. In Miami's South Beach area, pastel pink became part of the late art deco palette for holiday homes and hotels. Pink exteriors can look ridiculous in places far removed from the equator but look good where there is sun and sand and sea, where the sunsets are huge, and pink echoes the palette of shells and coral.

In the 1950s when women entered the workforce in large numbers and gained purchasing power, pink became more popular than ever. Besides a plethora of pink angora sweaters and the pink prom dresses that still abound in vintage clothing stores, there were pink food blenders, pink hairdryers, and pink Princess phones. In bathrooms, pink vied with turquoise as the hot colour for tiles and fixtures. (Survivors are starting to look vintage and quirky rather than just awful.) Even cars were pink. The faded colours of 1950s family happy–snaps and home movies made with the popular 8mm cameras where the reds have faded most of all means those times are associated with a palette of cyan blue, yellow–green, and pink.

During the 60s Sweet Sixteen pastel pinks shared the spotlight with unisex, psychedelic magenta pinks before pink was relegated to a Barbie Doll colour for little girls and dismissed as too feminine to be of interest to half the human race.

Magenta is the bridge between red and pink. An artist–house–painter, David, was painting a huge baronial home but he and his clients were stalemated over the colour for the two–storey entrance hall. Above the wood–panelled lower section they had tested red – too dark; yellow – too frisky; and all manner of greens – not a good blend with the warm wood. Blue would not give a warm welcome. I thought I was being rather original when I suggested magenta, strong enough to echo red but light enough to look less predictably traditional – like red with a playful twist. The next week I saw images of a nineteenth–century dining room in a British castle and there was "my pink" (so much for the novelty of my idea). The colour looked grand; not fluffy, not feminine – just good.

Pink is flattering to most skin tones. It is nurturing and pleasant to live with but men are often ambivalent toward it because of its feminine association. In my experience, many men like pink and don't at all object to their wives choosing it. I have had boys want it for their room or an accent wall, and it is their mothers who dissuade them from the "odd" idea. Some mothers would do well to suggest it to their energetic sons since it is known to be calming.

Many prisons in the United States have cells painted with a bubble–gum pink called Baker–Miller to calm aggressive inmates. Weightlifters cannot do as many bench presses in a pink room as in a red one. The University of Iowa painted the locker room used by visiting teams pink to give their teams the advantage. In 1999, prisons in Arizona expanded pink from walls to bars, bedding, underwear, and slippers as a way of humiliating prisoners. Maricopa County Jail has found that the pilfering and selling of prison–issue, logo–sporting underwear, an underground fashion item, has been reduced now they are pink. A preponderance of pink has also reduced the number of repeat offenders!

Before World War II pink was for boys because it was considered to be red's baby brother and more masculine than light blue. Light blue was the girlie hue because it was daintier, prettier, and associated with innocence and purity. In Germany in the 1930s the two colours did a gender reversal, and so the Nazis forced the wearing of pink triangles on homosexuals and sex offenders.

In the fickle world of colour, wearing pink has a flip side. Thailand was awash in pink when the world's longest–serving monarch, the popular King Bhumibol Adulyadej celebrated his eightieth birthday. A few weeks earlier, he had come out of hospital sporting a pink blazer and T–shirt. Royal astrologers said it was an auspicious colour for anyone born in the year of the rabbit and pink might bring him better health. To show their love, followers of the popular monarch bought up over forty thousand pink shirts and wore the colour in his honour. Royal guards wore spectacular pink busbies and military outfits, giving a new spin to the notion that there is nothing like a man in a uniform – even if it's pink.

In Britain, Moss Brothers, a retailer of men's clothing on Oxford Street, London, says pink is the fastest–growing colour in shirt sales. In America, pink has a split personality: the colour of male humiliation in penal institutes is also the epitome of male conservatism if the pink is a Brooks Brothers oxford cloth shirt. Perhaps it keeps businessmen calm under the collar in a high–powered corporate world.

WHY ROSES ARE RED AND VIOLETS ARE BLUE

COLOUR CONSTANCY AND IMPRESSIONISM

By the late nineteenth century, painters had colours bold enough to attempt painting not just an object but the effects of light on that object. Because light moves and changes quickly, Claude Monet (1840–1926) worked on a dozen paintings at a time of the same cathedral or hay stack just to keep up with the way it changed. Painting styles became looser and more spontaneous than before. To many, it looked rough and incomplete and, by way of an insult, it was called Impressionism.

We believe that a colour is a colour is a colour and that objects are the same colour all the time. Yet clients often ask me why it is that a colour they used in one setting looks so different when they use it in a new one. The reason is light.

Colour and light can still be an infuriating combination, as Geraldine found out when she asked me to help her choose an exterior colour for her pink Georgian–style house. Geraldine wanted something elegant and classic. We picked out a few candidates from the historical section of a paint company's palette including a grey–beige, putty colour. We walked around the house analyzing the colour in the north light and the south, the east and the west, in the shadow and the sun. I suggested she do a lighter tone on the front, the north side, and a darker version of it on the back. She was a little surprised that her house would not be one colour.

I explained that the two colours would look more like one colour than one colour would because the light was so different in each direction. Also lighter tones make an object appear bigger, and darker ones do the reverse. Lighter at the front would make the house look bigger, give it more street presence. Darker at the back would reduce the bulk and leave the focus on the garden. The sides would be darker still so they did not draw attention. (This was a bit like Leonardo da Vinci's *sfumato* colour strategy.) Using more than one tone is never noticed if the change occurs at a corner. Flat planes set at angles to each other are never the same tone if one is getting the light and the other is in shadow. If painted differently, our brain assumes, incorrectly, that the change of tone is just a change of light.

As it turned out, Geraldine's house required more than one change. The garden side needed to be greener to blend into the foliage, and the front, less green to suit the neighbouring homes.

We chose a few variations on her putty colour to be tested so she could watch what happened as the light changed with the time of day and the weather. After a few days, she called in a panic. The putty colour looked greenish when she tested it on the front of the house. The problem was easily solved. "Just keep painting," I said. The colour looked green because she was seeing it against pink.

Every colour casts some of its complementary colour onto its neighbours, a phenomenon called simultaneous contrast. This was the phenomenon that Impressionist painters loved. It meant they could add strength to their colours if they put complementary colours side by side – patches of yellow and orange sunlight bouncing off blue water.

Pink's complementary colour is light green. The pink of the house was throwing greenish–ness onto Geraldine's test patch. Geraldine wanted less colour and she wanted "her" colour. Its changeability was annoying and difficult. Colour is not constant. It is always part of a relationship. It changes with light and context. With the pink gone, the putty looked right again. And with only the greens of the landscape around the house for comparison, that putty would seem completely void of greenness.

By the time the painting was finished, Geraldine had three colours on her house and a fourth on the pool changing hut. To her, like most people, using different colours seemed like an odd idea. But if light kept making the same colour look different, why not use different colours to make them look the same? Colour is not just the colour we know it is but the colour it looks. If you asked an Impressionist painter to tell you the colour of Geraldine's house, they would ask if you meant the colour here or there or the way it looks now or ten minutes ago. They knew colour and light were a challenging changing combination. And embracing that challenge led to an outpouring of the most colourful paintings the Western world had ever seen.

Part of the appeal of Impressionist paintings was that they seem to be done so freely and colourfully with an in–the–moment directness that is easy to love. You don't have to know your Bible. You don't have to remember the who's who of mythology or understand an iota of symbolism to enjoy brightly coloured sunsets, flowers, sailboats, bathers, dancers, and friends doing whatever they were doing – lunching out, drinking absinthe, going to horse races, hanging with ballerinas, or getting out of the bath. The brushwork was quick and the colours often straight from the tube, unmixed: all part of the rush to capture the life and light in its colourful present tense. Impressionists painted what they saw as they were seeing it with a vibrant intensity that we enjoy today, no homework necessary.

The irony is that what looks so vital and informal was the result of artists trying to achieve something rather scientific in idiosyncratic ways. They were tackling fluctuating optical colour. They were not only painting what they were seeing, the object, but also how they were seeing it, colour perception.

This was the back end of the nineteenth century. Scientists were making lots of new colours – of the twenty pigments most commonly used by Impressionist painters, twelve were new synthetics. They were also discovering how we perceive colour. Artists wondered if scientists, colour authorities, had insights that no art school or academy was going to teach them. Impressionists' homework became the writings of scientists, chemists, and colour theorists. This was their reading list.

Theory of Colours (1810) by Johann Wolfgang von Goethe (1749–1832) reached the Impressionists largely via the artist Eugene Delacroix and scientific genius Hermann von Helmholtz, who thought the book represented a new and important way of thinking about colour. Goethe was a writer and poet who said, "I am the only person in this century who has the right insight into colour." (Goethe, who took over fifty-seven years to complete his poem-drama *Faust,* thought *Theory of Colours* the most important work of his entire life even though the scientific community thought it was just a lot of pseudo–scientific rubbish and his peers thought the book an act of eccentricity.) *Theory of Colours,* a work that sowed the seeds of colour as a subjective phenomena, explored complementary colours and observed that shadows were full of colour.

On the Laws of Simultaneous Contrast of Colour (1839) by the French chemist Michel Eugene Chevreul (1786–1889) was written as a guide for paint and dye manufacturers but artists were its most avid readers.

Chevreul had been made director of the Gobelins dye works in Paris in 1824. The company made fine carpets and tapestries but the colours were dull. In trying to find out why, Chevreul discovered the problem was not the dyes; the colours were actually bright and clear. They looked dull only because of how they were juxtaposed when woven. Colour, he noticed, was not a constant. It was an active ingredient that changed with the company it kept. Chevreul realized, as Aristotle, Leonardo, and Goethe had before, that colour is an optical interpretation. Colour placement could make or break colour's intensity.

Juxtaposing complementary colours made each colour brighter, more luminous. Juxtaposing analogous colour dulled or "contaminated" each. Chevreul called this the law of simultaneous contrast. This theory had a huge impact on how the Impressionists laid out their colours. To get light's brightness, they put colour opposites next to each other to create a brighter buzz.

But there was a catch. The complementary colours that look so vibrant close up get mixed optically at a certain distance and neutralize, or grey each other, especially if the colours are applied as small dots rather than larger daubs. This did not occur to the twenty–five–year–old Seurat as he painted *Un dimanche après–midi à l'île de la Grande Jatte* (1884–86). He thought that, according to Chevreul, tiny dots of complementary colour side by side should make his colours luminous. Working in his small studio at arm's length from his huge canvas, he must have thought it the most splendidly colourful work ever produced. Today, if you stand at the far end of the room where it hangs in the Art Institute of Chicago, the colours soften and blend into a misty haze, the opposite of his intended effect. Nonetheless, twenty–five years later, Chevreul's book, revised, translated, and renamed *On Colours and Their Application in the Industrial Arts,* was the most widely read colour manual of the nineteenth century. It stayed on the top of the Impressionists' must–read list for thirty years.

It took ten years for Hermann von Helmholtz to complete the most definitive nineteenth–century text on vision, *The Manual of Psychological Optics* (1867). This was because he was to nineteenth–century science what Leonardo da Vinci was to the Renaissance: an all–rounder who seemed able to do anything and succeed at everything. This German physician, physicist, mathematician, and scientist made contributions in hydrodynamics, electrodynamics, and meteorological physics, while grasping the physiology of acoustics and figuring out how vowel sounds are made. Artists liked the fact that, unlike Chevreul, Helmholtz referred to specific pigments.

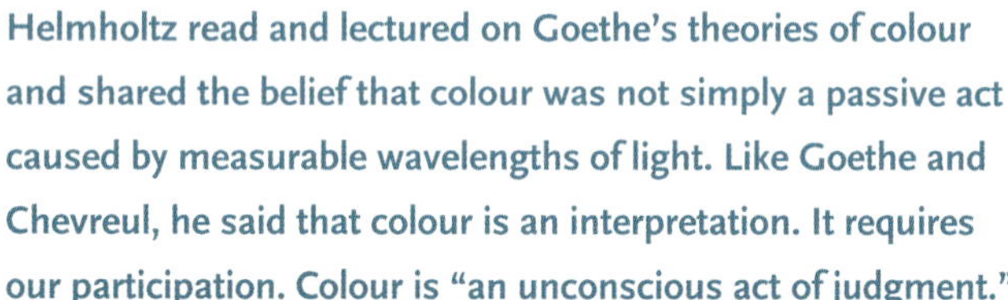

Helmholtz read and lectured on Goethe's theories of colour and shared the belief that colour was not simply a passive act caused by measurable wavelengths of light. Like Goethe and Chevreul, he said that colour is an interpretation. It requires our participation. Colour is "an unconscious act of judgment."

Helmholtz solved a colour riddle that had confounded everyone from Newton to Goethe: that light was an additive system and pigments were subtractive. Also, because he was researching sound and colour at the same time, he wondered if sound's three qualities – timbre, pitch, and volume – had colour equivalents. Applying the rules of music to colour hadn't always worked but Helmholtz was onto something. Colour's timbre was hue. Its pitch was value (darkness and lightness), and its volume was brightness or saturation. Colour was a three–dimensional phenomenon that could not be mapped out on a two–dimensional wheel.

Helmholtz also realized that while the ear can differentiate the various sounds that make up one complex sound, the eye cannot discover what colours make up a mixed colour. Colour is received as a single sensation with its components merged.

Helmholtz, like Chevreul and Goethe, saw that a colour's brightness was affected by its neighbours. Because of simultaneous contrast and after–image effects, neighbouring colours could intensify each other. He advised artists to heighten colour contrasts by juxtaposing complementaries to capture nature's vivid colours more effectively than any single pigment could do. It would bring light's dazzle to the canvas. Impressionists jumped on the idea.

Impressionists read *Grammaire de l'art decoratif* (1879) by Charles Blanc (1813–1882) a politician, art critic, editor, and a professor at the Ecole des Beaux Arts when Seurat was a student. Blanc thought of colour as a necessary evil, feminine, wild, primitive and to be kept in check or "like Adam to Eve, art would fall to temptation." Blanc believed that drawing was hard and colour easy if artists studied how science had worked it all out, or looked to Delacroix and his use of colour for practical applications. Even though Blanc's *Grammaire de l'art decoratif* was largely a regurgitation of Chevreul's ideas with examples drawn from Delacroix, it was studied by Gaugin, Seurat, and van Gogh. It is still on the shelf in Cézanne's studio.

Modern Chromatics with Application to Art and Industry (1879) by Nicholas Ogden Rood (1831–1902), an American physicist, theorist, and amateur artist, tried to apply physiological optics to colour to take away the guesswork and organize it into a precise system. He combined information from Helmholtz and mathematical wizard James Clark Maxwell with lots of tedious experimentation. Impressionists, especially Seurat, were fans of the book but Rood, being an amateur artist with more traditional leanings, hated all their paintings.

Impressionists also studied how French Romantic painter Eugene Delacroix (1798–1863) took up Goethe's colour ideas, especially coloured shadows. He was using loose brush strokes and unmixed colour to paint the transformative effect of light on colour half a century before the Impressionists. He complained that his peer, Ingres, did not know the difference between colour, which included light and its reflections, and colouring, the inherent colour of objects. Ingres, he said, painted things the colour they were, whereas he himself painted them the way they looked. In Delacroix's opinion, this total disregard for the reflections and effects of ambient lighting left Ingres' work looking crude and his objects isolated in their setting. Like ambient light that would later give Monet's work its colour *enveloppe,* light was, for Delacroix, what unified a scene. Impressionists read copies of Delacroix's journals.

After Delacroix's death, Degas bought several colour palettes that the older artist had painted onto long, thin strips of canvas. They showed how Delacroix organized his pigment choices before starting a painting. Sometimes there were as many as fifty–six hues, laid out from dark to light in complex sequences that intrigued Degas, although he found them hard to understand and harder still to apply to his own work.

Their scientific homework did not provide easy answers to Impressionist painters' colour queries. The information was hard to grasp and harder to apply and resulted in almost as many styles as there were artists.

Degas read widely, did colour experiments of his own, and kept a colour journal that included chemical colour "recipes" and colour descriptions. He also painted colour combinations that caught his interest into the journal.

Impressionists followed Chevreul's and Helmholtz's advice about juxtaposing complementary colours to make them vibrant. Straight–from–the–tube colours were applied in daubs to be mixed optically to make them as luminous as possible. The brilliance of juxtaposed colours, however, depends on how big the colour areas are and from what distance they are viewed. And so the pointillist canvasses of Seurat and, for a time, Pissaro and Signac lost their colour brilliance and became muted at a longer viewing distance. Pissaro and Signac gave up the pointillist technique because it seemed too confining. Monet and Gauguin never liked what Gauguin referred to as "a pile up of little dots." Van Gogh and Monet used the energy of the brush stroke to add to the optical intensity. Van Gogh varied his brush stroke size, direction, and rhythm to evoke the sensation of light, heat, the shifting breeze. His entire canvas seems full of energy and movement.

By the end of the 1880s, science and art were awkwardly aligned. By the beginning of the twentieth century, it was time for a separation, perhaps even a divorce. But for the few decades in between, painters' efforts produced brilliantly coloured and widely diverse results. Gauguin, Cezanne, Seurat, and van Gogh became categorized as Post–Impressionists, each one leaving behind any preoccupation with the fleeting colours of light to focus on colour's expressive, spiritual, or enduring qualities.

Van Gogh's letters to his brother, Theo, indicate a deep understanding of difficult colour concepts. Seurat was obsessive, read everything, and became convinced that technique was the most important part of painting. His nerdy attempts at what he called Chromo–luminarisme, what we call pointillism, didn't achieve his scientific colour goals but led to fascinating failures.

Gauguin was more of a DIY kind of guy. He read Blanc's *Grammaire* and chatted colour theory with van Gogh until they had their falling–out in Arles, but he was more interested in leaving science and civilization itself behind. He was inspired by a combination of spiritual and primitive influences he found in Brittany and the South Pacific. His colour interests became increasingly Expressionistic: his grass would be red and tree trunks purple if it felt right.

Paul Cézanne (1839–1906), unlike most Impressionists, wanted to create art that was solid and durable "like the art of museums." But this was not something to be done, as in the past, by taking studies done in nature back to the studio for working up into a painting. Memory deleted too much colour, evened it out, and generalized it. He needed to look intently at a scene, dividing up and painting it as small colour patches, like big pixels or a colour mosaic. He was not painting the colours in a scene moment to moment but inch by inch. His blue sky would be full of daubs of many variations of blue. The road meandering through the landscape would be many patches of orange and tawny colours. "Light," he claimed, "does not exist for the painter."

Colour Constancy

To paint the fluctuating optical colours caused by light, Impressionist painters did not realize that to do so they were struggling against *colour constancy,* the brain's habit of trying to delete them.

We see that lighting changes the colour of things but we hold on to the idea that the colour of every object is fixed, locked, and "real." Roses are red and violets are blue. This was made clear to me one chilly grey summer day when I was tucked up inside an old log cottage with family and friends. A few determined little outboards motored by the front of the small island as we settled into our rainy–day activities. Out came the Scrabble board, cards, books. My daughter laid out her paint set and brushes, a jam jar full of water, and a small canvas. She decided to paint a landscape, the view at the front of the cottage. But it was cold outside so she sat at the dining table and painted from memory. With blues and whites she made her big sky. With blues and whites she laid in the lake below. In between she added a slice of rocky shore in grey with a few pine trees in green. All in all it was a lovely piece.

I looked outside. If I had summoned the bravery to paint the scene as it actually was that day, what colours would I use? The sky was not blue. It was grey, almost white. The water was not blue. It was molten silver. Why did the colours in my daughter's painting from memory seem so right? Why would a grey landscape not be the one we hold in our memory?

To understand why, let's play our own colour memory game.

We are sitting at the edge of the lake at the end of a glorious day. We look out across the water at a raft that is gently rocking in the distance. We spent the afternoon diving from it and sunbathing on its white painted boards. Time passes. Now we are on shore, and beyond the distant raft the sun is setting. The sky is turning magenta. The sun's warm rays bounce off the water and dance over the sunny side of the raft. The other side is in deep shadow. I ask you what colour the raft is. You reply, "Well, you are the colour person. You know it's white." As we look at it I say, "Okay. But what if you were an artist, what colours would you need to paint it?" You pause. You realize the answer is different. You could not paint what you are looking at if all you had was a tube of Titanium White. No two surfaces are the same colour. The shadow side is blue, mauve, and perhaps grey. The sunny side is magenta, peach, and yellow. The top is a combination of all the colours. Pink would be a handy hue to have on hand, maybe an orange. White would probably be the one colour you would not need.

So what colour is the raft? Is it white because it was painted white or is it many colours because it is tinted by the reflected colours of the sunset? Is it the single colour a house painter would use to paint it, what we might think of as its fixed colour? Or is it the many colours an artist would paint it, a range of colours that changes from moment to moment as the lighting changes? What is real when you sit there at sunset and look at the raft: the colour you *know,* like Caroline's blue sky and water, or the colour you *see?*

Fast forward. We are driving back to the city and, I ask, "What colour was that raft?" As you picture the raft in your mind, you activate the colour cells in your cerebral cortex. They are the same cells you use when you are seeing the raft. They start firing off signals as if you were actually looking at the thing. You are rather surprised at the question. "Not this again, Ms Colour Expert? You know the raft was white!"

In your mind's eye, there is the raft out on the water and without a doubt it is white. The reason you are so sure is because white, the colour it was painted, is the colour the brain has chosen to store in memory what it believes to be the real and relevant colour. What it stores is the colour it would appear under clear white light. If I asked you what colour the shadowed areas were, you would say grey. The colours in shadow don't help us know the object we are looking at – raft, tomato, car. They only help determine depth, size, and placement in space. Our brain does not store the colour in the shadows.

Light itself is a colour but because the colour varies, an object's colour varies. The brain sees this and chooses to ignore it. Light that has all colours equally represented is clear or "white" light. It does not tint or bias an object's colour in any particular direction. In this light we see the truest colour. Sunset has more red wavelengths, fluorescent light has fewer. The brain has neither the room nor reason to store a series of variations. Wisely, it chooses to store the white light version of an object's colour. Our memory flattens colour, tames its wild side to make it sensible, functional, and efficient.

This *colour constancy* is the reason most of us are lousy photographers. How often does it happen that we take pictures fully expecting the results to match what we are seeing – a potentially wonderful shot? Then we get back the film or check the images in the back of the camera. Bright daylight shots look right. The ones taken in other lighting conditions are usually dreadful – Junior blowing out his birthday candles looks yellow. Friends dancing at a club look red or like dark blobs. Artificial lighting does weird things that we just don't note. The sunny shots are best because that *white light* is full spectrum; every wavelength of colour is equally present. We don't notice that light's colours change until we see the proof – dreadful photographs. It is not your photographic skills that are to blame. It is your brain colour correcting to make everything look normal, rather than accurate. Cameras are accurate because they don't make the mental adjustments.

In the 1950s, Edwin Land, inventor of the Polaroid camera, used his awareness of the disconnect between eye and camera to study colour constancy. He realized that what we see and what we photograph are different because the eye and brain together are dealing with colour and light in ways that the camera isn't. We know a white shirt is a white shirt no matter whether we are inside or out, in the sun or in the shade. A camera doesn't. Land found that a white shirt looked white when photographed under tungsten light and looked light blue outside under a blue sky. If Land adjusted the film so it looked white outside, then it looked pink under tungsten. A camera registers colour in a literal manner without sorting out the colour of the light from the colour of the shirt.

In 1957, Land concocted an elaborate experiment to test for colour constancy or what he called the *retinex theory of colour*. On a big board, he organized multicoloured squares in a colourful checkerboard pattern, then he set up three projectors directed at the board. Each shone light through a different colour filter. One was long wavelength (red), the other middle wavelength (green), and the third was short wavelength (blue). Land kept all three projectors on all the time but he adjusted the strength of the light coming from each. When all three projectors were set at the same level, the colours looked exactly the way they would in daylight, white light. When he bumped up the level of any one projector, the entire surface took on the tint of that particular filter. The surface turned greenish, reddish, or bluish. No surprise there. But what was interesting is that within that tinted light it was still clear which square was what colour. It didn't seem to matter if the red light were beefed up or the blue or green one. As long as all the projectors shone even a little bit of light onto the board, all the colours of the Mondrian-like image were recognizable. It was not that they didn't change. It was just that if everything changes in the same colour direction, then we mentally delete the tint. The red square under the green light became brown. A spectroscope would register brown. If we went up close to that square and could see no others, had no colour comparison, we would see it accurately and see that it looked brown. But colour is always a comparison. We never see only one colour, and if we do we are technically colour-blind. Looking at all the squares, we notice when one colour is tinting all colours. By looking at many squares tinted with green light, we know that the brown square is, *by comparison,* still the reddest of squares. We conclude that it is a red square under a greenish light.

Land specifically chose to use abstract squares instead of a landscape or any recognizable objects for the experiment because he didn't want the results to be biased by what we know to be true. Knowing leaves are green and the sky is blue might skew things. But his squares continued to be recognized as their daylight colour and illumination was discounted. He did the experiment on fish. They were trained to go to a particular colour of square for a treat. They too discounted the changes of illumination and found the right square. Like us, fish see colours as an interpretation and not as a wavelength.

Our eyes gather lighting information accurately, in the literal manner of spectroscopes. If our brain were not tinkering with the eye's signals and translating them into our notion of one-object-one-colour, then we would be aware that the colour of things changes all the time. Colour would flicker, which would be irritating and confusing. Colour constancy helps us see what we expect to see and gives us our strong, if bogus, sense of stable colour. Ignorance is bliss.

If we know what colour a colour is, does it matter what colour it looks? It did not matter when we were living in nature and not decorating and doing colour–specific things. It didn't matter when we weren't responsible for selecting colours from thousands and arbitrarily applying them to all manner of objects. In nature, where all colour is useful, it was no big deal that lots of colour nuance went unnoticed. But the ambient colour that our brain so tidily ignores is the colour that gave Claude Monet's paintings their individual colour unity. If you or I were driving along a country road at sunset, the gravel surface might be mauve but we probably wouldn't notice. It's all gravel grey to us. But if Claude Monet were in the passenger seat, he might be insisting we slow down or stop the car so he could take in this beautiful hue, one of his favourites. Our brain is intent on having us keep our eye on the road, not on its colour.

Keeping pace with the changing colour in light forced Impressionists to forgo meticulously drafted compositions in favour of more spontaneous improvisations done on the spot. Artists had painted outside before. What was new was that these hasty works were now considered the real deal, the finished piece and not just a preparatory study to be worked up into a more polished painting back at the studio where it could be big, belaboured, and, with luck or talent, serious enough to be worth a packet. Seurat was the exception. Spontaneity was not his style. As one of the few Impressionists to have any classical training, he never dropped the habit of preparatory drawings. For his large *Un dimanche après–midi à l'île de la Grande Jatte,* he did twenty–five drawings and painted three studies before tackling the real thing. In order to attract a buyer, Degas sometimes worked a quick piece up into a more polished studio piece.

Helmholtz remarked that it would be more accurate to call studio artists Impressionists because they were the ones who painted from memory, an impression left in their mind. Traditional artists painted *local* colour, the fixed colour of things. They knew that to paint your red shirt they would, of course, need more than red. Like the medieval artist, they used white tints, highlights, to bring things forward in space. Like the Renaissance artists, they added black and dark brown to recede parts into shadow. Like baroque artists, they might add a brown glaze to even the colour so none stood out. But your red shirt would look very much like you remembered it, like my daughter painting her blue landscape. Impressionists would stare so intently at your shirt that it would dissolve into abstract patchworks of many colours.

> *When you go out to paint, try to forget what objects you have before you, a tree, a house, a field or whatever. Merely think here is a little square of blue, here an oblong of pink, here a streak of yellow, and paint it just as it looks to you, the exact colour and shape, until it gives your own naïve impression of the scene before you.*
>
> – Claude Monet

Monet believed that to see clearly was to see innocently and objectively, uncluttered with the information added to perception by experience, memory, and habit. He sometimes wished he had been born blind and had his sight restored later so that he would see in that totally naïve way. Then he could paint with the eyes of a child.

Monet did as little work as possible back at the studio. (For years he denied even having a studio. However, he did more in the studio than he admitted.) To stay with the light moment to moment, he painted several versions of a single subject from the same view point. He painted over thirty versions of Rouen Cathedral, so he could keep changing to the canvas that matched the lighting conditions. Sometimes he would work for only ten minutes before shifting again. When he was painting the River Thames, he cursed if he woke up and the sun was shining. Without haze creating the consistent colour over a scene, he could not continue. The colour of haystacks and cathedrals and the buildings along the Thames didn't change but every painting had different colours because they were paintings of light's effects.

Once Monet was working on an early spring landscape when he had to go off to Paris. When he got back a few days later, he saw to his dismay that the tree in the middle of his scene had sprouted leaves. Because he was trying so hard to paint only what his eye saw and not to use his imagination to fill in or take out anything, he was flummoxed. He paid the farmer for permission to hire two men to take two days to remove every leaf. Then he continued.

Sadly, the qualities of colour and spontaneity that make Impressionist paintings look so appealing to us were the very qualities that spelled disaster for them. Impressionists were rebels. With no patrons to dictate what to paint and no academy teaching them how to paint, they were free to explore and experiment and, as it turned out, free to go broke. To sell a painting outside a circle of friends and family, it had to be exhibited at the annual public art salon. Paintings approved by a jury were hung on the walls from floor to ceiling. The catch for Impressionists was that all the jury members were from the art academies and advocates of traditional painting. Their taste was stuck in the late Renaissance. Subjects were to have a certain gravitas and polished technique. Compositions were to be formal, and the colours muted. There was no way that Impressionist paintings would get past the door. They looked like unfinished sketches of banal subjects in colours that were a vulgar assault on the senses. To the middle–class collectors who wanted museum art, these looked like rough studies and not the finished pieces.

In 1874 Impressionists were shown in their first independent show, the Salon dés Refusés. It was a disaster. Impressionists were not just criticized; they were reviled and derided. Ten years later, they held their first group show in a photographer's studio. (Paintings were not stacked up on the walls from floor to ceiling as they were in the official salons. They were hung at eye level with space between.) It was not a success. Another group show in 1876 was equally disastrous.

When Impressionism was at its creative peak from 1860 to 1870, the painters were almost invisible to the public. Occasionally a private collector would buy a painting but sometimes only with the proviso that the colours be toned down with a brown glaze to look better hung with the rest of their collection. Degas and Cézanne survived because they had money by other means and lived long enough to gain acceptance. Gauguin abdicated his day job as a stockbroker and left his wife, his kids, and his country to live in a hut in Tahiti and paint, thereby joining the ranks of the impecunious. Monet was constantly on the verge of being thrown out into the street but he and Renoir eventually reaped the benefits of belated recognition. Seurat and Lautrec died young. Van Gogh, by the end of his short and troubled life, was painting up to three canvases a day if he was well enough and could afford paint. In the fifteen months ending in May 1889, a year before his suicide, he produced two hundred paintings and more than a hundred drawings. In his short and intense career, he produced perhaps the largest outpouring of work in the history of Western art. Yet in his lifetime, he sold one painting and lived on an allowance from his art dealer brother, Theo. One of the many portraits he gave away to a sitter as payment became the siding on a chicken coop.

By the 1880s when Impressionism splintered into smaller groups with different goals, the style came to be appreciated. Ambroise Vollard, a young art dealer and one of the first to see merit in this work, bought it up cheaply and sold it for ever increasing prices. His timing was perfect. When he gave Cézanne his first solo show in 1885, the public was ready and the obscure and reclusive Cézanne became an overnight success. Vollard needed patience with van Gogh's work. At both posthumous solo shows, Vollard sold nothing. It was only in the early twentieth century that Dutch and Russian collectors started to buy them. In 1990, his portrait of Doctor Gachet (1890) sold for $87 million U.S. and set the record for the highest amount paid by a private dealer for an Impressionist painting and third highest of all paintings.

Colour is always comparative, and by the turn of the century the Impressionists' brilliant colours began to seem tame compared to a newer group, the Fauves. In 1905, the brilliantly colourful paintings of Henri Matisse, Maurice deVlaminck, and André Derain were hung together in room number seven of *le salon d'automne.* Inspired by an exhibition of Gauguin's work, the colours of their landscapes were not only bold and brilliant but bore no resemblance to nature. Colour had become expressive and not imitative. The public were so affronted by the "orgy of pure colour" that they said the works were brutal, primitive, and violent. The room was nick–named "the cage" and the artists were called Fauves, wild beasts. Almost simultaneously, collectors across Europe and Russia started to pay skyrocketing prices for Impressionist works. Vollard, not the artists, made most of the profits. Colour had finally been set loose.

YELLOW, THE COLOUR OF HAPPINESS?

Oscar Wilde walked into Eugene Whistler's dining room, took in the yellow walls, and exclaimed, "This is the colour of happiness." Many of the most vibrant people I know live surrounded by seriously bold yellow, the sunshine maker, the energizer, the intellectual stimulant.

Elena, who describes herself as passionate, a risk taker, curious, and engaged with her surroundings, grew up in Venezuela, two degrees of latitude above the equator. When she moved into her home in Toronto, yellow walls were an antidote to the greyness of the north. She tried white but without the strong light of the south it always looked grey. Yellow was not a choice but an imperative. "What I wanted was pure yellow, the real hue and not a shade of it." That was sixteen years ago. She is about to paint again, and she says she will be using exactly the same yellow. Often yellow is avoided because it is not flattering to the skin. Yellow clothing gives a jaundiced appearance to light or mid–tone skin. Elena's response to this is "Oh, I couldn't wear it if my life depended on it! It makes me look like a sick dog." But nor can she live without it. Over the years its domain has expanded from the living room and dining room to the halls, the kitchen, and more recently her bedroom.

Yellow is more joyful than mysterious. It is the colour of optimism and confidence, warmth and abundance, high self–esteem and an entrepreneurial spirit; the colour of honey, spring flowers and autumn fields and Kodak holiday moments. It is rarely chosen as a favourite colour. Maybe its in–your–face visibility is too pushy for non–extroverts.

Ochre and sienna, abundant earth pigments, were used in cave paintings in Arnhem Land, North Australia, about fifty thousand years ago. In Egyptian hieroglyphs, men's flesh is painted red but women are distinguished by yellow–coloured skin.

In the Roman Empire, saffron was a colour that only the wealthy could afford to wear. It made a strong and lasting dye but pollen from the stamens of over ten thousand purple crocuses were needed to make one pound. In China, yellow was associated with fire and power and wearing saffron robes was the exclusive right of the emperor. Tibetan monks, conversely, wear yellow robes as a sign of lowliness and humility. However, their robes were dyed with turmeric, a plentiful earth pigment. In India, turmeric yellow is the colour of Krishna and love and fertility, the marriage colour. Vietnamese used turmeric as a bronzing cosmetic to give their skin an amber glow. Turmeric was affordable but faded fast so it made a better dye than a paint pigment. Turmeric–dyed garments could be put through regular colour baths, like a rinse cycle, to replenish the yellow. In India, pomegranate skin made the colour more permanent. Sometimes decorative patterns in turmeric were painted on cloth for a specific occasion and then washed off.

Many of nature's yellow pigments are highly toxic. Artists found orpiment was hard to use because its gold tones blackened when it came in contact with many other pigments and it had a high arsenic content. Naples yellow, which was used by artists since Greek and Roman times and was the pigment Reubens used to add a healthy glow to flesh tones, became a banned substance in the nineteenth century because it is a toxic mix of lead and antimony oxide. Gamboge, a pigment made from resin that takes a year to ooze out of the tall Garcinia trees of Cambodia, was also a powerful diuretic.

In medieval times, yellow fell from grace in the West. Yellow, the colour of bile, jaundiced skin, and sulphur, was the Devil's colour. At a time when a colour's merits were determined by its price, gold held all of yellow's positive attributes as the colour of the sun, divine light, glory and goodness, and inexpensive earth yellows were considered to be like a dirty or tarnished white. Yellow clothing signified traitors, sinners, and non–Christians. In Christian paintings, Judas, the traitor, was given a yellow robe. In parts of Italy, Jews and Muslims were forced to wear something yellow, a hat or a patch. By the thirteenth century, yellow was also the signature colour imposed on assassins, heretics, and fallen women. Put with green, it was a sign of madness. Its only value was as a dye bath for cloth that had already been dyed blue to turn it green. Yellow with black, one of the most visible combinations, signifies a safety hazard. In nature it warns of the wasp's sting. The Renaissance restored yellow's value because in realistic art, yellow painted the look of gold more realistically than gold itself.

Yellow interiors were popular in ancient Greece and the Roman Empire until red took over as the favourite interior colour. Egyptians painted orpiment over burial chambers and sarcophogi because yellow was the colour of divine light. In the eighteen century, it was a fashionable wall-paper colour. By the nineteenth century, neo–classical decorating schemes liked yellow's way of enhancing the sense of sunlight. And it has been a popular wall colour for the same reason ever since.

The exterior of Van Gogh's little house in Arles was painted bright yellow.

One side of my main hall is yellow with a touch of green and a bit of dirtiness to it. It is as close as I have come to one I fixated on in a sculpture by Anthony Caro in the retrospective at London's National Gallery, one that was also used in 1940s advertising signage. I find most people prefer buttery yellows to these slightly bilious hues but to me their slight off–ness gives a magic twist to any palette, that touch of the ugly that makes beautiful things more beautiful.

Yellow walls are not good for everyone. They are a happy thing only if we are happy and can be very irritating if we are not. An art gallery in England that toured schoolchildren from disadvantaged neighbourhoods found that more vandalism occurred in the yellow rooms than in those of any other colour. To those suffering from depression, yellow can seem as unsympathetic and off–putting as someone who stays chipper and cheerful when we are in a bad mood.

Yellow is an intellectual stimulant. It should probably be used more often in boardrooms and classrooms and less often as a bedroom colour for hyperactive children.

Pretty yellow paint chips when expanded to a wall colour let out a surprising volume of energy. The kick is often reduced to tolerable levels when all the furnishings are put back into place and the art is rehung. But it can take time for the eyes to adjust to the intensity of the brightness and the body, to its energy.

Comfort yellows are the muted country colours of dried grasses, straw, and oiled pine. They are easily overlooked in the paint chip displays because they seem boring, dirty, and almost beige. These are the colours that turn drywall into an earthy, warm, natural material. They can soften and warm even the most functional spaces, as I found out when an architect hired me to design colours for some new schools.

Since I have been known to use half a dozen colours in one room, I found it a real challenge to do an entire school in the eight–colours–plus–one–for–trim limit set by the Catholic Board of Education. Those eight colours – and white counted as a colour! – had to handle everything from the gymnasium, library, and washrooms to classrooms, the principal's office, the cafeteria, places for kids with learning disabilities, and long hallways and . . . and . . . and . . .

But the floors were not included in my eight–colour limit so when it came to the gymnasium, I chose yellow for the main area, the basketball courts and a grey–blue for the surround.

I presented my design to Wolfgang, a bureaucrat from the board, my grand inquisitor. He made sure the number of colours and their distribution met the board's expectations and limitations. Wolfgang had a smattering of architectural training and was pretty good at grasping what I was trying to achieve but the yellow gymnasium floor seemed perplexing to him. I picked up the little yellow linoleum sample and placed it on his maple boardroom table. The colour matched. The yellow, I explained, would be warm in the largely white and fluorescent–lit space but more importantly, it would make the gym floor resemble a more expensive and more traditional wooden floor. I later learned from the architect that Wolfgang made that yellow the default colour for all future gym floors.

But for those like Elena who crave the jolt of light that only a saturated yellow can bring, maybe they should follow interior decorator Basil Ionides' lead. In the 1930s he was bold enough not just to use a clear sunshine yellow in the dining room of actress and socialite Lady Diana Cooper's London home but he had the daring to do it in high gloss!

COLOUR GETS MOODY

WHISTLER, EVOCATIVE COLOUR, AND SYNAESTHESIA

I love designing room colour around art. Empty rooms are hard to do because colour inspiration has to be imagined or wrestled from the client's verbal descriptions, my reading of his or her personality, and clues in the physical space. Full rooms are hard, too, because so many colours vye for attention, finding one that will make everything look its best is challenging. But give me a room with only art and a few things in it and I am immediately up and running, dancing into colour possibilities.

In the presence of art, the palette doesn't need to be designed, just discovered. It is as if an expert has already done a significant part of my job and all I have to do is balance the context, so the room works to enhance what is begun. Not everyone has paintings, but favourite objects, things that hold special meaning, become the next best source of inspiration. I would rather build a colour palette by looking at a handsome carpet, a vintage textile, a ceramic vase, or a hand–knit sweater than a pile of spiffy magazine images and a bunch of paint chips. If colour were music, the paint chips provide some good notes but in art and artefacts the colours are already making the music.

Not having an art collection does not prevent us from stealing great palettes from artists. I always feel like a kid in a candy store when I go to a gallery and see how artists use colour. I stole my studio colours from an Andy Warhol show – not the art but the colour of the gallery walls. When I was working on a palette of exterior colours for houses in the Bahamas, one cold grey winter day, I absolutely had to open my book on Mark Rothko to infuse myself with the brilliant colour combinations in his more joyful colour–field paintings, the ones done before depression took over and his colour succumbed to a dark, achromatic gloom. I had to see what accents he used when his main colour was yellow or orange or how he balanced the magic in a touch of lime, a band of mauve, and a section of pink. He showed me not just what colours to use but in what proportion. Rothko made me brave.

Just walking through any gallery makes me want to paint. At least my job gives me the chance to put some of these colour epiphanies to work for others. Without this release, I think I would burst. Creativity for me is taking the frisson of a wonderful colour combination and transforming and translating it into something entirely new – the colours for a room or a house. I would love to use Rothko's colours in a school that imposes no colour restrictions, or the palette from a medieval fresco on the white interior of the church up the road from me. Ideally colour design does not start with looking through the eighteen hundred colour chips in my kit. Eeny, meeny, miny, moe.

Artists themselves discover rather than invent their colour combinations. It is just that they have an eye that is better trained at seeing colour palettes everywhere – a bowl of fruit, London smog, a face. The French Post–Impressionist Edouard Vuillard, who lived with his seamstress mother until he was sixty, found them in her printed cotton fabrics. Henri Matisse travelled to the hot climate of Algiers to find colour more intense than in grey Paris. Van Gogh had only to go to Arles for the same brightening effect on his palette. Artists also look at other artists' work for colour inspiration. Delacroix looked to Titian, Degas looked to Delacroix. Why invent the wheel if you can just pick one up?

A room does not usually start with a work of art, quite the reverse. Too often, a room is furnished first and art comes in to finish it off, which means it will have to fit in. Artists and galleristas can get a bit uppity about art being coordinated to a room, and the relationship issue can be contentious. But the room and the art have to make each other look great.

Galleries don't have the art–decor dilemma. With no furniture and the other necessities of life imposing, white is the easy solution. In homes, we don't have that blank slate so wall colour can be a mediator. Galleries also don't have to worry about the emotional content of the art. In galleries, the art has its own voice. In rooms, it should ideally bring the appropriate emotional tenor. The wall colour can add to its power or calm its strength. Wall colour harmonizes the room visually and emotionally and sets the atmosphere. And for this, my inspiration is James Abbott McNeil Whistler (1834–1903), the artist who knew how to select that one colour to harmonize all the others, and the one colour that would most evoke the right mood. However, when Whistler was given the job of choosing a colour for the dining room of his most loyal patron, Fredrick J. Leyland, the result was artistic success and a decorating disaster.

The Leylands wanted his opinion because he had both refined taste and a brilliance with colour. Before starting a painting, Whistler would analyze the colours in the scene then edit them down to the one that would pull it all together and evoke a specific mood. He was an Impressionist in style before the French Impressionists but he doesn't usually get the same attention. Whistler pared colour and shape down to the poetic minimum, the essence of the Symbolist style but before most Symbolists did it. He was part of a circle of painters, poets, and musicians who gathered to exchange ideas hoping that if one art could share secrets with another then their combined forces would resonate feelings more powerfully. Whistler said he wanted his colour to sing to the emotions like music.

Whistler was born in Lowell, Massachusetts, but the family lived for a time in St.Petersburg, Russia. Even as a young man he was too urbane for his all–American hometown. In 1855, he sailed to Europe, became fluent in French, and made up stories of a more interesting past. He hopped back and forth between London and Paris and led the life of an aesthete. When Monet fled to London to escape the Franco–Prussian War, Whistler introduced Monet to Turner's way of dissolving subject matter into light with loose brush strokes and brilliant hits of colour. He showed Monet the artistic potential in smog and the way it softened edges and cast a veil of colour over London scenes, methods that became essential to Monet's own work and the foundation of Impressionism.

In Europe, artists started using colour more freely and less literally. Emotion and not realistic detail was gaining importance. Whistler's colour choices never left the real world entirely. He didn't change nature's colours so much as reduce them. Nature presented too many for them to be painted note for note. Whistler warned artists that copying nature's colours would be a cacophony, like a composer thinking he could write music by sitting on all the piano keys rather than selecting the right notes. Finding the one "true note" was, he said, the hardest part of painting.

> Much of my colour design is dealing with the same challenge, how to create harmony and atmosphere in the presence of colour chaos. It is a mistake to think that if there is a lot of colour in a room, the last thing the room needs is more colour. Actually if I can find that one true note that adds cohesion, then it will blend and calm the existing random colours. Mood

cannot be made from too many unedited colours. With too many colours there can be no atmosphere, just a fuzzy, busy feeling that leads people to think that colour is tiring. Colour isn't but colours can be. The right one quiets the yappy bits, pulls them into line, and helps them sing with one voice.

This seemed counterintuitive to Sandra, a client who told me that when she walked through the front door after being away for any length of time she always felt bombarded by all the colour information. She had lots of colourful paintings, carpets, and furniture. Her curtains were pink. She had just reupholstered a wingback chair and large ottoman in gorgeous red leather. There were burgundy needlepoint pillows next to red and pink cushions. Of all the colours, red, which is the boldest colour, was the most dominant. So as not to compete, her wall colour was a pale grey. I began with the logical solution. Might she consider editing out some of her things? She made it clear that she liked them all. Sandra was not critical of her beautiful things. She just wanted a more harmonized feeling.

The solution was obvious. The pale walls had to go. They were too timid to do the job. The other colours were running riot. The most dominant colour, magenta red, was needed on the walls to pull all the reds and pinks forward. With red on the walls and all the red-based hues pulled forward, the chaos was swallowed.

Whereas Impressionists used their vivid colours to capture light, darkness and smog helped Whistler edit them back. These acted like a veil that muted hues and shapes in the landscape and made even the ugliest industrial settings look beautiful. "Poor buildings lose themselves in the dim sky and the tall chimneys become campanile and warehouses are palaces in the night and the whole city hangs in the heavens and fairyland is before us." In paintings like *Nocturne in Blue and Gold: Old Battersea Bridge* (1872–77), his colours meld into an almost abstract monochromatic harmony in indigo.

When Whistler exhibited his almost abstract, almost black painting *Nocturne in Black and Gold: Falling Rocket* (1872–77) at the Grosvenor Gallery in 1878, it was the right thing at the wrong time. Londoners were in the thrall of the super–realism of the Pre–Raphaelite painters. Unlike Whistler, the Pre–Raphaelites tried to depict every detail, each blade of grass, with a verisimilitude not seen in painting since the Renaissance (hence their name). The Gothic period was the Pre–Raphaelites' source for Romantic subject matter – knights in shining armour, maidens in distress. They were emulating the era of jewel–like colour. Using contemporary pigments but the early Renaissance colour techniques of Jan van Eyck, the Pre–Raphaelites suspended their colour in glazes applied over a white ground, making it almost translucent. Whistler meanwhile was influenced by Japanese watercolours that were being imported into Europe. He avoided purity, preferring mixed and muted hues. Nor did he start with white. Whistler primed his canvas with a tint of the main colour of his composition and built up thin layers of the key colour, letting other "imprisoned colour" show below the surface.

John Ruskin – British art critic, writer, connoisseur, the man whose opinion on matters aesthetic was always the last word – stumbled upon an exhibition of Whistler's paintings, and *Nocturne in Black and Gold* in particular, while on his way into the Grosvenor Gallery to see an exhibition of the realistic and colourful works of the Pre–Raphaelite artist Edward Burne–Jones. Ruskin had been the first to champion Turner's work and to see the beauty in even the vague and evocative late paintings that inspired and informed Whistler's own. Whistler had hoped to curry Ruskin's favour. But the day Ruskin came upon Whistler's paintings he was in the mood for Pre–Raphaelite works. Instead of embracing the nebulous, Turner–esque beauty in Whistler's art, he was affronted. The paintings were, he complained, "about nothing." He thought *Falling Rocket* was an "ill educated conceit" and that it was "Cockney impudence" that the maker would expect to be paid two hundred guineas "for flinging a pot of paint in the public's face."

When Ruskin's comments were quoted in the press, Whistler took offence and sued. He locked horns, arguing that it was the right of the artist to decide what his subject matter would be. It was the right of the artist to decide when a work was finished. And it was not the artist's job to paint only religious or historical pieces. A moral lesson was not a prerequisite, aesthetic value was enough. This may seem logical today but it was Whistler, in an act that would benefit artists for all time, who first argued "art for art's sake."

He won the battle but he lost everything. He was awarded one farthing and a lot of bad press. He went bankrupt. Gone was his house, his much–loved collection of blue and white Japanese porcelain, and a lot of his feisty, urbane joie de vivre. It took several years and time away working in Venice before he came back to London and was treated as a star.

Whistler was defending an aesthetic he shared with French Symbolist artists, poets, and musicians. Art's new intent was to ignore details and focus on an inner reality that existed in the space between knowing and feeling. It was not literal, specific, or defined. One of the ways to do this was to leave bits out so imagination would be involved in completing the idea, sound, or image. From now on, the artists would expect us all to fill in the missing pieces. The human mind cannot resist completing incomplete information. We can't resist finishing each other's sentences. We make whole things out of parts. Symbolist and Impressionist paintings engage us in the way unfinished works – Michelangelo's *Slaves,* Pre–Raphaelite painter Ford Maddox Brown's painting *Take Your Son, Sir (1851)* – always do. This was the beginning of modern art.

In the best rooms things are not entirely complete. Nor is everything a perfect match. French art deco designer Jacques–Emile Ruhlmann said his rooms were not finished without people in them. If they are perfect without us, they don't invite us in. And if everything is complete and matched, then small evolutions in the details are not possible and the room becomes rigid, turgid, dead. On the other hand, as a designer, it is hard to resist not taking a room to completion, like a painting. When I come back to a room I have designed I can't help arranging the pillows or objects on a shelf or mantel, and removing a few knick–knacks. Client filling–in can be a mixed blessing.

Colour became less predictable as it became emotionally expressive. In 1884, Gauguin wrote in his *Synthetic Notes* that colour gave enigmatic sensations and that artists use it not to define form but for the musical sensations that "spring from it, from its peculiar nature, from its inner power, its mystery, its enigma."

Colour and emotion are inseparable because colour is directly linked to the emotion centres in the amygdala of our old, or limbic, brain. That is why colour is a personal experience in a way that texture and shape are not. And because this area of the brain is used for urgent or reflex actions, colour response is triggered so fast that we feel it before we are aware of seeing the colour. We respond to colour before we can even think "landscape" or "living room," let alone have an opinion about them.

One sense can trigger the desire for more input from another. What we see, we want to touch. Haptic urges can be especially strong for things like puppy fur, silky hair, oiled skin, satin lingerie, velvet drapes, moving water, the icing on the cake, and absolutely anything that has a notice next to it saying "Do Not Touch!" At the Museum of Modern Art in New York, I noticed that in one large room full of colourful twentieth–century paintings, a single canvas had a "Do Not Touch" sign beside it. It was a large, totally blue Yves Klein with a surface pigment that looked like indigo velvet. It begged to be touched. Touch enhances our visual experience, like smell enhances flavour. One sense enhances another and the combined experience is heightened. Romantics coined the term synaesthesia for this effect and artists tried to bring it into their work.

People with strong connections between one sense and another experience synaesthesia. Synaesthesia, from the Greek for "joined senses," is the results of wiring from one neural sense module being crossed with another. Tastes have colours; sounds are coloured. For many synaesthetes orange is the colour of pain. Because synaesthesia affects the X chromosome, it is six times more common in women than men. (For some reason synaesthetes are often left-handed, have good memories and a lousy sense of direction.) When synaesthetes have their wires crossed between the neural centres that handle numbers and letters and the colour centres in the visual cortex, numbers and letters get colours. (Tests have shown that when synaesthetes and non-synaesthetes are shown a page filled with row after row of 5s and with a few random 2s thrown in, synaesthetes can spot the hidden 2s much more quickly because they are a different colour!)

Unfortunately, not all synaesthetes see colour the same way. When he was seven years old, Russian novelist Vladimir Nabokov (1899–1977) complained to his mother that the letters on his wooden building blocks were all the wrong colours. Because she too was synaesthetic, she agreed with him. However, she disagreed about what colours they should be.

To some degree we are all synaesthetic, linking sounds, colours, moods, feelings, and associations into a complex and personal experiential soup. We don't really know what we have in common and what is our own idiosyncratic take. Are my responses like yours? Minor keys seem sad and full of longing but, for you, is the sound of the cello maroon, the violin orange, the trumpet yellow, and flute green or is that just me? We don't question the idea of music called the blues but to me there is nothing bluer than the sound of Joe Henderson on sax doing Billy Strayhorn's "Blood Count" or the vivid weightless underwater indigo I get when I listen to the choral works of the medieval nun Hildegard von Bingem.

> In pre–MP3 days, I was driving my six-year-old son to a friend's house with an orchestral piece playing on the radio. He said, "Mum, I sort of feel like I am in a movie and this music is the music for my movie." The car, the scenery going by, his frame of mind, and the music all combined into the experience of the more synaesthetically enhanced moment.

For three centuries, we have been aware that synaesthesia existed but it was only in the nineteenth century that the mixing of sensation became a theme of importance and a goal for artists. (A taste, especially in France for the sense enhancements of hashish among artists and intellectuals may have been one reason.) Artists wanted to trigger heightened emotional response by connecting sound and colour and meaning. Concert halls started performing colour music performed on instruments that would simultaneously play musical notes and project colour. By 1893, artist Alexander Wallace Rimington had patented a colour organ. Some composers were synaesthetes or pretended to be. Franz Liszt was. He had *colour hearing* and must have had a few members in his orchestra scratching their heads when he asked them to adjust their playing to make it sound bluer.

Russian composer Alexander Scriabin (1871–1915) thought himself a synaesthete. He said he saw the keys of the piano in colour and heard in colour too and complained that fellow composer and synaesthete, Rimsky–Korsakov, had the colours of his musical keys all wrong.

Composers like Claude Debussy and Richard Wagner were combining sound and image and composing in a style called *chromaticism,* sound painting. Debussy's works were *tone poems* with pictorial names – *Le Mer, Sunken Cathedral, Au Claire de Lune.* Melody and traditional structure were dissolved and notes, like colour, evoked an image in sound.

In 1876, Richard Wagner, who said he did not compose operas but music drama, created the ultimate synaesthetic master work. *The Ring Cycle* had been twenty–five years in the making. Wagner's goal was a union of music, theatre, and visual art into one all–encompassing art form, what he called his *gesamptkunstwerk.* Impressionists took note. Degas and van Gogh were fans. Renoir went to hear his opera and painted Wagner's portrait.

It has been said that Wagner's music is better than it sounds but having had the good fortune of "doing" the Ring in one week at the opening of the new Toronto opera house, I came to realize that it sounds better as one gets used to a different kind of listening. There would be no sing–along tunes as in Mozart, Puccini, or Verdi. With Wagner, like Debussy, the timbre of each instrument was a sound colour. Traditional structure and organized musical patterns were gone and individual notes unfold in a fluid and evocative soundscape. Rather than predicting what is coming, it was time to go with the flow, be in the moment, feel it.

To enhance the power of the music by controlling the visual effects, Wagner redesigned the way concert halls and opera houses should look. He was the first to have the house lights

dimmed and the orchestra lowered into his new invention, the pit. It is hard to imagine not hearing the Ring's first deep resonant note, D minor, slowly rumble and build like an immense force out of darkness – like the beginning of all creation.

At the same time artists wondered how they could mimic music. Music is inherently abstract and evocative and revealed over time – just what they wanted their paintings and poems to achieve. Whistler laid out his colours on his wooden palette in two scales, red to black and yellow to blue, and always placed them in the same sequence so they would be ready to use, like the keyboard of an instrument. Then he said he "played out his harmonies like a musician playing on a beautifully cared–for violin," painting with colour the way a composer used notes.

It was his patron, Leyland, before their falling–out over the famous dining room, who first suggested he use musical terms in the titles of his paintings. Nighttime images that were originally *Moonlights* became *Nocturnes*. His musical titles show the importance Whistler put on the abstract qualities of colour. His most famous painting (not my favourite), the portrait of his mother, is called *Arrangement in Gray and Black: The Artist's Mother* (1871) and the portrait of his mistress, Jo Hifferen, is *Symphony in White No. 1, Girl in White.*

Whistler's *gesamptkunstwerk* was The Peacock Room he created for Leyland, and like Wagner, once he got into it, it was difficult to know when to stop. Leyland was a wealthy shipowner from Liverpool and Whistler's prime patron. The decorating debacle began when Leyland's wife, Whistler's lover (Leyland was generous in more ways than one), asked the artist to pick a colour for the trim and window shutters that would suit his painting, *La Princesse du Pays de la Porcelain* (1863). It was prominently hung in the room that had just been designed and executed by interior architect Thomas Jeckyll. Leyland and Jeckyll considered the project pretty much finished.

Jeckyll had designed an elaborate Gothic ceiling hung with unusual lantern lights. Most of the walls were covered in intricate shelving in a Japanese manner housing Leyland's collection of fashionable blue and white Oriental ceramics. What wall was left was hung with antique leather–embossed panels. The furniture was in place. Whistler said he would choose the colour and do the painting himself. Leyland went back to Liverpool. Jeckyll went on to other projects. Whistler, in their absence, went overboard.

As always, he chose one colour to establish the mood of the room. As if it were a canvas, every surface in Leyland's dining room became part of *Harmony in Blue and Gold: The Peacock Room* (1877), a work in three dimensions with a Japanese flavour, a peacock theme, and a turquoise and gold palette.

Whistler glazed Jeckyll's new ceiling with a Dutch faux gold leaf, using copper resinate as an adhesive because it added a greenish tint to the gold. On the walls, his blue–green was glazed in layers that added a translucency, not unlike that of peacock feathers themselves. He added the circle pattern of a peacock feather glazed in gold. He covered the floor with a large peacock blue carpet. He covered Jeckyll's new walnut shelving with numerous layers of gold glaze. Whistler was on a roll. Nothing would stop him from completing the room, his composition, in its entirety, even if that meant painting and glazing over the leather hangings that some claim were sixteenth–century pieces that once belonged to Catherine of Aragon.

Whistler was so delighted with how things looked he wrote Leyland suggesting that he not return until everything was finished. That way he would get the full effect. As he was nearing the end of the job he wrote again with his customary lack of humility, "You can have no idea of the ensemble in its perfection gathered from what you last saw on the walls than you could have that of a complete opera judging from a three finger exercise."

To finish, he painted large gold and silver peacocks on the walls, doors, and shutters. It was so magnificent, or so Whistler thought, that he printed off dozens of invitations for a public viewing and distributed them to clients, artists, and friends and then left a stack of them in the shop Liberty, to give the room broader exposure.

When Leyland returned and found out what Whistler had done and how much it cost, he went berserk. He refused to pay a cent more than the set fee for the work. Whistler, as always, stood his ground and lost his most loyal patron forever. To his credit, Leyland did pay up although he subtracted from the £2,000 the £1,000 Whistler owed and to further show his displeasure, the businessman paid Whistler in pounds instead of guineas so the total was ever so slightly less than the agreed–upon amount. Whistler said the world would know of The Peacock Room long after they had forgotten about Lord Leyland and he was right.

To show his indignation in perpetuity, Whistler painted gold coins thrown at the feet of fighting peacocks (one of which has a forelock that resembles Whistler's own hair–do), then he left the room, and never saw it again. In 1904 just after Whistler's death American art collector Charles Lang Freer had The Peacock Room dismantled and saved. It moved several times before being ensconced in the Freer Gallery at the Smithsonian in Washington, D.C. It took $300,000 to restore the rather modestly scaled room to its original glory because Whistler had achieved his original colour harmony by using up to thirteen layers of Prussian–blue paint, gold leaf, gold, and platinum pigment.

For me, being in the room is like being in the presence of a star, live and in person. What I wouldn't give to be able to walk through any of the homes Whistler decorated for himself. Whistler's own studio–house at 35 Tite Street, London, was designed by E. Godwin in 1877 and was considered a landmark in the new direction for residential architecture.

(It was torn down in the 1960s.) The artist and illustrator Charles Ricketts took over the lease of Whistler's Chelsea house, The Vale. He said that Whistler had created subtle and sometimes surprising colour harmonies. One room was a glazed green. Another was the bright yellow that Oscar Wilde loved.

Whenever possible, Whistler and Degas specified wall colour to harmonize with the mood of their paintings. They weren't the first. Turner built his own gallery. Before visitors were allowed to see his paintings, they had to spend time in a dark anteroom letting their eyes adjust. When they came out into the light and his colours, they were dazzled – literally. Degas used a yellow wall colour for one show and occasionally sought advice on wall colour from an interior decorator named Belloir. In 1877, when electric lighting was being pioneered by Jablochkoff and Company, Degas was one of the first to make inquiries. The colour of ambient light affected the colour in the painting. Artificial lighting seemed like a good way of controlling this relationship. When Degas tried it he invited his audience to two openings. They should see his work by daylight and again in gaslight since the effect would be quite different.

When in the 1880s Impressionism fragmented into smaller groups, Post-Impressionists and Les Nabis, a group of avant-garde artists, pursued the Symbolist theory of colour as emotion but they wanted to push it further to add a spiritual power. Paul Gauguin (1848–1903) found spirituality in the more primitive and naïve styles of rustic Brittany and later Tahiti, where he painted and played the organ in his thatched hut every day until he died. *Vision after the Sermon: Jacob Wrestling with the Angel* (1888) was the beginning of his work in a style he called *Synthetism*. Following a path antithetical to Impressionism he advocated painting from memory. Intuition and not observation allowed an artist to devise colour harmonies more emotionally powerful than nature's own. Colour had synaesthetic powers, a deeper reality. Colour was "the voice of the earth singing the harmony between man and animals and plants . . . a primitive force." He told his students at Académie Julian to push their colour instincts to their very limits. An exhibition of his paintings at the turn of the century inspired Fauve artists to push colour farther than it had ever been pushed before. And since colourful is always a comparison, once the Fauve's palette had gone beyond anything previously done, Impressionist works started looking pretty tame, almost conservative, and definitely worth buying.

Gauguin's influence rubbed off on the young Vincent van Gogh, who often referred to himself as "the arbitrary colourist." Like Whistler before him and Matisse after, he chose "suggestive colour as a vehicle of self–expression." The correct surface colour was not important. He juxtaposed complementary colours, not to mimic the optic buzz of sunlight as older Impressionists had done, but to capture inner emotion and its turmoil. *Night Café* (1888), he said, was the ugliest painting he had ever done, one that expresses "the terrible passions of humanity in green and red."

Van Gogh considered his portraits, not his landscapes and sunflowers, his most important works and the place where he pushed colour to add a spiritual elevation to the ordinary and the mundane. A postman, a doctor, their wives, and children became iconic. By bending and intensifying colour van Gogh made each look less like a real person and more like a spiritual presence. He wanted portraits to have the power of religious icons.

He wrote Theo that he always began realistically but gradually let his colours loose. They became more "arbitrary" in order to express himself more forcibly. Photographic accuracy did not interest him. He was using "our knowledge of and our modern taste for colour as a means of arriving at the expression and the intensification of the character."

In van Gogh's backgrounds, colour could make an ordinary wall into an other–worldly infinity. In front of the most intense blue he could find, the sitter became '"like a star in the azure sky." Intense colour elevated the physical to the metaphysical and imbued his sitters with a "touch of the eternal." Even if they were his doctor or his postman, colour gave them the heightened other-worldly effect that halos gave figures in medieval art.

Van Gogh tried to convince Gauguin and others to make a pilgrimage to Arles where they would experience the intense light and blue skies over bright yellow fields that he was sure would cause them to give up their "tame Northern colour habits." They would "express something with colour itself" and this alone would revolutionize painting. It was not until the twentieth century that artists realized his vision. And I have the luxury of opening up my gloriously coloured art books when trying to push my colour ideas. It may not be as good as seeing the painting in person or travelling to the Bahamas when designing a palette but it helps.

By the time of Whistler's death in 1903, colour psychology was trying to find out whether specific colours did in fact trigger specific emotional or physiological responses. Were there universal responses, and when responses differed, how did they and why? Did colour have a language that we all speak? And how did the senses overlap?

Russian artist Wassily Kandinsky was synaesthetic so he was sure there were links. He tried to put sound into his paintings. He believed that shapes had specific colour associations. The circle was blue, the square was red, and the triangle yellow. Blue was the symbol of the earth, and water covered most of the earth and is key to life. Red is heavy and strong, which suited the solid, immobile nature of a square. Yellow is light, the sun, the spirit, and best suited the triangle with its association with the Holy Trinity. (He surveyed a thousand people and the results, coincidently, agreed with his theory.)

But Kandinsky didn't understand that not everyone saw or felt things the way he did. To him the sound of the trumpet is yellow; the flute, light blue; the cello, dark blue; and the organ even darker. The violin ranges from green in its mid–range to red when it is "clear." Achromatic colours, white, black, and grey, were different kinds of silence. Circles in blue radiated outward and in yellow radiated inward. Every line or mark had the power to convey emotion and content. A line angled up from left to right was positive. Lines that seemed to point downward were sad, negative.

"The psychological effect of colour calls forth a vibration from the soul" and artists could use this spiritual language. Through the selection and arrangement of colour and shape, specific emotions and the inner essence of all things was communicated. To Wassily Kandinsky synaesthesia was a sign of spiritualism. The more one could see interconnections between colour and shape, sound and emotion, the more elevated the soul. Synaesthetes' higher levels of awareness let them see the interconnections and the signs of a universal harmony and order that were invisible to the less enlightened.

I have to admit that although I enjoyed a retrospective of Kandinsky's paintings at the Tate Modern in London, his colours did not vibrate with me the way Whistler's do. Giving one colour a chance to speak can evoke mood in a painting or a room in ways that Kandinsky's many do not. I got the feeling that what he thought he was expressing with line and colour was not clear. It was in a language I didn't understand. I am sure he could not imagine anyone not experiencing colour and line in the ways that were so obvious to him. The gap between us reminded me of the frustration I can feel when I try to imagine the world through the eyes of my colour–blind clients, so clear but only from inside.

WABI-SABI, BEAUTY'S ESSENTIAL IMPERFECTION

Colour is more fundamental and therapeutic than decorative but my clients still call me because they want a beautiful room. So what makes a room beautiful? Are there qualities that all the wildly diverse beautiful rooms in the world have in common? For six years I wrote a monthly newspaper column called "Rooms That Work" to explore what made a good room. Lots of natural light and good proportions are important. Beyond that, was it size or cost or coordination – professionally done? Was it the colour?

In the beginning, I thought style was key so I wrote columns about different ones – Victorian, Modern, Colourful, White, Minimal, Cluttered, and Flea–Market–Find. When it seemed like I was running out of possibilities, I realized it was not style that was important. It was personality – what a room revealed about the people who used it and how it served their lives. Beauty was in the harmony between the person and the place. There are no golden rules of aesthetics, no demands of style, nor any colour laws. The foundation of what makes a room a good room is very simple. Good rooms are functional, personal, and used.

Form without function is too silly to be attractive. It doesn't matter how pretty a room is, if it doesn't do its job, it is a bad room. Good rooms are not saved for guests.

Rooms that speak of the person do not happen overnight. They evolve. Any room put together in short order by even the most talented designer can be handsome, comfortable, and aesthetically pleasing but it will always be second best to the not–so–perfectly matched room that grows out of lives lived and things loved. Some over–designed rooms make people seem like clutter, and change an imposition that ruins its aesthetic integrity. The best rooms have balance and order but are loose enough to admit change.

Finally, and perhaps most surprisingly, good rooms are used and it shows. They are just a little frayed, a little worn, and marked by life. Like that first scratch on a brand–new car that takes away the curse of unsullied perfection, signs of use are signs of life and they let us relax and feel welcome. Our marks make our rooms unique and, like ourselves, not perfect. What all beautiful rooms have in common is wabi–sabi.

Not to be confused with the sinus–clearing green mustard that comes with your sushi, wabi–sabi, meaning poverty–loneliness, is an old Japanese aesthetic philosophy begun in the fourteenth century that believes a flaw or imperfection is essential to beauty. If something seems perfect, you are not looking closely enough. Wabi–sabi began as a reaction against ostentation, a rejection of the Chinese love of rich materials, lavish colours, and elaborate ornamentation. It was originally associated with the Japanese tea ceremony so its practitioners were often tea masters, monks, and priests who followed the ways of Zen Buddhism and Taoism. One of them, Sen no Rikyu (1522–1591), revealed the meaning of wabi–sabi when he was asked to rake the courtyard of his superior. He carefully raked up every single leaf. With this accomplished, he went over to a tree growing in the corner and shook it. A few leaves fell to the ground and he put away the rake.

My wabi–sabi story is about an interior designer. Her grandchild came over every week to play. He particularly liked arts and crafts. One day, unbeknownst to her, he put paint–covered fingers on the side of her white linen sofa. She discovered the hand prints, dried and permanent. Rather than re–upholster the sofa, the next time he came over she asked him to initial them.

Another designer replaced her cedar shake roof with an artificial one. The fakes looked too perfect to be real so she had a few shakes of a slightly different colour mixed in. The roof looked more attractive because the imperfection made it look real.

The quintessential wabi–sabi characteristics were inherent in teahouses – modest in scale, undecorated, minimally appointed, and built of humble materials. Their message is have less and enjoy it more. Rather than hoard possessions for a special occasion, things should be used every day because every day is special. My great–aunt, even during the war years, used the best china for family. "If it's good enough for the guests," she would say, "it's good enough for us." Use it or let it go. Clear out the clutter but know that the book on the coffee table or the slippers by the bed are life and not clutter.

Wabi–sabi teaches us that value is personal and beauty is in the eye of the beholder. I will never dissuade a client from having an Ikea paper lamp on an inlaid mahogany antique if it looks nice. I happily build a room design around a piece of furniture that is loved no matter what it looks like. These are the inspiration and not the impediment to design because something that is loved, is always beautiful. It cannot be otherwise. If I don't see the beauty in my client's object of desire, then I am not yet tuned in enough to my client.

Wabi–sabi sees everything as waxing or waning. Life never stays still. Beauty is in the ephemeral – tulips on the verge of opening are more beautiful than those that have. A misty morning when everything is still vague and full of potential has more wabi–sabi than the sunny afternoon. Poetry that leaves space between the meaning of the words is more wabi–sabi than prose. There is beauty in a newborn and in the old face upon which life has written its story. Wrinkles, scars, scratches, wear and weathering, dents, tarnish, and rust are all signs of life, and these marks make something unique and so more beautiful. An old leather chair that holds the contours of our grandfather's body and the worn place where he rested his head is more individual and attractive than a new story–less chair. I continue to use and love a pair of carved wooden salad servers that my husband and I have had as long as we have known each other. One has a broken prong where Blake, our grown boy, used them as drumsticks when he was a toddler. Flaws are stories.

Introducing hand–crafted or natural things is a way to infuse wabi–sabi into the cold uniformity of cookie–cutter places decorated with the sameness of mass–produced objects. These things may seem crude and raw at first glance, but the beauty in unsophisticated, plain, or primitive objects reveals itself over time. The artwork of a child is more beautiful than a Picasso poster just as the crumbly cookies baked by a friend look (and taste) better than any packaged perfection.

Wabi–sabi is so relevant today that it seems strange it was almost forgotten. In 1906, Okakura Kakuzo wrote *The Book of Tea* to describe it in contemporary Western terms and it became a cult classic. The book explains the principles of wabi–sabi in great detail without once using the term! More recently, Leonard Koren summed it up in *Wabi–Sabi for Artists, Designers, Poets and Philosophers* as an appreciation of the beauty in things imperfect, impermanent, and incomplete.

It is the element of incompletion that prevents a room from being locked in time. It is the element of beauty that many interior designers, with a zeal for aesthetic control, can thwart. Was it wabi–sabi that led artists like Michelangelo and Leonardo to leave more and more of their artwork unfinished toward the end of their lives? Perhaps their intention was to bring them to a more polished conclusion but they sensed a greater potency in the incomplete. What is left out engages us. Incompletion involves us. It is part of the attraction of the paintings of Turner, Whistler, and the Impressionists.

Artists are often consummate wabi–sabi practitioners when it comes to pulling together rooms that work. Stringent budgets are no impediment to beauty when you have an eye for it. With creative ingenuity and a curatorial eye, beauty is discovered in humble objects – wishbones, branches, scrapyard salvage, and a garage sale chair with great bones, art of their own and friends – artfully organized and arranged. Artists have a feeling for colour and when to use it and where.

To take a closer look at an artist's way of making a room that works, I wrote one of my columns on the semi–detached Victorian home of Toronto artist Kai Chan and his partner, Glen, a place which embodies wabi–sabi ways. They bought the house, and like artists priming a canvas, they painted it white to purge its rooming–house past and establish their blank slate. In came their assortment of furniture: an old sofa that was too comfy to part with, a brown vintage chair, and an antique Quebec table bought cheaply because the dealer was in the middle of sanding it for refinishing when Kai bought it as was. An indigo blue coffee table was a desk Kai made in a furniture course that wouldn't fit up the stairs to his studio so he cut down the legs and used it in the living room instead.

The attitude toward the furnishings was laissez–faire and relaxed but, because of his curatorial eye, Kai was obsessively particular about placement. Two large square canvases – one red, one yellow – that Glen painted are hung inches above the baseboard. A row of African masks hangs at a low height just above low shelves. Hanging the pieces low makes the room taller, more spacious. Arranged on the shelves are ceramics and art by friends and colleagues. His own sculptural pieces are fragile – humble materials threaded together into skeletal structures of bamboo, garlic stems, cinnamon sticks, and dogwood branches from the garden. They come into the decor from time to time although, he says, "by the time they are finished you have had enough of them."

Kai and Glen might have lived happily ever after in their white space were it not for two colour events. They painted French doors leading from the kitchen to the back garden a deep periwinkle blue and the greens of the garden through the blue doors were so appealing, they craved more of the combination. Then they paid a visit to the Modernist galleries in the Art Gallery of Ontario where paintings by Picasso and Braque hung on walls of green and deep indigo blue and looked terrific.

Soon their main staircase wall was indigo, which made the rest of the house look dull. Next, three walls of the living room became a custom–tinted green suspended in glaze. The glaze made the colour lighter, more transparent, and slightly mottled. Then the fourth wall, between the living room and the indigo hall, was painted a vivid azure blue, the colour of a clear tropical sky. The blue made the green more lush.

Finally the ceiling became green, erasing defined edges between it and the walls. This expanded the dimensions of the room. At night, according to Kai, "the green ceiling gives the feeling of being in the enclosure of a forest or being underwater." Colour made the white display shelves too stark so they sanded off some of the paint to make them look older, worn, and more natural. Friends started asking if this or that object was new. Colour changed the visual experience of everything in the room.

Upstairs, except for a bright yellow bathroom, everything stayed gallery white because the contrast between the upstairs and the down makes the colour all the more striking. Kai and Glen made their rooms beautiful by using and re–using things loved, by surrounding themselves with handmade and simple objects, and by letting the space itself and their intuition direct the evolution of the colour. Price tag and brand name are not part of wabi–sabi or essential to beauty. And no matter if we live in a monster mansion or one–room flat, what makes our rooms work is how we bend them to serve our daily needs, reflect our unique personalities, and bring comfort to our imperfect selves.

THE TWENTI

TH CENTURY

THE DARK AGE OF WHITE

THE MODERN WORLD

With the arrival of the twentieth century, colour burst out beyond the artist's canvas and onto walls. It could be bought by the bucket and had by all. Chemistry made colour bountiful and affordable. Steam power delivered it. A bulging middle class bought it. Colour came home.

Twentieth–century tastes for interior colour went on a crazy ride but it was white that always seemed to drive the bus. White, as in whitewash, had been commonly used in the countryside for centuries because it was a cheap disinfectant that adhered well to stone, brick, or wood. The calcium in the lime had a wonderful sparkle but more importantly it was a protective coat that made building materials stronger. In small outports white was a popular colour for the clapboard houses, not for aesthetic effect but because it was a way to use up leftover boat paint.

But that would change. Canadian author Farley Mowat in *Bay of Spirits: A Love Story* describes how the houses in fishing villages became more spectacular than any rainbow after Newfoundland joined Canada in 1949 and family allowances and pension and welfare cheques turned money into paint. "Purple, yellow, magenta, orange and scarlet seemed to be the favourite hues, but some were like layer cakes, horizontally banded by two or three blazing colours. . . . [And] the outports looks like bowls of jelly–beans."

The official year of the birth of white house paint is 1921 thanks to titanium dioxide. Before this time, there was lead white but it was expensive and poisonous. Artists had survived its use for centuries because they didn't lick their brushes enough to make it a hazard. Sadly, women who applied it to their faces for the fashionably ethereal look of the Victorian period or geishas who whitened their skin with it to contrast their gall–blackened teeth were often not so lucky (many lipsticks even now contain lead). Death by lead poisoning was not pretty.

Zinc paint was used but it was not as white a white and was too expensive to be mass–produced for slathering over walls. Along came titanium. Titanium dioxide was discovered at the end of the eighteenth century but it was not until 1916 that it was made into white paint. It was opaque and it was cheap. By 1921, most artists had switched over to it, and in Norway and New York paint manufacturers worked out how to make it in bulk. By the 1940s, it dominated paint sales and by the end of the century it seemed to have whitewashed the world.

There were several reasons for white's rise to chromatic dominance. When colour became affordable, it lost its cachet. In gaining access to colour the masses gained access to what the wealthy had enjoyed for centuries, and so for the wealthy it was time to move on, rise above. White interiors and black clothes became chic. Other factors also played a role – the discovery of germs, the rise of interior decorators, and the post–war need for quickly built, no–frills bulk housing. White proliferated as the interior colour for mass–produced houses even though, more than any homes ever built, they desperately needed colour.

White is the colour of cleanliness, which, by the twentieth century, was becoming an obsession. Germs were discovered at the end of the nineteenth century. Getting sick was no longer bad luck, an act of God or the result of being around too much foul air. In the 1860s, after Louis Pasteur and others proved that the culprit was micro–organisms, a.k.a. *germs,* it was not the medical men but women, home economists such as Catherine Beecher and Harriet Plunkett, who spread the news about germs to housewives. Self–help books with must–read titles like *The American Woman's House* (1869), *Women, Plumbers and Doctors* (1885), and *Home Sanitation: A Manual for Housekeepers* (1887) put cleanliness next to godliness. According to Plunkett, "obedience to sanitary laws should be ranked . . . as a religious duty." In the days before vaccinations and antibiotics, every mother was terrified that her loved ones might be stricken at any moment with diphtheria, scarlet fever, tuberculosis, cholera, or typhoid. Hygiene *was* a matter of life or death. To combat germs that had been lurking in household dirt and dust, interiors changed. Using light colours that reveal deadly dirt would start to seem a lot smarter than the dark colours traditionally used to hide it.

By the turn of the century, factory jobs had depleted the supply of women wanting to be domestics. "The woman of the house" was suddenly running the show. Self–help books about household management, decorating, and hygiene were as popular as today's television decorating and cooking shows. A taste for heavy and often masculine interiors waned. Interiors full of decorative bric–a–brac were also not as appealing if you were the one doing the dusting. The smart choice became rooms less densely furnished and lighter in colour, rooms in which the air could circulate and dastardly dust and dirt be kept at bay.

This is the mindset that led to the huge success of two books by Swedish watercolour painter Carl Larsson, *My House* (Ett Hem) (1899) and the sequel, *At Home with the Larssons* (1902). They were to the housewives of the early century what Martha Stewart's *Living* was to many of us at the end of it, simplicity made beautiful. Larsson's watercolour images of the interior of his home showed rooms that were colourful and casual, full of kids and life. It was Larsson's wife, Karin Bergoo, who was really responsible for a style that looked so effortless and simple, like a breath of fresh air. She was an artist who, as their seven children were born, applied her creativity to the home. Besides designing and making the kids' clothes (which could have been a full–time job!), she designed textiles and much of their furniture. She wove her crisp checks, stripes, and geometric patterns and made them into drapes and upholstery for the furniture she painted white or bright colours. The wood–panelled walls and ceilings of bedrooms were whitewashed. The bright rooms, sparsely furnished in a folksy manner became the quintessential Scandinavian style and precursor to the Ikea aesthetic of today. Larsson's images inspired colour and decorating ideas and a packaged *life style* – the happiness to be found in modest homes that were casual, family friendly, and full of colour and light. Simple was good.

In England in the 1880s, the Arts and Crafts movement favoured light wall colour and simpler decor. (Oh, that we might all live by the dictum of its founder, William Morris: Have nothing in your homes that you do not know to be useful or believe to be beautiful.)

By the Edwardian era (1901–1910) Arts and Crafts architects like Charles Francis Annesley Voysey were paying a lot of attention to interiors. Previous architects, usually gentlemen dilettantes of discerning taste who studied historical models and drafted up their own variations, had concentrated their efforts on exteriors. "Upholsterers" were businessmen with taste, who took care of everything inside. They began with upholstery, carpets, and curtains but over time expanded their services to include furniture and anything else to do with interiors. For those who could not afford upholsterers, large department stores such as Liberty and Fortnum and Mason were happy to outfit entire homes. Because sales were as important as aesthetics, this arrangement led to densely appointed interiors.

Voysey's new style of architecture rejected the usual mishmash of historical styles and the Victorian penchant for every kind of elaborate decorative detail. It turned nature's curved lines into a simplified, streamlined art nouveau. No furnishing readily available for purchase matched the new style so Voysey, like other Arts and Crafts architects, designed everything himself so it would match – the furniture and light fixtures, door knobs and wallpapers, carpets and even the fire tongs and dinnerware.

Pastel shades became popular. Dining rooms were often kept a deep colour, commonly red, but most rooms took on more ethereal tones – muted greys, greens, blues, or whites. Wallpapers remained popular but shifted from densely coloured and patterned to small pastel florals and dainty stripes. Wood was no longer covered with a dark and heavy stain. High-gloss white trim paint was invented (and has been overused ever since).

White was the signature colour of architect Charles Rennie Mackintosh (1868–1928), famous for his redesign of the Glasgow School of Art in a style that fused art nouveau and Arts and Crafts styles and for his Hill House chair, the tallest most uncomfortable ladderbacked chair ever made. Although Mackintosh gets the credit, many of his projects were done as part of an artist–architect group called The Four, which included his wife, Margaret MacDonald, an artist and textile and metal work designer; her artist sister Frances; and Frances's husband, architect Herbert McNair.

Their style was simple and organic like Voysey's, but the decorative elements by the MacDonald sisters had a more feminine art nouveau feel. In 1898, The Four began with white in bedrooms. Soon white expanded into living rooms, various tea rooms they designed in Glasgow, and, most radically, into the boardroom in the Glasgow School of Art. Apart from gesso art panels and some decorative motifs, everything was white – white walls, white woodwork, white fabrics. Often their white rooms were furnished with white lacquered pieces designed by Mackintosh and embellished with a decorative rose motif or female forms. Often, a Mackintosh chair in black finished the room. *The Studio,* a magazine that published only work in the avant–garde style by designers from many countries, spread the fame of the white rooms by Mackintosh and The Four throughout Europe.

In 1904 Mackintosh's Hill House was built just outside of Glasgow for the wealthy industrialist Walter Blackie. I visited one summer and, much as I love art nouveau and am intrigued by the Mackintosh group, I couldn't help but find the white living room and bedroom delightful but cloying and over–designed. Because everything matched – curtains, carpets, cabinets, chairs, built–in cabinets – all were white, and all had the signature decorative floral motif, the Mackintosh–MacDonald rooms felt like stage sets or storybook settings. They looked as if anyone or anything in the rooms would interrupt the look. Heaven forbid that there be a pair of slippers or a magazine left lying about. Forget about wanting to hang a painting or buy different bed linens after a hundred years! An art nouveau room had more room to breathe than a typical Victorian one but in the rigour of its unity, there was less room to live. I have concluded that when everything matches, no matter how exquisitely, it becomes a great place to visit but you wouldn't want to live there.

The ultimate white room was the one Syrie Maugham designed for herself in the 1920s. Syrie was the wife of writer Somerset Maugham. The white living room in their Chelsea mansion on Kings Road, London, uses the clean lines and luxurious materials typical of the new art deco style. This is the room that designers still use as inspiration for their own white rooms.

Syrie married into wealth (twice). To nab her second husband, Somerset Maugham, the most celebrated author of the day, she had to dump husband number one, chase Maugham across two continents, and become pregnant with his child – a challenge since he was sexually inclined in the other direction. Her determination paid off. Their messy divorce many years later left her with their house (fully furnished as only she could do it), a Rolls, a tidy stipend, and child support. When she died Maugham cheered, disowned "his daughter," legally adopted his secretary and travelling companion, Willie, and lived happily ever after.

Syrie was one of the first interior designers at a time when there were few careers available for ladies beyond painting or opening a little shop. The first interior decorators were wealthy women with flair and a circle of rich friends to draw on as clients. Syrie opened shops to sell items of good taste on both sides of the Atlantic and counted the Duke and Duchess of Windsor among her clients. Syrie's business practices were sometimes dubious (passing off reproductions as the real thing, doing a bit of smuggling to avoid paying duty) but she was a huge success. Her ideas were adventurous and often theatrical. She started a craze for special paint finishes, lacquers, crackle techniques, and white. It didn't matter if it was a valuable antique or her baby grand piano, if she wanted something to be white she had it painted.

Syrie did not use white to avoid colour. White was her colour. Hers was not that awful no–frills white used on walls regardless of what is going on in the room. Her own living room was the luxurious, impractical, "chic" of an all–white room. The carpet was two tones of white woven into a fashionably modern deco pattern. Two long clean–lined tuxedo sofas were upholstered in white satin and embellished with skirts of white silk fringe. Her whites were reflected in the mirrors of a floor–to–ceiling accordion–folded screen. And, to complete the room, Syrie added her signature, a spectacular floral arrangement in white. Syrie's room had the look of money and glamour, the as–good–as–it–gets ideal.

Another colourful lover of white was Syrie's peer and competition, Elsie de Wolfe (1865–1950), who is credited with being the very first interior decorator. De Wolfe had a combination of design skills and fashion savvy that were cultivated while she was acting and staging theatrical productions. She got her big break when the architect Stanford White commissioned her to decorate several rooms in the Colony Club in New York, the first women's club. Its well–to–do members became de Wolfe's clientele. Hiring her signalled their own good taste. De Wolfe parlayed this into a hugely profitable career and a client base on two continents that also included the Windsors as well as Ann Vanderbilt, Anne Morgan, and American industrialist and art patron Henry Clay Frick.

Decorators were a spirited force to be reckoned with. In *Glass Houses* by Eleanor Gizycka published in 1926, the main character says: "All lady decorators are recruited from the ranks of the great misunderstood. You know what we say in America about them. Is she happily married or an interior decorator?" De Wolfe had a colourful life. She was considered one of the best dressed women in the world, not surprising since she admitted to spending $15,000 a year on clothes (about $138,000 today). For over thirty years she lived happily with

the wealthy heiress and one of the first theatrical agents, Elizabeth Marbury. Then in 1926 she abruptly left to marry the wealthy Sir Charles Mendl.

Besides opening shops in London and New York, de Wolfe published a ghost–written piece of self–promotion, *The House in Good Taste,* in 1914 and still in print. De Wolfe's idea of style, which she called "Old French," has never ceased to be popular for anyone in the Western world with money: simple lines, no clutter, pale walls, fine fabrics, good craftsmanship, and a mix of new and old – preferably French. Like many designers today, she had a signature style or formula that she knew worked. But she paid attention to light and never got too stuffy. She mixed in reproduction furniture, especially if it was more comfortable. She added funk, like chintz with a black background or faux animal skin prints. And she played with interesting colour combinations, using greys with pale sage greens or greens with mauves. (Mauves, she thought, were delicate and evocative of a vanished past.) Rooms, if not white, were always light. She took one look at the Parthenon and shrieked with delight, "Look. It is my colour – beige!"

To augment light and space, like Syrie Maugham, Elsie de Wolfe used lots and lots of mirrors. This was particularly helpful in making skinny New York Victorian homes look wider. She kept window coverings simple, just enough for privacy, but not so much that they blocked out the light. She advocated new homes be built with as much lighting as possible. I wish building developers today would try to understand how important lighting is to life and that sticking one light in the centre of a room is pathetic tokenism.

De Wolfe thought white walls juxtaposed well with colour in fabrics and furnishings and gave the feeling of brilliant colour better than coloured walls. She used white to set off dark furniture with clean lines and the fabric patterns she loved to use. She said rooms need "no actual color save the blue sky framed by the windows and the flood of sunshine that glorifies everything." And I agree totally with her observation, "We can carry this white paint idea too far. I have grown tired of over careful decoration, of plain white walls and white woodwork, of carefully matched furniture and over–cautious colour schemes. Homeyness is lost if the decorator is too careful."

In the first half of the twentieth century, white was only one of the many colours used by high society in their interiors. In France especially, decorating and fashion were two sides of the same coin. *Vogue* magazine often featured interior decorating spreads. De Wolfe was a dedicated follower of fashion and her work was frequently featured in fashion magazines. It is not surprising that she got the job of decorating the Park Avenue apartment of Condé Montrose Nast, the owner of *Vogue* and *Vanity Fair.*

Paris fashion designers, like Paul Poiret and his Atelier Martine, were designing interiors and a line of home furnishings. Interior decorating was for the home what haute couture was for the body. Fashion and home decor both got colour inspiration from the art world. The large group exhibitions of work by Gauguin, Matisse, and the Fauves and Picasso sent bright colours into fashionable clothing and interiors. The same artists also fuelled a taste for the exotic. Picasso was buying African artefacts, and in *Les Demoiselles d'Avignon* painted one of his female figures with a face like an African mask. In the 1920s Josephine Baker, the exotic and erotic "African" dancer and singer (right off the boat from America), caused a sensation in Paris, performing in only a skimpy skirt of bananas and a bead necklace. Poiret started designing jungle–themed rooms. De Wolfe started using animal prints.

When Russian impresario Sergei Diaghilev brought le Ballets Russe to Paris in 1909 the bold, exotic colours of the costumes designed by Leon Bakst became suddenly popular. Even Syrie gradually tired of white and became partial to greens, hot pinks, and reds. Poiret turned his hand to Arabian Night themes, rooms with richly coloured walls and mounds of big cushions in silks and satin and cut velvet with huge tassels. For artistic types or people with disposable wealth, interior decoration was, like fashion, something to change with each new trend and a deluxe vehicle for self–expression.

In London in 1913 Roger Fry, an art historian, artist, and enterprising member of the bohemian artistic circle, the Bloomsbury Group, started the Omega Workshop. Fry's concept was to set up an artists' collective to bridge the gap between art and home decor. Artists would anonymously design and make furniture, textiles, and ceramics. Members included Bloomsbury's Vanessa Bell (Virginia Woolf's sister and Fry's lover and protégé); Wyndham Lewis, writer, painter (and briefly Vanessa's lover); and Duncan Grant, Vanessa's housemate, soulmate, and creative partner (they had a daughter, Angelica, although Grant was homosexual and Vanessa was married to Clive Bell with whom she had two boys). Three years earlier Fry organized the first–ever London exhibit of Post–Impressionist painting, That year the Bloomsbury circle saw both the works of Cezanne, van Gogh, Matisse, and Picasso and the Russian Ballet. Immediately the colours in their art, ceramics, and textiles acquired a bold, expressionist palette. The workshop collapsed in 1919 because of the war and Fry's archaic business practices but the Bloomsbury style and its penchant for colour carried on.

When I see the way some people agonize over adding a bit of paint colour here or there, I wish I could send them off to Charleston, the country home in Sussex that Vanessa Bell and Duncan Grant shared with husbands, lovers, children, and friends. Bell and Grant were DIYers with artistic skill and graffiti–like urges. Wherever they lived, they coloured their walls with decorative painting. Sadly, with the exception of Charleston, to appease landlords they returned the walls to their original state when they moved. Their style was unpretentious and often whimsical and if ever there was a place where art and life met and married, it is at Charleston. Beside the walls, much of the furniture is decoratively painted, and curtains, carpets, and upholstery fabrics are Grant's designs.

As I walked through the rooms at Charleston, I noticed that the colours are a free blend of every colour but bright white. Its absence is so relaxing and so appropriate to country life. Upholstery prints are muted. Some of the wall decoration has greyed because the pigments were cheap and became faded and chalky but the bathroom is a bold bluish–green; the powder room, a vivid swimming pool blue. The dining room is black with a geometric stencil pattern of grey–blue. Vanessa painted the table and repainted it when it looked shabby. Each version became more geometric. It still shows more wear in the spot where she dished up meals.

Their daughter, Angelica Garnett, described Vanessa's studio as a place of peace, tranquility, and creativity but not a studio "where the artist wrestled with personal demons . . . insulating himself from daily life, but an eminently civilized place, half devoted to pleasures of the eye and half living room. It contained of course easels, canvases, brushes and turpentine, of which it smelled deliciously, but it was also here that Duncan and Vanessa did their accounts, here that Vanessa ordered a leg of lamb from the butcher."

The feeling in these rooms is so different from Mackintosh's Hill House. There is an essential looseness to the unity that makes each room unique, personal. Like Carl and Karin Larsson's rooms, they don't just accommodate life, they are part of it. Things do not match but mingle – comfy chairs; books and art written or painted by each other and friends, things that matter gathered over time, and everything well used. The house is a testament to the comfort and beauty of being surrounded by colour and handmade things – even the radiator cover is macramé and hanging light fixtures look like upside–down Bloomsbury pottery bowls suspended on strands of glass beads.

Standing in the dining room and looking out through wildflowers that frame the front window, one can almost believe that Vanessa's boys still float boats on the small pond or that Virginia might come up the lane for tea. Vanessa's colour–filled studio still has her paintbrushes in a jar near the easel. I would have been happy to recline on the chaise near the painted screen surrounded by the art and creative bric–a–brac, looking through the French doors to the little walled–in over–grown garden, sipping a cup of tea, reading one of Virginia's books and never, ever leaving.

Not just artists enjoyed working with colour. Virginia Woolf's friend Vita Sackville-West had a mother with colour flair and the funds to play with it. Lady Sackville loved to decorate her huge home. In 1911, Vita's bedroom was done up in a colour scheme that makes me feel like I dwell in the land of the chromatically timid. I would love to have seen the emerald green walls topped with an apricot ceiling, sapphire blue furniture, curtains in blue with a yellow lining, salmon and tomato red cushions and lampshades, six orange pots on the mantel, and lots of art. I wonder what colour she chose for the trim because I am sure it would not have been white.

Modernism begins . . .

World War I curtailed the demand for extravagantly creative interiors and luxuriously designed and crafted rooms and created the need for modest living quarters for those with limited means and often no home at all. It was time for a simple and affordable style called Modernism and what, at first glance, seemed like the tyranny of white.

When modern, white, box–shaped buildings designed by Modernist architects first appeared, they looked as though they had been dropped down to earth from an alien planet. They still do. In 1923 in Holland,

Gerrit Rietveld's Schroeder House looked like a three-dimensional Mondrian in white and grey with geometric colour accents stuck onto the end of traditional, dark brick, three-storey row houses. In 1925, in Dessau, Germany, the new Bauhaus buildings by Walter Gropius were white, grey, and glass with bright red doors. The white Villa Jeanneret-Roche (1925) and the white Villa La Roche (1925) by Swiss-born artist and architect Le Corbusier cropped up in a Paris neighbourhood. His white Villa Savoye (1931) landed in a field in Poissy, just outside of Paris.

White boxes proliferated. In America, Austrian-born Richard Neutra was doing white houses in California in the 1920s. In 1933, Edward Durell Stone designed the white Mandell House in Bedford, New York. Leading Modernist architects fled Europe in the 1930s, accelerating white's spread across the United States. In 1951, the white Farnsworth House, designed by Mies van der Rohe as a retreat for Dr. Edith Farnsworth, settled into a forest an hour south of Chicago.

Modernism didn't start out being white. In 1909, America's own Frank Lloyd Wright designed the first "modern" homes, his Prairie houses. He applied concrete and steel construction to residential architecture and created the first open-concept layout. Walls became floating partitions flexibly arranged, instead of being relegated to the boundaries of the roof they had to support. He developed an architectural vernacular that we still think of as modern – flat roofs, horizontal windows, cantilevered balconies, radiant heat, and the car port (his term).

His work was published in Europe and caused a sensation. Wright was not using white. He used natural materials because, unlike the white-box architects, he felt homes should blend into their natural settings. His original paint colours were often autumnal. When the Museum of Modern Art in New York launched an exhibition of bold new Modernist architecture, which they called International Style, the work of the forty-three-year-old Wright was included but only peripherally. It represented the roots of Modernism. He was classified as a pioneer but also an out–of–date has–been! In the years following the show, it was the Europeans – Gropius, Mies van der Rohe, Moholy–Nagy – who won the commissions and plum teaching positions at Yale, Harvard, and the Armour Institute in Chicago.

Under their tutelage, students would learn the beauty of the white box. Wright, meanwhile, teetered on the brink of bankruptcy and didn't know that his most productive and successful years were still to come. Between the age of sixty–eight and his death at ninety, he was at his most prolific. His last major project, finished in 1957 two years before his death, was the Solomon R. Guggenheim Museum on Fifth Avenue in New York. Its sky–lit white inner space is a spiral around a central void. The exterior colour Wright had suggested for the spectacular piece of Modernism, shaped like a vast rounded mollusc, was in fact, a Mexican rose red. I can't say I mind that he was overruled. If you design a building in opposition to its context and one of such striking shape, then it might as well be the colour that emphasizes that shape most of all, white.

Modern architecture bore no resemblance to anything that had ever been seen before. From the cave to classical Greece and Rome, from Gothic to the present, there was nothing like these flat, straight, pristine, white structures. They seemed just as jarring in an urban setting as in a natural one.

An infatuation with The Machine was the root of Modernism. Previously in architecture, engineers took care of function, and architects added the decorative niceties. But the decoration that had been handcrafted by skilled specialists was, by the end of the nineteenth century, often mass–produced at great speed. Frank Lloyd Wright and others felt it was time to replace bad or fake versions of old styles that had become irrelevant. New times and new techniques needed a new design language, one that was appropriate and honest. Things made by machine should look like they were made by machine. Modernists agreed. They were already working on their pared–down, streamlined style when World War I broke out and accelerated everything. Modernism changed from a style to a cause, a mission to do good for the masses. Housing, shelter, and rebuilding vast areas that had been destroyed required new building techniques that were fast, cheap, and easy to replicate – like flat boxes.

Artists–turned–architect wanted architecture to "start from zero." It would be anti–bourgeoisie. To erase the tastes and idiosyncrasies of princes and politicians, it would become impersonal, homogeneous, and standardized. Decoration served no purpose. Anything that smacked of luxury was unnecessary and decadent and had to go. Peaked roofs, eaves, trims were abolished. It didn't matter that they were more practical in wet or snowy climates, they were gone. Colour? Colour was decoration, ergo, "Gone!" Now all materials had to be honest – concrete, stucco, steel, and glass had to look like concrete, stucco, steel, and glass.

The curse of Modernism is that it could easily be copied by those less talented than its pioneers. Bureaucrats and developers could say that they were building in the new style but what they were doing was building in a faster, cheaper way. Modernism went from being a socialist design style to being a technique for erecting banal buildings with no style at all. But that was not in the summer of 1925 when Modernism was vying with art deco for public attention.

That summer L'Exposition des Arts Décoratifs et Industriels Modernes opened in Paris. It was the definitive home show. Buildings devoted to what was the latest in home decor covered seventy–five acres. This was where the austere, colourless working–man's style Modernism met its alter ego, the luxurious and very French style, art deco. Both advocated new, streamlined shapes. Both were thought to be the hot new trend but no different from others like neo–rococo or chinoiserie.

In art deco pavilions, white was just one of many colours. Jacques–Emile Ruhlmann's oval boudoir was a medley of mauves, the softest on the walls, stronger ones for curtains, carpet, and upholstery. Shiny, slim–lined black lacquer furniture gave it a stylish edge. A dining room by Poiret's Atelier Martine was blue but with lots of mirrors and a geometrically patterned floor in black and white marble. The smoking room by Francis Jourdan had a dark grey carpet but every wall surface was yellow, very, very bright yellow (think canary then turn up the volume). Deco rooms sported any and every colour. If one colour was essential it was black. Black was graphic, clean, and a more dramatic accent than white.

Art deco was a style suited to the French and the wealthy. It also suited Americans. The effects of war were minimal in the United States so their love affair with The Machine was untarnished. By the end of the nineteenth century, engineers and architects led by Louis Sullivan joined forces and built vertically. In the 1920s and 1930s, thanks to the invention of the elevator and the revolving door, buildings shot to the heavens. Reference to Gothic, Renaissance, even classical architectural styles gave way to the style of airplanes and ocean liners or the geometric shapes of newly discovered Mayan temples. Everything from skyscrapers, to ashtrays, armchairs, and refrigerators adopted these deco motifs. Colour's importance was secondary to streamlined shapes and shiny surfaces.

Art deco was short–lived. The Wall Street Crash of 1929 was the death knell of residential luxury. The 1930s brought hard times. Decorating was scaled back. Old furniture was reused, reupholstered in new colours. Furniture and accessories were pared down and walls were painted white, off–white, or pale grey. Hanging nothing over the mantelpiece gave a room "the new look." If there was a place for colour exuberance, it was the floor, where the latest thing was wall–to–wall carpeting, often in bold colours. If kept neutral, small handmade rugs were layered on top. Deco's clean–lined airplane aesthetic prevailed in home accessories from ashtrays to lamps and sofas. Art deco continued to be used for public buildings – banks, hotels, and movie cinemas – to evoke a luxury that was in short supply. And Modernism, because it could be proliferated quickly and cheaply, became, for better and worse, the architectural lot of the future.

Le Corbusier declared that "homes should be machines for living in," living spaces should be treated with the less-is-more, practical manner of work spaces, not furnished but equipped. His clients didn't always agree. Pierre Savoye, an insurance administrator, and his wife, Eugenie hated their now iconic house in the middle of a field in Ville de Poissy.

It was not just because Le Corbusier didn't approve of Mme Savoye's notion of putting some comfortable furniture in "his" living room. She may have even liked the sink stuck in the front hall. Le Corbusier had been in the Orient and liked the Japanese ritual of cleaning away the dirt of the outside upon entering a private space. The lack of storage cabinets in the kitchen may not have driven Mme Savoye nuts even though the house was hardly down the path from the local shops for a daily stock-up. She could probably live with Le Corbusier's bare light bulbs hanging on cords as light fixtures and the large tiled chaise surface in the bathroom that was too cold and hard to ever use.

Call her fussy but what really bothered Mme Savoye was that the flat roof leaked constantly. The entire family got colds and their son developed a pneumonia that had him hospitalized for a year. Living in the house was so insufferable to the Savoyes that they would have sued Le Corbusier except that World War II broke out and they had to leave France altogether. Looking like a machine did not translate into working as efficiently as one.

At first glance it seems that colour had no place in Modernism. The surprise is how important it was, how widespread its use. It was not obvious to passersby because most of it was inside. It wasn't obvious to those of us who studied architecture because we were shown slides and photographs in black and white. It was not obvious because many of the iconic white–box Modernist buildings became dirty and derelict (cheap white buildings do not age well) and what colours there had been were badly faded. But Le Corbusier, the architect I blame for imposing white on the modern world, used colour in ever–increasing quantities and in ways that were more like the ones I use than anyone I have ever encountered.

When Le Corbusier wrote *Towards a (New) Architecture* in the early 1920s he would have had us believe that colour was as frivolous and as useless to architecture as curlicues and fancy trimmings. His book, the bible of Modernism, has an entire chapter on surfaces and light playing off them but not a mention of colour. He argued that colour was "suited to simple races, peasants and savages" but he was not being honest. Le Corbusier laid down the rules for colourless buildings but used colour masterfully in his paintings *and* more and more of it in his architecture.

Le Corbusier's first buildings were relentlessly white. The purge was necessary because, he complained, a wall's main purpose seemed to be to hold up wallpaper and decorative bric–a–brac. However, once colour was gone, Le Corbusier found himself looking at a blank slate, the primed canvas. He realized it was pattern that should be rejected as ornamentation but not colour. In 1924 colour crept into the studio home that he designed for his friend, colleague, and fellow Purist painter, Amédée Ozenfant. In 1925, he used lots of colour in the Villa La Roche, designed for a Swiss banker and collector of avant–garde art in Paris. He insisted the colour – red, teal, black, grey, pale pumpkin, and white – was just an experiment. It was one that lasted a lifetime.

Le Corbusier not only coloured the walls in the dining room in Villa La Roche, the apricot wall colour was added to the ceiling. He said, "If the same tones are on the ceiling as the walls, the impression is totally modified; from one categorical thing one moves to something very softened, calmed, entrancing: it is like being under a dome. I have closed up the space." Closed–up should not be confused with compressed. It is rather a sense of completion. He had rid the room of what I call "the white lid effect."

By 1927 Le Corbusier admitted that an entirely white house "looked like a cream jug." The exteriors of two housing units, designed for Weissenhofsiedlung, an exhibition of new housing in Stuttgart, were soft green and pink. In 1931, he was designing the first of two wallpaper collections for the Swiss company Salubra. Twenty–seven solid colours he called *Clavier de couleurs* or *Colour Keyboard* were organized from light to dark and in two groups – colourful and un–colourful colours.

Architectural colour was becoming increasingly important for this champion of white, and colour technology was making it easier to have. Emulsions, paint as we know it, were premixed and sold in cans. As a result, synthetic colourant was sold by the gallon and powdered pigments no longer had to be mixed with oil into custom formulas on site. But because colour matching was not as precise then as it is now, wallpaper was Le Corbusier's way of getting his exact colours applied like paint by the roll.

He complained that most industrially produced colours were acidic, sharp, dynamic, and tiring and that trying to be original with colour led to "misadventure." He took pains to mimic nature in palettes called Velvet, Sand, Landscape, Sky. Then he turned to something very new, colour psychology, as the guide to how colour mood and colour perception manipulated space. Sky and sea colours were soothing, and they dissolved structure and expanded space. Reds and brick colours were more imposing, emphasized structure, and compressed space. Browns and oranges had weight and fixed the exact position and dimension of the wall. Colour could accentuate or camouflage and make any room into what Le Corbusier called a "rectangle elastique."

The one–room–one–wall–colour decorative system was less interesting and less appropriate to architects working with another new influence – the open concept. Steel and concrete construction techniques freed walls so interior space became a loose and fluid arrangement of partition walls. Colour turned walls into what Le Corbusier called "the carriers of ideas." White became the perfect foil against which colour's effects were most strongly experienced. White was servant to the master, colour!

To this day open plans seem to present a huge colour dilemma for people whose homes are modern but whose colour ideas are Victorian. Open plans have so many colour possibilities that are more interesting than the one–room–one–colour of the past. They invite flexible colour placement and make it easier to get just the right physical and emotional colour balance in a room. This is harder to do in traditional homes where boxy rooms do not invite colour blocking, zoning, and loose transitions that follow the dictates of the heart and not the walls.

Until 1931, blue–green dominated Le Corbusier's colour accents. Then it was reds. After 1945, his colours stopped evoking natural materials and, like Mies van der Rohe, he used more unpainted, raw material. Wood was not painted. Concrete was left bare instead of being given a skim coat of white plaster. Black was introduced and strong colours defined structural elements, organizing them into visual rhythms. Interior sliding doors were often strongly coloured. By 1959, he did a second series of wallpapers, expanding the range to forty–three colours, some much stronger. He even let a few little geometric patterns creep into the series to be used sparingly as accents. Colour was no longer an add–on decorative element, but was like a building material and conceived of as an essential part of the design process.

A Toronto architect recently told me that when she studied architecture not a single colour course was taught. She now teaches architecture at the same university and still there is no colour course. And when architects submit scale models for design competitions, colour is not usually allowed. The monochromie Le Corbusier praised at the beginning of his career but soon left behind is perpetuated by others.

Modernist artists–architectures had utopian goals: homes that would be affordable for all. Inside, works of art would add colour. It was no coincidence that interiors looked like art galleries waiting for the art. Art was to be as integral to a home as a chair, and a chair would be as well designed as art. Bauhaus under Walter Gropius took as its mission "Art and technology – the new unity." Artistic skills applied to industrial techniques would mean good design could be had by all.

Architects were excited by the concept and happy to teach courses at the school in cabinetry and millworking. Gropius and architects Mies van der Rohe, Marcel Breuer, Lazlo Moholy–Nagy all taught this course at one time or another. Students were challenged to design chairs, tables, storage units, carpets, lights, wallpaper, textiles, and other decorative arts that met the following criteria: functional, long–lasting, cheap to make, attractive to look at, and suitable as prototypes for possible mass production. There was no interior design course. What they did was "interior architecture" – rooms were 3–D art projects not just a space in which to live. Many students would rather have been painting than learning industrial techniques and colour theory and preferred the idea of art as self–expression and not socially useful design. They were told to forget everything they had previously been taught because at Bauhaus, everything started from zero.

Artists, including Wassily Kandinsky, Paul Klee, Johannes Itten, and Josef Albers, taught colour theory and each had his own version. The wall–painting workshop was led by colour designer Hinnerk Scheper (1897–1957). No distinction was made between wall painting and easel painting, and much of the students' time was spent painting Scheper's colours on the halls and walls of the new Bauhaus buildings. Sometimes they were allowed to be more expressive and improvise by throwing sponges soaked in coloured paint at a wall. They were also taught the hot new topic, colour psychology, the effects of colour on space perception.

Recently the Bauhaus building has been restored to its clean and colourful brilliance. As with all good Modernist spaces, sunlight pours in through huge curtain walls of glass onto bountiful white surfaces. Scheper's bold colour accents define structural elements and give rhythm and orientation to the interior spaces.

They are a delight for someone like me who loves to block colour anywhere and everywhere that it feels right. He blocked a wide horizontal colour band along the top of a wall. Instead of stopping at the corner, he continued around the walls and extended his colour partway along the next wall. Colour seems to draw visitors through the space. There are indigo blue vertical blocks, red end walls in stairwells, charcoal grey and black accents. Many of the rooms have shiny charcoal black linoleum floors that give crisp contrast to white walls and reflect light.

Ceilings are divided up by boxed ductwork so Scheper turns them into Mondrians in red, white, and yellow. Door trim is not white but a charcoal grey that extends into the floors pattern. Every surface is part of one colourful and cohesive rhythm balanced by big areas of white.

A 1923 colour illustration of the director's office shows white walls, and a white and grey ceiling. There is the essential large window. But the cubic chair designed by Gropius himself is upholstered in a bright yellow. A cheerful area rug, no doubt made by the Bauhaus weaving class, is multicoloured squares in blues and yellows and looks just like the square paintings Itten used to demonstrate colour theory. But up at the top of the walls behind the desk is a sassy band of canary yellow that wraps a corner and stops in the middle of both walls. You can't tell me it has anything whatsoever to do with structure or rationalizing anything. It speaks to me of a freedom that is not inhibited by the dimensions of a wall and a creativity that makes a room into a 3–D art piece. Colour, it says, can be used in whatever way and in whatever amount the heart desires.

Gropius wrote articles about using colour to protest austerity. Paint had become cheap, and colour almost free. And although I do not have the same socialist aims as Bauhaus, I do appreciate colour for its power to do universal good. It does not matter if my client lives in a flat or a mansion, the colour choices are as vast. If you can afford the paint, you have the colour. A gallon of deep colour might cost marginally more than a pale hue but it is nothing like the difference between, say, a sofa from Ikea and one from B&B Italia. I never have to say to a client, "Look. I know you would really love a magenta dining room with a platinum grey ceiling but I am afraid you will have to settle for pastel pink walls and white up top." Colour is about following your heart's desire, and for some that is what makes it both delightful and difficult.

Modernists realized that when times are hard and funds are short, colour becomes a design essential. Prussian–born architect Bruno Taut

(1880–1938) put it into practice using colour full tilt inside *and* out. Because colour doesn't photograph well in black and white and black and white photographs were used to spread and popularized the look of Modernism, Taut's colourful work was sidelined before it could blot the page.

Taut's obscurity is not because he was a minor player on the scene. Like many of his peers, he was an established painter before he became an architect. He was as prolific a writer on architecture as Le Corbusier but little has been translated. He was responsible for about ten thousand housing units in Berlin alone. He was just as politically engaged, or more so, than any of the Bauhaus group. In 1919, he established the Arbeitstrat fur Kunst (AFK) to lobby the Weimar government to put architects in charge of the post–war restructuring plan. That same year, Taut published "Call for Colourful Buildings," which was co–signed by many leading architects, including Gropius. It advocates using colour to put an end to joyless housing, the concept Gropius took to Bauhaus. Taut said all other decoration – fancy trims and moulding, luxury materials, art – was costly. The rich could have it and the poor could not. Colour was democratic. "As it can be provided with limited resources, we should, in this present time of need, particularly urge its use on all buildings which must now be constructed." For him, the use of colour was not about aesthetics but ethics. Colour was the social equalizer.

As city architect for Magdeburg, Germany, Taut built several thousand workers' housing flats with brightly coloured façades. Between 1913 and 1915, he designed the Falkenberg Housing development. The 128 houses were so brightly coloured it became known as the Paint Box Estates. Berliners who moved there from their grey city flats thought the colours insane and often remarked that whoever was responsible should be locked up. (A developer is about to tear down those that remain.)

Several of Taut's colour schemes in Berlin have been restored. Some have vertically zoned areas of primary colour – a bold red section flanked by two in indigo. Some have soft, muted colours, resembling the palettes of his early pastel landscapes. One apartment block is like a layered cake – each of its three storeys a different colour: cherry red, banana yellow, and indigo, reminiscent of colourful buildings by the zany Viennese artist–architect Friedrich Hundertwasser (1928–2000). Taut never imposed a fixed set of colour rules on buildings, and he never used the same palette. Every situation was unique. He analyzed the conditions and developed the colours accordingly. But they were always bold.

Taut was never daunted by the flack caused by his colour; he just kept on doing what he did thinking that others might come around. In 1924, he worked in Berlin with city planner Martin Wagner on developing over ten thousand colourful flats integrated into a garden complex. Contact with gardens and nature was an important component of his housing developments. Taut believed that colour, unlike white, fit buildings into their natural setting, and in grey urban settings lacking nature, bright colours acted as the next best thing, nature's substitute.

The façades of the Horseshoe Estate in Berlin were several tones of bright yellow, a pink, a blue, and a burgundy red. In 1930, a journalist looking at Taut's work said perhaps his colours couldn't, on their own, bring happiness but they certainly invited one to be happy. Taut disagreed with the idea that bright colours suited only tropical climates – colour was good everywhere. If it looked wrong, the bland context was the problem. The more colour there was, the better it would look and the happier everyone would be.

Mies van der Rohe did not agree. In 1927, Mies was put in charge of the Weissenhofsiedlung, the exhibition of housing that gathered together all the great Modernist architects. Each architect would do a housing unit. Participants included the usual suspects: Le Corbusier, Gropius, Behrens. Bruno Taut got a house on lot 19, right across from Mies's own. Taut set about doing what he liked to do best, colouring all the surfaces inside and out in primary colours. The day before the opening, Mies, in his capacity as art director, came by and told Taut that he did not think the colour worked. Taut promptly replied that the problem was not his colours, it was that all the other buildings looked unfinished.

One can only imagine how infuriated Mies must have been when the sunlight reflected off Taut's primary red exterior wall onto his housing unit, turning its white bright pink–red. One day the fire brigade was called because someone saw the bright colour and assumed the building was on fire.

Taut explored functional uses for colour. He analyzed visual ergonomics and what colours best suited which kinds of work. He experimented with colour and energy efficiency by painting the exterior of his home black on the east side to absorb heat in the morning and white on the west side to reflect it in the afternoon.

When Modernist architects fled Germany for America, Taut, always the loner, went the other way. After a short stint in Switzerland, he left for Japan, where he wrote two books on its culture and architecture. He died in Istanbul, Turkey, in a house of his making that looked like a three–tiered pagoda on the side of a ravine. And the colour? Hot pink.

By the 1930s the White Gods of European architecture were in America. Wright's concrete construction and open plans were much copied but not his richly coloured and nature–inspired style of Modernism. In 1939, the wealthy industrialist Edgar J. Kaufmann commissioned Wright to design a weekend retreat in Western Pennsylvania, a project that would bring the architect out of bankruptcy and launch his second career. Fallingwater, built on top of a waterfall, was voted the best building of the last 125 years by the American Institute of Architects and is considered the most famous house in the world.

Its colours were drawn from nature and the natural material he used: stone walls and flagstone floors that run uninterrupted from the outside in, the wood surfaces of furniture and built–in shelving Wright designed to prevent any decorator or homeowner from having their way with the interior. The windows are autumn red. Large flat balcony terraces that tier down the side of the hill, cantilevering out over the waterfall, are of ochre–tinted concrete, the colour of dried foliage. If Wright had had his way, they would have been finished with gold leaf to look even more like dried leaves. However, the budget for the house had been $35,000 and the actual cost, without gold leaf, was three times that (the standard Wright budget over–run) so it's easy to understand why Kaufmann nixed the idea. (The cost of the house was later viewed as a bargain compared to the cost of keeping the whole thing from collapsing into the water. Whether it is true that Wright did not listen to his engineer's advice about using a heavier gage steel to reinforce the balconies or that the engineer added thickness to the balconies that Wright had not specified, the results were almost disastrous.)

Unlike Wright, many American modernists through the forties and fifties were happy to use white because it still looked new. They shared his desire to merge the inside and out as seamlessly as possible and since their exterior colour of choice was white, so too were the interior walls. Colour was restricted to the natural materials, upholstery fabrics, and mostly the grand views of nature seen through floor to ceiling glass–membrane walls.

If you were to ask me what house of all possible houses I would choose to live in, I would decline Wright's brilliantly articulated but cramped ones in favour of one by Richard Joseph Neutra (1892–1970). Neutra seems to capture the best of Modernism – European sophistication with more relaxed American ways. He was born in Austria but was so enamoured of the work of Louis Sullivan and Wright that he moved to America in the 1920s. He studied very briefly with Wright then moved to California, where the climate and laid–back lifestyle perfectly suited architecture that used window walls, clean horizontal lines, and white. In California, "less is more" was not about austerity but about easy living. Neutra used white but relieved it by using natural materials. Bedrooms and living rooms open onto terraces and swimming pools. His sunbathed minimalist homes seem relaxed and sexy rather than overly conceptualized and cold, the right amount of shelter and nothing more.

In 1942, designer Russel Wright (1904–1976) – no relation to Frank Lloyd – and his wife, Mary Small Einstein Wright, knew the value of nature and a laid-back lifestyle and so they were, not coincidentally, very enamoured of colour. They designed a home called Manitoga on a deforested and over-quarried wasteland near Garrison, New York, that the Wrights turned into a nature preserve using indigenous plant life. Ever since the late 1920s, Russel and Mary had been encouraging others to lead a modern lifestyle – casual and informal (a recurrent theme in twentieth-century America). In the 1950s, they gathered their ideas into an illustrated book that is still available, *Guide to Easier Living,* with tips on everything from designs for his-and-her closet spaces to stain removal and division of domestic labour – who does the dishes and who walks the dog. Planning and good design that worked out things like how to reduce the number of footsteps from the dining table to the kitchen sink saved time and effort. Instead of keeping up with the Joneses, readers were encouraged to care less about how things looked and more about how they worked.

From the thirties through the fifties, Russel Wright designed textiles, appliances, and a hugely successful line of basic family furniture, but where he made his biggest mark was with dinnerware and his radical notion that it could be casual and colourful. His shapes were curvaceous and his colours changed like fashion. Wright had an obsession with colour and meals. Food and the plate upon which it was served were to be a pleasing colour combination. His china was so successful that not so long ago it seemed to be in every North American country home or cottage. Then tastes changed. It began to show up in garage sales. People didn't bother to take it when they moved. It was his colours – avocado, melon, olive, butternut, turquoise, and so on – that seemed so dated. But tastes have changed again and those colours, their flaw, make them retro collectables.

I love the fact that at Manitoga the Wrights changed their colours with the season. Bedding, the curtains, carpets, and cushion covers changed, so did the kitchen. In winter, the cupboard and drawer faces were white to match the landscape and maximize light. In summer, they were switched to red to balance with nature's greenery and more colourful palette. By the 1950s, walls may have been going white but everything else in the home went colour crazy.

Toward the end of the twentieth century, new architectural styles reacted against Modernism's bald and colourless functionalism. Post–Modernism began in the late 1960s and took as its mantra American architect Robert Venturi's retort "Less is a bore." The style embraced bold colour, playful decoration, and historical references. Over–sized architectural elements like pillars and pediments looked like Brio building blocks on a monumental scale in red, turquoise, and ochre.

Brutalism was a style of building that massed together bulky, plain concrete forms often confusing in orientation, minimal in fenestration, and lacking in colour. Its name comes from the French word for concrete but I think of it as coming from brute, meaning unpleasant, harsh, irrational, and loutish. I was not surprised to see that the cave–like lower parts of a 1970s' edifice, the National Theatre on the South Thames in London, are covered with graffiti and used as a hang–out for skateboarders.

In adroit hands, Modernism evolved into the refined, almost monastic Minimalism of British architect John Pawson (1949). His approach, he says, is not about self–denial or doing without. It is about having what is essential and no more. His aesthetic is as edited and distilled as any Modernist could desire. Pawson used natural and artificial light together to sculpt and animate his unembellished surfaces. The light, lighting, and exterior views provide the only colour. Whether designing his home in London, a monastery in the Czech Republic, or retail stores in Manhattan for Calvin Klein, he achieves a sublime harmony of proportion and light. His spaces seem to invite one into a state of stillness and quiet meditation so I would love to visit him at home in Notting Hill and find out how his wife and two boys manage. Does living in such a disciplined place change us or thwart us? Is it possible that Le Corbusier was right and we would love living with less if we were re–educated? Or would we always struggle against our messy, informal selves? If I look around my studio, I am sure that there is no hope of re–education for me but amelioration would be good.

Dirt has usually been a bane of the white exteriors. By the end of the twentieth century, there was a fix. American architect Richard Meier, one of the reigning masters of white, as any visitor to the Los Angeles Getty Museum discovers, uses a cement tile with a self–cleaning coating on his exteriors. Developed by the Swedish company Cementa, this self–cleaning surface material also cleans pollutants out of the air around it (near Milan a 75,000–foot stretch of highway was painted with it and the air above became up to 60 per cent cleaner). And the magic ingredient? Good old titanium dioxide, the same ingredient that makes paint and toothpaste white. In the cement, it causes a catalytic reaction when it is

exposed to ultraviolet light from the sun. This stops dirt or bacteria from sticking to its surface. A little water or rain and the white become pristine. The only catch so far is whether builders will feel that reduced cleaning costs will balance out the 40 per cent higher price.

Modernism usually didn't work at home. Le Corbusier did not live to see us "re–educated." Wright railed against the "mobocracy" – everyone who could not understand what he was doing. Homes continued to be built in the ways Wright and Modernists hated, as a pastiche of historical references but without the craftsmanship or the rules of harmony and proportion that made the old beautiful. Exteriors were bland. White and its cousins, off–white and beige, took over the interiors. And for renters, white was not choice but the rule of law. White became the default colour used by people who didn't realize white needed light, texture, or luxurious and beautiful furnishings to bring it to life.

Taut was right. Surely colour and not white is the best way to put the welcome into walls, to put back something when all the trimming has been stripped away. And that something is joy.

Ironically, throughout the century, advances in paint technology made colour easier and easier to use. At the turn of the century, car paint took ten days to dry hard. By 1930, it took ten minutes. In 1927, an alkyd binder was added to house paint and it became quick drying. In 1953, artists started using water–based acrylic emulsions. They dried fast and opaque. Even thinned with water, they did not lose their punch. Brushwork could become invisible, which suited the 1960s' penchant for bold, flat colour.

In the 1940s, the epicentre of the art world shifted from Paris to New York. Old school artists who tended to paint "normal"–sized canvases still liked oil paint. But Abstract Expressionists who discarded recognizable subject matter in favour of colour alone wanted their colour to be big – big and cheap. And because rules of colour theory were also discarded in favour of more random combinations, any colour would do. Jackson Pollock started using high-gloss house paint to drip and splatter over his large action paintings. For a time, Frank Stella's palette was whatever the paint store was getting rid of. Robert Rauschenberg bought unlabelled cans of house paint for five cents a quart. His colour rule was "use up what you have before you buy any more."

Colour was freed from narrative content and became the subject in its own right. Gerhard Richter thought paint manufacturers' colour charts showed how to organize colour into isolated squares free from all rules of colour theory. He did his own version of colour charts making them so monumentally large they span up to thirty-one feet. He said his colour choices were random "like bingo" but looking at them at the Museum of Modern Art's show Colour Chart: Reinventing Colour from the Fifties and Beyond only confirmed my suspicion that colour intuition, free from rules, is the best guide to gorgeous colour combinations. Rather than using random colour, French artist Yves Klein used his signature IKB in random ways. In 1958 he had women cover their naked bodies in his signature blue then press against large sheets of paper, creating action art. He painted blue canvases, tied them to the back of his car, and drove around Paris until the trip had added its effects, making each unique. But he also painted a lot of IKB (International Klein Blue) canvases and sold them for different prices, cheap to someone on the street, expensive to art collectors. If art was idea, and the idea was colour, what was it worth? And was it worth more to some than to others? Did value depend on who was buying?

If things were not confusing enough, the notion that art and life might marry in every home was further thwarted by the fact that colour-filled art was getting bigger and new housing smaller. Mark Rothko argued that colour was not decorative, it was transcendental. However its effect worked only if the colour fields were so big they overwhelmed you. Rothko said it was not that he was especially interested in colour but if you took away line, what was left? He felt his compositions required no explanation because if they were any good they would speak for themselves. Big colour had the power to trigger a sense of the sublime. But big is relative. He would not be happy had he lived to see his big paintings reproduced as pretty little postcards and wall calendars. Nor made small by hanging them in a large gallery space. He painted his large works in a small studio, six feet by eight, and he wanted viewers to experience his big paintings in the same small space and hung close to the floor so viewers would be, as he was, confronted and commanded by colour, overwhelmed by it. In the right space, he was sure we would all want to fall on our knees in front of his work because we would have the same religious experience he had when he was painting it.

Abstract Expressionist Barnett Newman (1905–1970) shared Rothko's colour attitude. He did huge fields of flat colour interrupted with a slim vertical line or lines of another colour that he called "zips." He said that if others could see his works properly, then global capitalism would come to an end. I stood in front of one of his red paintings the size of a huge wall at the MOMA in New York City. And I did get a buzz from it. It made me giddy, like a person who giggles when an emotion is too big and confusing to hold in. But it would be a long stretch to hook my response to anything outside of me and the colour and the moment. Newman and Rothko remind me of Kandinsky thinking that colour would speak to us in exactly the way it spoke to him *if* we were tuned into it properly, spiritually. But where colour actually speaks most clearly is to the non–specifics of raw emotion.

It is too bad Newman did not live long enough to comment on the huge public outcry when the National Gallery of

Canada bought his large painting *Voice of Fire* (1967), a red band down the middle of a blue background, in 1989 for $1.8 million. It might have been a sweet vindication for an artist whose only success came late in life. In the 1930s he failed the test required to get an art-teaching licence three times. (He got 15 per cent the first time and was only at 33 per cent by the second.) By the age of fifty he had sold only a few paintings and all but one to friends. He made a little money reviewing art but lived subsidized by his wife's teaching salary for decades. He sued a fellow artist Ad Reinhardt for referring to him in an article as "an avant-garde-huckster-handicraftsman." The case was dismissed. And to all those who look at his paintings and say "Oh, I could do that!" I say "Why don't you?" Why don't we take a page from the book of abstract expressionism and get out paint and rollers and make big colour fields of our boring walls? Not to call ourselves artists but to explore and enjoy the power and mystery of being in the presence of big colour.

Rothko was like Leonardo da Vinci when it came to being so in the orgiastic colour moment that he paid too little attention to what concoctions he was using. Sometimes following centuries-old recipes written up by Cennino Cennini, he boiled up buckets of animal glue and mixed it with egg and pigments. Sometimes he thinned his paint so much the canvas looked stained rather than painted. He used oils and acrylics in the same piece or so much pigment with too little binder to hold it on. He was obsessed with how his colour looked and not what it took to get there. It didn't take long for streaks, cracks, and fading to occur.

In 1962, Harvard University commissioned Rothko to do five huge vertical panels as a mural for a penthouse space used for entertaining. Rothko liked his colours to be seen in dim light or against a subdued background but there were large windows on two walls. To darken the space, he advised on curtains and suggested a wall covering of olive green fabric. Still the light poured in and the murals began to fade almost immediately. Five years later, the dark reds had become blue–purple, other colours faded to grey and white. By 1979, they were wrapped up in black plastic and put into storage.

A series of nine paintings intended for the Four Seasons Restaurant in New York met a better fate. Rothko spent time in the space but after watching wealthy patrons eat he became disgusted with the idea that his great works would be like wallpaper for the elitist setting. He cancelled his most lucrative commission and sent them to London's Tate Gallery, where they arrived the day of his suicide. Now they have a room to themselves at the Tate Modern and are shown the way Rothko would have liked. In the small room the light is so dim that viewers can't rush. It takes a few minutes to even see the work emerge out of the gloom. It felt to me like being held captive in a big underwater pool of red surrounded by large, nebulous creatures. Visitors become quiet. They move slowly. The large colour presence is felt.

In 1969, Ken Newland was trying to make colour what he called "the generating force" by doing hard–edged paintings that looked like bar codes or targets. He was trying to get rid of anything but colour. Sol de Witt got rid of the canvas and painted his colours onto gallery walls. By the end of the century, American artists Dan Flavin (1933–1996) and James Turrell (1943) transcended paint by working with coloured light. Then Turrell explored colour at its purest. He opened up an oval void in the ceiling of an art gallery and a rectangle in the ceiling of Live Oaks Meeting House, a Quaker church. Views of the sky itself in a perpetually changing range of vivid blues, indigos, or blacks, nature's own colours untouched by man, become the subject. Colour has journeyed back to where it all began – with light.

WHITE, THE HARDEST COLOUR OF ALL

When Christopher Wren selected Portland limestone for Saint Paul's Cathedral around 1700, there was an outcry. It was too white. No church worth its salt looked so pristine, so colourless. They were supposed to look more like Westminster Abbey which was made of French limestone. Wren said there was no need to worry. London's dirt and pollution would soon tone it down to suit public taste. At the moment, it is being cleaned and it looks almost surrealistic, a ghost of a building. But it no longer looks wrong. What makes a white right?

White, white, white. I get really tired of white.

I tried to find out from paint manufacturers what percentage of paint sold was white but the difficulty was to determine what range of light neutrals could be classified as white. All said, whites accounted for more than 70 per cent of total sales.

It isn't that, as a colour designer, I don't like white. I really love white when it is used well. The trouble is, it so seldom is. White is hard to get right. The slightest tilt in the wrong direction and white goes wrong. With a red or a green it is comparatively easy to judge what is what but white and very light pastels, which I call whites, have nuances that are exceedingly subtle. If I am asked to build an all–white palette for clients, it is as if my eyes have to sharpen their colour tuning and come into a tighter focus. An entire spectrum has to be discovered within the range of white. It requires care and caution. It takes time. Used well, it is the height of elegant simplicity. Used badly, it is sterile, clinical, unwelcoming, and hostile.

White, like black, is a beginning. It is like the silence before the music, the space that is full of possibility. White is associated with the purity and innocence of a new life and with fading, sterility, and death – bones, dust, driftwood, shed skin. For Hindus, white is the colour of serenity and detachment. In many cultures it is the colour of enlightenment and, by extension, God, and so it is worn by those considered close to Him or trying to be – the Pope, since the sixteenth century, monks, nuns, and pilgrims. White is used for rituals marking life's passages and symbolizing a new beginning – funeral shrouds, wedding awnings, and, in many African initiation ceremonies, body painting. In sixteenth–century Spain, it was the colour of mourning. In nineteenth–century Europe, brides began wearing white wedding dresses to symbolize the innocence of an unconsummated union.

White was not always easy to achieve. Chlorine's bleaching powers were not discovered until the end of the eighteenth century. To whiten fabric, cloth was laid out on the grass and kept moist while the sun bleached it. But, like tanning in reverse, the white soon faded and the fabric lost its sunny whiteness. In Europe, royalty made their mourning clothes look less yellow and more white by contrasting it with wardrobe elements in mauve, grey, or black; clergy used gold. *Bluing,* rinsing white laundry in water tinted blue, was another way to brighten white.

We were never meant to live in a white habitat. Living in a snow-covered landscape requires adaptation. But nature's white is full of colour. Big skies full of changing hues are reflected off the transparent surface of snow and ice. Unlike paint, nature's white – snow, clouds, orchids and blossom, animal fur – is made with light. It catches and reflects colour. Vermeer's most luminous whites were made with ground alabaster and quartz that refracted light. The lime in the whitewash used on humble homes refracted light beautifully. Most white paint cannot come alive unless natural light plays across it.

Imagine a beautiful white room. It will always be filled with light. Perhaps it is in a house in Malibu: open plan and very modern. Californian sunlight pours in through a wall of glass. The beach and the breaking waves fill the panoramic view. Inside, everything is white: walls, furniture, curtains. The carpet is thick. Light bounces off the glass surfaces of a large coffee table and big lamps with white shades. The absence of other colours and the presence of light, texture, and sheen make it a beautiful white room.

A good white space can also be humble and not pristine perfection – a Greek fisherman's cottage or Mexican hut. The imperfect walls are whitewashed; the floor is of wide scrubbed planks, the furniture – wood or upholstered in faded fabrics – is minimal and well used. A few functional items like cast iron pots, an old tin bucket, a stack of old white plates, and woven baskets sit on open shelves. Implements hang from iron hooks. Through the window, a Mediterranean blue sky spreads out above a green tropical lushness. White is beautiful when it is simple and basic and set into a landscape of year-round colour brilliance.

The perfect white space can be urban – a SoHo loft. A large colour–filled painting leans against one of the white walls under a wood beamed ceiling. There is a wall of north–facing old factory windows. The furniture is still minimal but big and comfortable and the sofa set at an angle doesn't match the random chairs flanking it. Red wine in oversized glasses sit on the large square coffee table next to a stack of books. A bench holds state–of–the–art stereo equipment. What makes white work is basically the same: light, variety of materials, and if there is any colour, it is held firmly under control.

Good white rooms always meet three demanding criteria. They must have good light, harmonized proportions, and a few attractive objects artfully arranged. They are a kind of iconic ideal. This is why white rooms are a challenge, not to be taken on lightly by those not up to aesthetic discipline.

Adding colour to a sunny room is like putting makeup on a beautiful face, totally unnecessary. Besides, why have paint's one colour when you can have light's many? It is poorly lit spaces that need colour. White will look grey. White is typically used in basement rooms or in windowless or dark rooms in the misguided hope that it will make light but it won't, so get out the colour.

White is a snob that likes its own company best. Interest comes from a variety of textures and sheens and from natural or uncoloured materials – wood, stone, fur, metal, glass. It likes other neutrals and finds black, its colour complement, incredibly exciting. If other colours are pale enough, white considers them part of the family. If they aren't, the white tries to make them look bad: bold and boisterous, like vulgar intruders. Colour gets blamed for being loud but white is the mischievous culprit. White on ceilings and trim, for example, makes wall colour look too strong. White is what puts the kick into colour palettes. Taking it out or replacing it with beiges and tans immediately calms colour. White and colour com-

binations are suitable only for colour lovers who don't mind the intensity. Otherwise, leave the colour alone and tone down the white.

Stark white ceilings should be banned from all rooms with deep wall colour. They should either be softened by mixing in a percentage of the wall colour (25 per cent or more) or changed for a soft neutral tone. The effect will be light but not bright, subtle enough to make the fifth wall an integral part of a well-dressed room. In small rooms or rooms with sloping ceilings, the wall colour should extend over the ceiling to make the space more ambient and expansive. Why is it often hard for others to believe this?

White walls offer no place to hide, no camouflage. They create an art gallery effect, spotlighting attention on every object so each must be worthy. White walls highlight shape and colour and tolerate no chaotic mess. Each object is part of the composition and so has to be selected and positioned with a curatorial eye for arrangement. White walls are not the avoidance of colour. They are the embracing of the most demanding colour of all.

White, the colour of refinement, is overused as the colour of function and efficiency. Until the 1970s, white was used in hospitals to make them appear antiseptically clean but it also made them clinical and sterile. In high-traffic areas or functional spaces, it is not the most practical colour. White walls are like white clothing. Unless the dry-cleaning budget is huge and the body perfect, we are best to avoid them. They show all the dirt and wear and tear, every blemish.

Bad white spaces are those where white is not used as a colour but in the misguided notion that it is the avoidance of colour. This is when white looks bald and empty, cheap and unfriendly. Or it can look unfinished, a beginning still waiting for something to happen.

I empathize with a little girl who could not bear the sight of the perfect white wall that her mother had just finished painting. It was huge and ran the length of the ground floor of their house. The paint was barely dried when the little girl took a black marker and drew a wiggly line from one end of the wall to the other. Needless to say, her mother was not amused. When she asked her daughter why she would do such a thing when she knew she shouldn't, the child answered, "I couldn't help it. The white made me do it."

White is aloof. Colour excites. Real estate agents should know that colour sells even to lovers of white. There are endless stories like the one about the manufacturer of plastic garbage pails who decided to boost sales at a trade show by adding a new pail, a raspberry red one, to their line. They showcased the red pails in the centre of the booth. The show was an astounding success. They never sold as many pails. The biggest seller? White. Seeing the raspberry red buckets got purchasers excited and that excitement extended itself to all the buckets, especially white ones.

My client Lynn loved colour and we used lots of it in her condominium. When a larger one came up in the same building, she sold her condo in two days, setting a record for her building. Colour made her furniture look good and the apartment different and exciting. Probably the first thing the new owner intended to do was change the colours, no doubt using more white.

Often the desire for white walls is really the desire to avoid colour. Neutrals, not white do that. Tan, beige, linen, sand, putty all dress a room without any colour commitment. They are white's understudy for those of us not disciplined in our belongings and our lives. After several years of colour consulting, I am brave enough to specify white but only for those who can deal with the rigours of such a demanding hue.

RULES ARE FOR BREAKING

COLOUR THEORY

No one, and I mean no one, uses theory to design their colours. If they do, they are amateurs. Colour theory explains how colour is organized. It is excellent for labelling what has been done. It gives us terminology for describing colour palettes. I might tell you that here we have an analogous colour scheme, hues from neighbouring or similar colour groups, and this is a complementary one. Over here we have gone for a monochromatic or a single–colour approach. And to really impress you, I might draw your attention to some split complementaries. Well lah–di–dah. You might think I design according to rules of colour theory. I can only categorize with them – after the fact. The funny thing about colour theory is how interesting it seems and how useless it is.

Colour theory has always seemed to me like the emperor's clothes. I was taught it in art classes. I confront it in design books. People in the know about colour seem to think it is important. If they sang its praises,

I hummed along. But the truth is that I never really understood how I was supposed to use it. I put colours together by feel.

We have always tried to solve colour conundrums with rules. In my experience, every rule about colour is a rule that colour will break, but this doesn't stop us from trying. Even when picking colours for their rooms, people cling tenaciously to colour do's and don'ts as if they were commandments written in stone. Colour rules, many I am sure made up by impatient house painters, usually don't make sense. For example, *ceilings must always be white.* It would be more correct to say ceilings should often be light. Or *dark colours will make a room feel smaller* is more correctly this: bold colour on four walls will make a room appear smaller but on one wall it can open up the box, and really dark colours make the walls disappear, which can create the illusion of more space. *Colour is tiring* is a common old axiom. Colour isn't tiring but too many colours can be. Reducing pattern and high contrast can relax colour and calm its effect. *Good colour schemes use three hues, the dominant which makes up 60 per cent of the colour, the intermediate 30 per cent, and the accent 10 per cent.* Hmmm. Who was the nerd that came up with that one? Not a designer. Most of us are not good enough at math to deal with ratios. The worst one is probably this: *putting complementary colours together makes colour harmony.* The truth is that, unless very judiciously apportioned, they make colour cacophony.

The rules of colour theory that we fixate on, the ones taught at every art and design school, are those that were espoused by Bauhaus in the early twentieth century. It was a time when rationalizing colour into a set of practical rules seemed like a necessary and worthy exercise. Artists, architects, and theorists were rationalizing everything – architecture, housing, city planning, education, social systems – why not colour, something that was literally and metaphorically closer to home?

Johannes Itten's *The Art of Color,* a book based on the colour course he taught at Bauhaus, was still compulsory reading when I studied art at university in the 1970s. He warned us in his introduction that "only those who love color are admitted to its beauty and immanent presence. It affords utility to all, but unveils its deeper mysteries only to its devotees." This kaftan-wearing oddball colour preacher continued, colour is a primeval essence, a "phantasmagorical resonance, light become music" but trying to rationalize it broke its spell and left us holding a corpse. So perhaps he should have stopped there instead of proselytizing to the colour uninitiated.

Itten believed that we who don't know colour like colours that blend rather than contrast. We like groupings of various tones and shades of similar colours. It is true. Think of the range and variety of greens in any garden. Together they blend into what we enjoy as one lush greenness. We do prefer colours that blend to those that bump or bang into each other. We like colour flow with controlled amounts of colour contrast: the floral border in that lush green garden.

According to Itten, this penchant of ours for analogous colours is a sign of our chromatic ignorance. If we knew better, we would like what we are *supposed* to like, and what we are supposed to like are *complementary* colours, opposites on the colour wheel.

Complementary colours, even though they are stridently contrasting, are supposed to be harmonious because they balance one another. The theory is that they balance one another because together they contain all three primary colours and, therefore, all colour. (They make grey when mixed together.) Hence, they are complementary or complete. Red's complement is green. Green is the result of combining blue and yellow. Voilà: all colour. Like others before and since, Itten confused what was complete with what was attractive.

I am sure I am not the only one who finds red-green living room schemes busy. A blue-orange one looks strident rather than harmonious. And purple and yellow – don't even think about it. But Itten used after images to justified the idea.

At the Barbican Art Gallery in London, I had a pleasant experience of the phenomenon. The main gallery has white walls, grey floors, and dark granite pillars and feels more like the cold, colourless atrium of an office tower than an art gallery. The show, Colour After Klein, infused it with welcome hits of colour but I was drawn toward a coloured glow emanating from a room opening off the far corner of the main space. Through its wide entranceway came a bright, lime green light. Inside was a Dan Flavin installation. Neon tubes shone bright lime green light onto one wall and yellow onto another. The rest of the room was filled with a reflected combination of the two. I stood there basking in the vivid yellow–green light. When I turned and walked back into the main space, everything was the most wonderful mauve–pink. After a few seconds it vanished. Like a child who wants to keep spinning around to get dizzy, I couldn't resist going back to the Flavin installation and getting my eyes saturated so I could turn around and get another blast of pink. And another.

The green cones in my eyes were absorbing so much green they became saturated. While they were recharging, they could see only in yellow–green's complementary, pink–mauve. Itten took successive contrast as optical proof that the eye seeks equilibrium so badly that it refreshes itself by making up the colour it lacks. It seemed logical to think that if both colours were present, the eye would not experience this overload, and colour would balance. This was thinking that led to one of the biggest colour mistakes ever conceived.

Who goes out into nature or sits in their backyard and feels that the green is tiring because there just isn't enough red! We don't want a few red trees scattered about to bring visual balance. Complementaries *compete* with each other. *They do not coordinate with each other.* There is no greenish–red or reddish–green because they are as far apart as two colours can be. They are colour opposites, chromatic opponents. They don't harmonize, they scream at each other. Besides, when it comes to interior design we don't get retinal fatigue from single colour overload because no one puts the same colour on four walls, the floor, and the furniture. Colour relief is something we intuitively build in.

Colour theory has never been as important for artists as we are led to believe. Naturalist or Realist painters did not need colour theory to paint what they were looking at in the most literal way possible. Impressionists paid attention to scientific colour theories but didn't know quite how to attach them to their work so they applied theory in their individual ways, which is the reason their styles are so varied. For Post–Impressionists and abstract artists, colour theory was not as important as feeling. Grass could be blue and the sky green if it suited. Madame Amélie Matisse did not think Henri's vision was impaired in 1905 when he painted her portrait and put a big green stripe down her face. Nor did she object to her face being colour coordinated to the walls – the left side was lime green because the right side of the wall was teal green. The right was pink to coordinate with the red and mauve on her left. Then came Abstract Expressionists who used a single colour, a restricted palette, or no colour as their aesthetic signature or for psychological effects. Yves Klein did not feel the need to add a dash of orange to his International Klein Blue paintings to achieve colour harmony. Op artists like Bridget Riley use optical effects and not colour theory to make the colours of her geometric paintings shimmer, flicker, and pulsate. She said that instability is the basis of colour and it should be allowed to breathe and play its own "wanton game." In art, as in decorating, there was one key colour rule: if it seems right, it is right.

In his book, Itten admits that his attempts to teach his students at Bauhaus that complementary colours are complimentary failed miserably. He painted a series of "colour harmonies" that were complementary colour pairs in lighter and darker tones painted as a patchwork of squares. The

students did not think the results were harmonious, in fact, they found them hideous. Itten suggested that they try the exercise themselves. Each would do a coloured–square painting using whatever colour combination they thought most harmonious.

When they were handed in, Itten noticed something interesting. He knew without looking at signatures which student had painted which colour harmony. He later photographed the students standing next to their paintings to record the fact that each palette matched the student's physical colouring. It also matched their personality. The outgoing Hispanic student used strong colours plus black. The quiet blonde did a pastel harmony.

Colour harmony is as unique as we are. Just as we know what smells and tastes good without anyone telling us, we know what looks good. Colour is like food. We know we don't want ice cream with pasta or mashed potatoes. We don't need anyone telling us why. We also know that, much as we might love those potatoes, on their own they get pretty boring. We prefer them with peas and gravy. We may love red but into that red room will come other colours, including a pinch of its opposite, green, to add spice. It isn't that complementaries should be avoided altogether, just balanced. We like variations of a single–colour family in a room. The farther apart another colour is from the main one, the less of it should be used. For colour calm and for a balance that is easy on the eye, the complementary should be used in the smallest amount of all. But who ever told us that?

Itten's colleague Josef Albers had a better approach to colour theory. He believed that rules of harmony were a worn–out idea and that no system could be flexible enough to deal with all the changing variables of colour.

In his book *Interaction of Color* (1963), Albers focuses on how colour behaves. According to him, if someone says, "Red" in a room of fifty people, everyone will imagine a different red. (For men the reddest red is usually a blue–red. For most women it is an orange–red.) If the colour term is more specific, "Coca–Cola red" for example, and those in the room were asked to choose it from a selection of red paint chips, each would still probably select a different one. Even if everyone were looking straight at a Coca–Cola sign, it is not possible to know that everyone is seeing the same red. (It is true that the smallest molecular difference between human beings, a difference in a single amino acid, can cause a difference in perception.) Albers wisely advocated forgetting about "recipes and rules." Forget about what colour *is*. Pay attention to what colour *does*.

Colour is changed by the company it keeps. The same colour looks different if the colours around it are altered. It is a comparative reality. Albers began work on *Homage to the Square*, a series of painted colour studies of a smaller square centred on a larger one. The centre square appeared to advance or recede and looked lighter or darker depending on the background colour. If the centre square was grey, it appeared tinted with the complement of the background colour. The colour we see is not what is literally being reflected from the square but what we do with what is reflected when the information reaches our brain, and in our head the grey square becomes coloured.

I thought being aware of the brain's trick would help me to outsmart the illusion. With the intention of proving that if we know the real colour we will not be fooled, I recreated some of Albers's experiments. I pasted pieces of the same colour into different colour settings. Even though I knew I was looking at the same colour against different backgrounds, I still couldn't *see* it that way. Our brain really does make up its own colours, optical colour. If your living room beige looks greenish on the wall between the red drapes, then no matter what colour you thought you were painting, the greenish colour you see is the colour you get. If you change the colour of your ceiling and drapes, your wall colour changes again. Combinations determine the colour a colour looks. Colour is a subjective illusion founded on objective facts. Colour is a verb, not a noun.

Colour is a shifting, changing chameleon. No amount of training helps us to overcome its trickster behaviour. Albers tested his colour experiments on colour experts, artists, and designers and found them no more capable than anyone else of knowing which colours were the same in changed settings and which were different. A musician would feel totally incompetent if he couldn't distinguish between higher and lower notes. Colours cannot be called up in exactly the same note–for–note, tone–for–tone sequence because they are seen in combination. So when people tell me they have a good colour memory, I know they only think they do.

Even describing a colour from memory skews our accuracy. Daniel Gilbert in *Stumbling on Happiness* mentions a study in which two groups of people were shown a yellow swatch, like a paint chip. When it was taken away, those in one group were asked to describe it. In the other group they weren't. Thirty seconds after seeing the yellow, they were all shown six yellow swatches and asked which one was the one they had just seen. Of the group that did not describe the yellow, 73 per cent picked the right one. Of the group that described it, only 35 per cent got it right! The description got in the way of colour memory. It "coloured" accuracy. Because colour is part external fact and part internal creation, never rely on the accuracy of your colour memory.

The difference between a colour expert and a colour layperson is not knowing about colour as much as it is knowing not to make assumptions or guess about what colour will do. One of Canada's finest architectural partnerships, Bridget Shim and Howard Sutcliffe, put two dozen deep blue test patches on a wall in their home and looked at them for a year, observing them at different times of day and in the different seasons. Then they made their choice.

But which colours interact in aesthetically pleasing ways? What makes some colours look good together and some not? Is it personal or are there laws? I have the feeling that I know when a combination makes visual music, colour harmony. And when I play with colour, putting palettes together, clients will sometimes ask if I have always been good with colour. I know practise makes me much quicker with colour but are we not all equally good at spotting harmonious combinations when they are presented to us?

In all my work I have had only one client who admitted she was completely tone deaf when it came to colour. My clients usually are very tuned into colour or they wouldn't bother calling. But Jill was in charge of a rental property, and a real estate agent had insisted she call me to get the colours done before putting the big old mansion on the market. When I was there building the palette, I asked her opinion about this or that tone and she said she really didn't know. She could see they were different. She was not colour–blind. She just didn't have the emotional trigger or colour response that would lead her to a preference.

I asked her what colour her house was. Beige. Well, how did she choose her beige? The painter chose it. As I did the colour for the rental house, her concern was mainly how many colours – the fewer the better. She did let me do some dramatically dark ones in a few places that needed colour to distract from unattractive realities. She had an appreciation for what I was doing, even called afterwards to say she was delighted. She simply could not engage with colour – good, bad, or indifferent.

Usually my challenge is to choose the best colour for harmonizing all the existing hues in the fabrics, the floor, the details. It is like being an artist who is handed a half–finished canvas and being asked to fill in the missing bits. I get out my colour chips and, almost immediately, a good colour seems to jump out. The random colours in the space will fall into line and the result will be a unified colour harmony. But what makes the magic?

Maybe Philip could lead me to the answer. He worked for a company that made portable spectroscopes using the technology found in every digital camera. He said that with his gizmo I could walk up to any material, your sweater or your neighbour's porch, and take an accurate colour reading. And this could be translated into a paint chip number from any paint company programmed into the colour reader. The spectroscope was developed by M. Ronnier Luo and Li–Chen Ou at the Department of Colour and Polymer Chemistry at Leeds University in the United Kingdom. Philip told me they had also done in–depth research into colour harmony and could predict what colour combinations make it. This seemed too good to be true so I contacted them.

In Li–Chen and Luo's experiment, seventy participants – British, American, and Chinese – were shown over five thousand colours and colour combinations. They had to put individual colours and then colour pairs in order according to preference. The purpose was to find out if there was anything consistent in what made colour pleasing and what combinations were harmonious. Did hue, value, or chroma have more effect? In a world obsessed with colour – red, blue, and green – and value – light–dark – one might expect those qualities of colour to be the big influence on preference. Surprisingly they were not! It was chroma – how dirty or clean the colours were that could make or break harmony. Value (the degree of contrast between two colours) made the next biggest difference.

Studies done in the 1960s by anthropologists Brent Berlin and Paul Kay at the University of California, Berkeley, to determine how colour is divided and named in over a hundred languages found all cultures see six basic colour groups. The six categories are the colours of the spectrum. Colour is also divided into two groups: chromatic – the spectrum – and achromatic colour – black, grey, and white. It is on the bridges we build between these two groups that our six basic colours fan out into a gazillion variations. In the nineteenth century when scientists such as Chevreul, Young, and Helmholtz were deciphering what colour was, how we see it, and how it behaves, this is when it became clear that the colour wheel was not adequate for mapping colour. Colour was a globe.

Coordinating colours into harmonious palettes requires balancing not just colour, but its three dimensions: hue, value, and chroma. And what the research in Leeds found out was that of the three, hue is the least important! Any basic colour is attractive. (It makes sense that evolution would have predisposed us to like every basic colour.) It is how they are played that counts. Coloured pairs are perceived to be harmonious only if there is some light–dark contrast between colours. They are harmonious only if the chromas match; dirty colours with dirty colours and clean with clean. Combinations that were dark and looked "heavy" were unattractive. When colours were viewed individually and not as a combination, clean or saturated colours were preferred over dirty ones. (This preference was especially strong for the Chinese participants.) Other studies found that we prefer small pieces of colour that are clean and bright. But Li–Chen and Luo found that dirtier or complex colours are easier to mix and match and easier to harmonize.

Wall colours should not be chosen by looking at a little paint chip on its own or we get too easily seduced by the clean ones that look "pretty." Increase them to the size of a wall or a room and they can seem like way too much of a good thing. High chroma colour is usually too strong a presence to be lived with. Low chroma colours grow into sophisticated and

elegant wall colours that are easy to have around. Choosing the wall colour as part of a fuller colour package, one that includes flooring and fabrics, helps us see the user–friendly beauty in a wider range of less saturated colours. I often have to get clients to like dirtier colours by asking them to think of them not as a colour but a material. "That isn't a dirty yellow beige, it is the colour of straw." "That is not a grey–brown. It is the colour of tree bark or stone."

So did the team at Leeds find the definitive answer to what makes colour harmony? They took their findings to a conference in Budapest where experts from around the world brought their research into colour harmony. Li–Chen Ou said that while the discussion was very interesting, there was no consensus. Everyone had a different idea. So I mentioned to Ou one of my own. Making colour harmony will never be an exact science because what makes the magic is putting together colours that seem to work well and then just bending one of them off course a little or dropping in a little bit of some odd–ball hue that makes everything get up on its toes and dance a little. It is the twist, dent, flaw, the mischievous blip that makes magic. How we bend the note is too personal to ever be formulaic. Ou did not disagree.

French artist Eugene Delacroix said, "Draftsmen may be made but colourists are born." I think we are all potential colourists. Like playing the piano, the more you do it, the better you get at it. I go through life making colour observations and connecting colour dots. I gather colour information because it is what I do. Am I a more gifted colourist or just more practised? According to research, women have more facility with colour than most men. We have had a few more million years of colour practice as gatherers, a job that requires a lot of colour skill. The guys, meanwhile, were hunting, a job for which colour blindness, which heightens awareness of movement and texture, is not disadvantageous.

For those of us who want to be better at colour and don't have a million years to practise, colour theory will not set us on the fast track. Good–bye Bauhaus. Good–bye rules. Colour, and those who love and work with it, hate rules. Like artists and designers, simply looking and feeling is our way back to an intuitive relationship with colour. We know which colours bang and bump together and which ones flow effortlessly, even if we don't know why. Balance, harmony, and what we like are things we know.

3054
1000 YDS.

THERE IS NO SUCH THING AS TOO MUCH COLOUR

I am a colour snob. I like to think that I use colour in many different ways but I never want to be accused of the cardinal sin: a design that is too colourful. Unless there is a good reason for it, what I don't do is "colourful." Bold colour where it does not belong looks ridiculous and juvenile. Good colour is appropriate colour. It makes a place feel good and function well. Whether strong or subtle, good colour has to set the right energy levels. It is always logical but not necessarily colourful. Colourful can be tiring; colour isn't.

I am usually called in to design colour for people who want more than they have and less than they need, so how much is enough? There is no rule of thumb, no norm because the equation depends on personality, place, and what is already there. Like decibel levels, "enough" is comparative. Sound technicians at most rock concerts build the volume to keep the music at the same level but they would do better to make it quiet and loud intermittently, like Beethoven does in his symphonies, to generate excitement without deafening everyone.

By not wanting colours to yell, I sometimes err on the side of safe. When people think they want neutrals, I try to be sure that they get the right neutrals. But sometimes the urge to introduce a bold chromatic hit is irresistible. When I was almost finished the neutral palette for David and Beth's new house, I suggested a bit of colour at the end of the long narrow hallway to the bedrooms. A pumpkin colour that related to the warm tones of the hardwood floor would shorten the hall's tunnel effect and create a focal point. They were reluctant. I said it would be so simple to delete it or change it if it didn't work.

A week later they called and left a message. "Please call us. We have a problem. It's the orange." I rolled my eyes thinking that they were probably overreacting and hadn't given the colour time to settle but I was wrong. When we spoke they said, "We are loving that colour so much, we needed more – lots more."

Colourful is not how much or how strong. It is only colourful in comparison to the context. In a white house, a red wall is colourful. In a green setting, red is colourful. But add red into a setting full of other reds, oranges, pinks, purples, or deep wood tones and it seems like a very tame addition. Reducing contrast reduces impact. Colourful is not the amount of colour but the amount of contrast.

I wondered if my abhorrence of being too colourful made me too colour conservative when I heard about another colour designer with a reputation for having no such inhibitions. It was a grey March afternoon when I went into her storefront business. I don't think of anyone who loves and works with colour as competition but rather a kindred spirit. I am always curious about how others use colour, how they "sell" colour, and what colours they like. Jane had a reputation for using colour with a capital C. As she and her husband–business partner put it, "We hate beige. Safe is not what we do."

When I walked through the door, the profusion of colour was astonishing. The place was full of furniture and accessories grouped into what is called, in the trade, "stories." Each grouping was themed to a particular lifestyle, labelled Classic, Exotic, Spa, and so on. Each was dressed in the appropriate colour palette. It was all very exciting – at first.

I browsed through a portfolio of their work, rooms full of canary yellow, orange, magenta, red, purple, and blue. Browns and taupes were scattered here and there. All the ceilings and trim were bright white. No colour was left unused. I talked to them about their clients and they sang the gospel of how colour brings joy into the lives of all who venture there.

But before long I started to feel overwhelmed. It was like having one too many helpings of a seriously rich dessert or being talked at by too many people at once. It was too much information. I had to escape. Re-entering the grey streetscape came as a relief.

In the shop, the colour information was compressed to fit the confines of the space. No home would have been so overloaded. Nonetheless, it presented me with an exaggerated version of what I think clients fear: that colour designers will impose too much and too many colours and the effect will be exhausting. What the shop showed me was that even for someone like me who thinks there is no such thing as too much colour, there can certainly be too many.

Next I paid a visit to Jane and her husband in their small but colourful home, a place where their design philosophy is very evident. Jane said that she didn't understand how people could move into a home with all their boxes and belongings but live in it like visitors. "We all need to take emotional ownership," by which she meant personalizing with colour. She wondered, "Why is it that people who invest thousands in fixing up a bathroom or kitchen, investing liberally in details like granite counters, don't spend even a little on infusing the house with personality?" By which she meant adding colour.

Jane divides colour into six palettes: Playfulness, Tranquility, Simplicity, Warmth, Power, and Elegance. She is not averse to a bit of mix–and–match. In her home, each room has its own colour story. "You are never going to make small rooms big by leaving them white," she said, "just boring. You might as well make them into jewels by using saturated colour, not dark but rich." In her home all the colours were the same depth or value, tonal unity to balance her chromatic variety. The bedroom is in passionate purple. The kitchen is orange–red. She never uses blue in kitchens because it suppresses appetite (although this might have its advantages). The back den is yellow–orange with big yellow furniture and bright cushions and bright art painted by herself and a brightly painted armoire. She said that in the evenings passersby often stop and look in, attracted by the glow of the colour, which is as intense as a burning fire. House guests gravitated toward the orange sitting room when the living room was white so she painted it red, from her Power palette. Major rooms, in Jane's opinion, should not be relaxing. They should be strong and dynamic.

And as if her colours are not intense enough, she always uses white ceilings and trim to beef up their strength. This strategy works for her and her husband because, as they told me, they thrive on colour "because colour gives everything life. It relaxes and invigorates. I'd feel unhealthy if I didn't have lots of colour around me." When they walk into their house at the end of the day, the strong colours are their relief from the bland urban settings.

Jane does not think being too colourful is possible. Her husband showed me a colour palette they were working on for one of their clients

– one colour after another was spread out before me, a full diet of hues, no chromatic stone left unturned. Could she be right? That no matter who you are and what your nature, bold colours will pull the vivacious and energetic "you" out of the woodwork? She has such faith in the energizing power of colour that when a client said she loved Jane's colour design but her husband didn't, Jane's advice was "keep the colour and ditch the husband." And she did!

I enjoyed my morning with Jane, her husband, and their colours. I admired her appetite for hue and her zeal for applying it. I do think in an ideal world everyone would have, at the very least, one totally exuberant room full of colour to go to as an energizer. But although Jane's house was very exciting to visit, I would not have wanted to live there. It overpowered me. There were too many decorative Me–Me–Me colours. I would find them as irritating on a daily basis as getting up to a person who is jolly, chipper, and smiley every day.

I do love it when clients push me to beyond my chromatic comfort level to get to theirs. But I am equally happy when my colours go unnoticed. My client Patricia's taste was fun and contemporary so for the main floor of her open–concept house we used white for the walls, ceiling, and trim. It kept things crisp, clean, and bright. Colour accents that could be changed like fashion accessories added the sizzle. They also broke up the space into more intimate areas.

First we tackled the big, boring main wall that ran from the front door up the stairs and beyond. Any art hung on it would have the impact of postage stamps. To make the wall shorter required a panel of unframed mirror glued to the first few feet of it, baseboard to ceiling. The next section of wall, about eight feet, would be olive black. This would punctuate the entrance area and create a reasonably sized gallery area for Patricia's black and white photography. Now the main wall was considerably shorter and the entrance more dressed. Across the room, the back of the niches on either side of the fireplace were aubergine. Farther down

the room, a section of wall the length of the dining table and chairs was dressed in red to make the area warm and cozy.

It took a long time for Patricia and her husband to paint in the colours, not just because they were doing the painting themselves but because they were timid about blocking so many different colours into what was effectively one big room. The darker the colour, the more terrifying they found it. The olive black went on last and predictably, in my experience, is the one they love the most.

To celebrate the completion of the painting, they invited friends over for dinner. The next day one of the guests called to say how wonderful the house looked. Patricia asked how she liked all the colours. "What colours?" was her friend's reply. The five colours were not experienced as separate from the room. In life we can so easily see things that are wrong but because what is right feels right, we don't pay it attention. Sadly, right is always less visible than wrong and colour is no exception.

Colour is more interesting than merely colourful. One of my clients said that I had done the colours of his mother's condo the previous year. "You used twenty-four colours in her place," he said. "I have looked really hard and I think I can see nine of them." So maybe it is not how many colours we use but how we use them that matters. I use lots of colours but rather than dividing them into colour stories and themes, I divide them into those to be seen and enjoyed and those to be invisible and do the work. The invisible colours are there to enhance the visible ones, not to compete for attention. The two complement each other in ways that are nuanced and complex because it isn't how they look but how they feel that is most important and that is much harder to see than colourful. As in nature, some of the most appropriate colours will seem so right you can experience them but hardly know they are there.

I am never fearful of adding a wall of colour here and there but I am usually opposed to bits of colour used as accents. I dislike wall tiles with little patterns on them – colour clutter. I dislike trim work that contrasts strongly against the walls and loathe it painted a punchy, decorative accent colour. A wall of red is big enough for red to add to its energy and its feeling to a room, but red as an accent on trim would be like a lot of lines and stripes and bits of colour clutter distracting us and making the room seem busy. Patterned fabrics, carpets, and art bring in colours that make music or noise depending on how they are orchestrated. If the colours in a room seem too colourful, reducing the amount of pattern, rather than colour, calms its. Adding colour to a wall also calms colour chaos. This colour brings itself forward from the pack, attracting focus to itself so that the rest of the room appears colour unified. Colours stand out against white but they nestle into a background of colour.

In my experience, the need for colour increases with the having. There is an Italian saying that the appetite increases with the eating. A small amount of colour can lead to a big addiction.

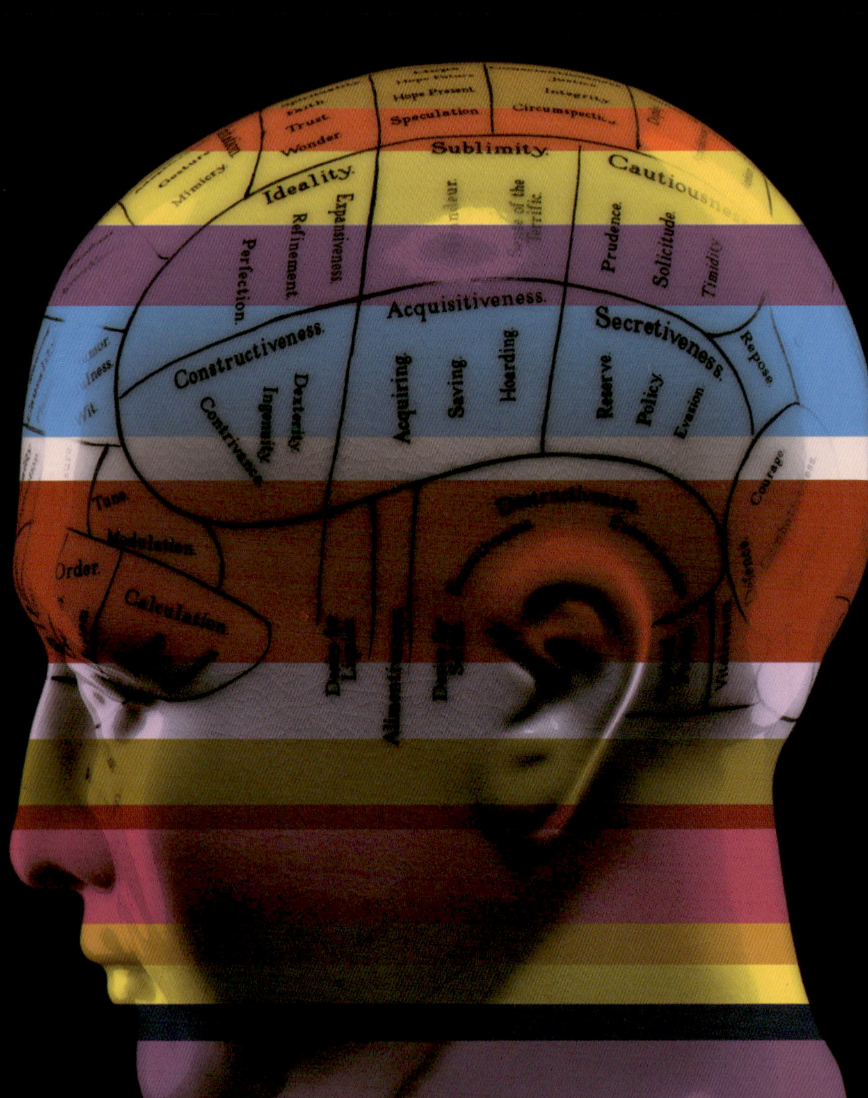

Hope Present
Speculation.
Integrity
Faith.
Trust.
Wonder.
Gesture
Mimicry.
Sublimity.
Ideality.
Expansiveness.
Refinement.
Perfection.
Sense of the Terrific.
Prudence.
Solicitude.
Timidity
Acquisitiveness.
Constructiveness.
Secretiveness.
Repose.
Dexterity.
Ingenuity.
Contrivance.
Acquiring.
Saving.
Hoarding.
Reserve.
Policy.
Evasion.
Wit.
Courage
Tune
Modulation.
Order.
Calculation.

SEEING RED, FEELING BLUE

COLOUR PSYCHOLOGY

I had the rather thankless task of being on the decorating committee at my tennis club. One day we had a volatile meeting over finalizing carpet colour. We were looking at the large sample of the one the architect was recommending. Everyone had a different opinion. The two guys on the committee admitted to being out of their depth. Theirs was a kind of "yeah, whatever" response. The manager was more concerned with timelines than aesthetics. An architect on our committee agreed with the architect doing the design. She thought that the dark brown and grey sample was very nice. However the committee member who was a decorator argued that the colours were blah, very, very blah, and appropriate for a hotel but not a friendly club. I said the colours were cold and corporate. The architect in charge of the design said they were warm and would look even warmer against the "warm" white walls.

Now you can call a black, brown, and grey colour combination against white a lot of things; "warm" just isn't one of them, which is what I said. We went round in circles. The decorator threw up her hands and stomped out. No consensus was reached.

How is it that what looks right to one person looks wrong to another? *Is* there a right and a wrong or is it personal? Are there universal truths? Don't we all respond to a particular colour in the same basic way? Red is warm. Blue is cool. Put together a bright combination of pink, lime green, and turquoise and it looks juvenile. Greyed tones are mature. Neutrals are sophisticated. Browns and greys are masculine. Pinks and pastels seem feminine. I could go on and on and on.

There do seem to be patterns to the way people respond to colours. Blue is the favourite colour of the world's population (35 per cent call blue their favourite). Red comes a close second while yellow is least likely to be called the favourite. But not having yellow as a favourite colour does not mean that you wouldn't be happy with a yellow room and, conversely, liking blue does not mean you want blue walls. A lover of blue who had an unhappy childhood in a blue bedroom would have a particularly negative response to the blue of that room. Blue lovers might also hate blue if it were for a sofa, a carpet, or nail polish. The right colour can become wrong depending on how and where it is used.

So how do we work our way through the morass of colour's complexities? How do we know right from wrong when picking a hue? Call in an expert to do it for us? As a colour designer, can I make intelligent assumptions about what will happen if I suggest a room be painted red?

If colour were entirely predictable, choice would be as easy as this. You want to be calm? Choose the colour of comfort and relaxation, green. You want to engage in lively discussions? Go with the intellectual stimulant, yellow. You want to get together with friends? Pick warm, sociable, and often underrated orange. You want to be excited? Choose the arousal and stimulation of red. You want sleep? Take the tranquilizer, blue. You aren't sure? The colour of ambiguity is purple. You hate colour? Choose grey. You want to listen to music, watch television, or hear yourself think? Then reduce visual information by choosing the quiet strength of black. You want to be alone and meditative? White is the colour of silence. It does not speak. It does not engage in friendliness. It is empty of content. Be sure that where you use white is a place where you feel comfortable and unthreatened.

We do seem to share a lot of responses, but if the meeting to finalize carpet colours was anything to go by, there are just as many ways that we diverge. This is the realm of colour psychology. Until the end of the nineteenth century, psychology only existed as a branch of philosophy. It evolved from an academic discipline into an empirical science in 1879 when German physician Wilhelm Wundt opened the first laboratory in Leipzig, Germany, to research psychology. For seven years Wundt had been assistant to scientific genius Hermann von Helmholz and Helmholtz's research on colour must have rubbed off. He began to connect the dots between colour and psychology. He recognized that colour responses were rooted in feelings, not intellect. He categorized colours as happy and sad, stimulating and relaxing and studied how colour could be used to reduce stress. In 1887 he published his two–volume *Physiological Psychology.*

William James, brother of novelist Henry James, published the discipline's next great tome, *Principles of Psychology* (1890). Even without the benefit of today's scientific understanding of the brain, James was able to think about thinking. He had phenomenal insight into the brain's idiosyncratic strategies and how conscious and unconscious thinking worked. James was to psychology what Shakespeare was to play writing, and Mozart was to music, and his book is still the bible of psychology.

By the end of the nineteenth century, interest in psychology, colour psychology, and chromotherapy was flourishing.

> **In the 1880s, Charles Frey was experimenting with chromotherapy as a cure for madness. Chromotherapy, or using exposure to different colours to cure different ailments, was practised in ancient times in Greece, Egypt, India, and China. It gained momentum up until World War I when advances in surgery and pharmaceutical treatments made these seem superior to the vagaries of chromotherapy. Science is still discovering how different colour vibrations affect different parts of the body on a molecular level, and no doubt chromotherapy will re–emerge.**

Fifteen labs like Wundt's had opened by 1890, and by 1900 there were sixty, mostly in Germany and the United States. By 1903, journals about psychology were being published. And by the 1920s, the United States was experiencing what was called "an outbreak of psychology."

Behavioural psychologists believe our behaviour is conditioned. Many responses are like unconscious reflexes. Basically we are fundamentally similar and predictable. Science, which brought such progress to so many areas of life, could be applied to our very selves. By paying attention to knowable patterns of behaviour, more efficient workplaces and social systems could be developed.

This was the thinking that convinced Le Corbusier and Bauhaus architects that colour could be rationalized into a set of universal laws and its effects predicted. Unfortunately, we humans are not all that predictable. As my carpet colour meeting showed, there was something very un–universal going on.

To find out more about how predictable our colour responses are, or aren't, I took the course required to become a member of the International Association of Color Consultants. It was taught by Frank Mahnke and as preparation I read his book *Color, Environment, and Human Response*. Chapter 4, called "Characteristic Effects of Major Hues," begins: "Color not only produces mood associations and subjective and objective impressions, but also influences our perception of volume, weight, temperature, time and noise. Collective findings have shown that there are basic reactions to color common to most people. It may be said that color is a universal language." This was good. Mahnke went on to say that even words that have no apparent colour link are hooked to common colour associations. I wrote down the list and put my colour associations next to them before looking at his results. (You might want to do the same.)

Love
Hatred
Peace / tranquility
Mourning / sorrow
Happiness
Joviality
Life
Luminous
Noble

I looked at his findings. My answers all matched! I was surprised and delighted.

Here are the colour associations for the majority of those surveyed by Mahnke. Love, no surprise, is red (or pink). Hatred, rather predictably, is black or red or red and black. Life is green. Happiness is yellow. Joviality is orange. Peace and tranquility are blue. Mourning is grey or purple. Noble is burgundy or purple, sometimes gold.

My daughter walked into the room. I asked her to tell me the colour of the same words. Hers matched. I was so excited about this synchronicity that I started quizzing everyone. Asking people for their colour associations became my favourite dinner game. When people did not give the expected response, I was disappointed at first. Then I began to notice a pattern. People departed from "the norm" when they had tagged the word to a specific personal experience. For example, my brother–in–law said happiness was not yellow but blue. "What colour blue?" I asked. Light blue. Why? He likes to escape the Canadian winter by going to the Bahamas. Light blue is the colour he sees when he lies on his back basking in the hot sun. Pink was the colour of life for a woman who had given birth to six children. Eli's colours were completely "wrong." It turned out his life was upside down. He was miserable and going through a messy divorce. Our colour sensibility is not entirely predictable because it is a nature–nurture combination. What makes our colour responses unique is how what we have in common is affected by our life experiences.

In the 1940s Max Lüscher (1923), head of the Institute for Medical Psycho–diagnostics in Lucerne, Switzerland, began devising what became known as the Lüscher Colour Diagnostic Test. His idea was that if we are all born with the same basic colour responses and our personal experience alters the common response, then how we depart from the norm should reveal much about our personality, our experiences, and our frame of mind. Taking the test involves putting twelve colour cards face down in order of preference several times. The results indicate twenty–three different personality traits. They identify personality strengths and weakness and which areas are causing psychological stress.

Lüscher's test assumes our colour "default" codes are still hooked to nature and our evolution in the wild. For example, yellow marked the beginning of a new day. The higher yellow is in preference, the more optimistic the personality. Darkness marked the end of the day and the approaching dangers of the night. Black is almost never the most preferred colour but if it is up near the top then there is rebellion and negativity going on. Red is blood. A strong red preference indicates impulsiveness, a will to win, and a strong sexuality. Green preference suggests a resistance to change. Brown in an upper position indicates the need for a secure environment. It is not just which colour is the favourite that matters but how the sequence as a whole is organized.

When I was studying colour with Mahnke, he dismissed the test partially on the grounds that the colours used would not be reproduced consistently enough and small changes in nuance could affect preferences. Our group included a Russian psychologist who had been using Lüscher's test for years. She was convinced that the colour test was consistently accurate. It opened patients up in a non–personal way because colour works on an unconscious level. The test tapped into a deep well and what came out never ceased to amaze her or her patients. Mahnke remained sceptical.

One day in the class, we were to do quick and free pastel drawings intended to convey our personalities. This was not to be a work of art. One by one, we showed our piece and described what we thought it revealed. Then the rest of the class had a turn to give their interpretations. Mine was a kind of spiralling cornucopia with bright colours bursting out of the top that Mahnke said he would have known was mine had he seen them all unsigned. I was one of those students who keeps wanting to ask and answer questions and who does get rather effervescent on the topic of colour.

An older designer's bold colours were all at the bottom of her page. She said she was not sure what it meant but as she spoke it came out that she loved her work but never felt she had reached her full potential and wondered if it was too late. Would her real talent stay latent, buried? Another woman used colours that were all pastel, mostly mauve. In the centre of the drawing was a large, squared–off horseshoe shape. Its open side tilted downward. Our Russian psychologist said that colour and open shape facing down indicated a lot of negativity or unhappiness and unresolved issues needing closure. Her pale mauve and blues were floating colours meaning she was neither asserting herself nor being held and supported by others. At lunch a little later, she shared with a few of us a heart–rending story of marital woes, a suicide attempt, and her hope that the worst was behind her.

It was a fascinating day. When it began, we were a dozen amicable people from around the world sharing a class for a few days. By the end, many of us felt like a united tribe of friends. Surely the power of such a simple exercise that only took a morning is something that could and should be tapped into more often as a way to share, learn, and understand.

Instead it is usually advertising companies that use our colour responses to communicate and manipulate and use colour psychology to sell products. They know that blue is associated with trust, loyalty, and authority which is why so many banks and corporations use blue. Trust is green or blue. Green, before it became so tightly linked to environmental issues, also implied efficiency, new growth and, in the United States, the colour of money. Leadership is red. Innovation is yellow.

With advances in colour printing, Kodak became one of the first corporations to use colour branding. In 1930, the company made its name red, the colour of leadership, in a box that was yellow, the colour of innovation but also the colour of sunshine and happiness, suggesting those holiday moments that everyone might want to capture using Kodak cameras and film.

Coca–Cola made use of white lettering on a red ground to give its brand visibility and associate it with winners, leaders, action, and passion.

American corporations began to make more use of colour symbolism than anyone since medieval icon painters.

Product designers should bear in mind that different colours are perceived to have different weight. Dark is heavy. Pale is light. There is a popular myth about dockworkers in England whose job was to unload cargo that was shipped in dark green crates. They complained constantly that the crates were too heavy. Finally they threatened to strike. The next shipment arrived and the same crates were pale yellow. Complaints ceased. Although they weighed the same, they were perceived to be lighter and the strike was averted.

Advertising companies know that colour preferences change with health, age, and personality. Pastel and soft colours are supposedly best for newborns. Young children like clean and vibrant colours, especially warm ones, and are more attracted by colour than shape. Their art reveals very consistent responses because personal experiences haven't had time to alter nature's innate default colour settings. Their favourite images are always the things that haven't changed since we evolved in nature: themselves, animals and flowers in full colour, especially the favoured colours of red, orange, and pink.

Between the ages of three and eleven, children acquire more rational behaviour patterns. Self–control is reflected in their art by stronger use of line and shape. Psychologists tell us blue is the colour of order and control and cool colours start to move into the childhood palette. A preference for warm colour lasts much longer for girls than it does for boys. Are they more emotional, less "cool"? Girls are better able to sort and group colours into different categories than boys.

By the teen years, colour has lost its prominence. It is considered normal development that the intellectual world of shape and form suppresses the emotional and undisciplined realm of colour. It used to be seen as a sign of immaturity or unintelligence if colour continued to be emphasized over form. Now we understand that it indicates a creative or right–brain thinker rather than a mathematical or scientific left–brain thinker. With maturity, colour in art can't just feel right. It has to look right – realistic and harmonious. As we become more self–conscious, we become inhibited and less spontaneously in tune with colour.

Our colour sensibilities are like music preferences, they change with age. We start by being sensitive to pastels like the gentle drone of a lullaby. Then our taste picks up energy. Crayon brights are like busy, cheerful kiddie songs. Then comes the teenage guy taste for unpredictable but strong personality–driven colour, including black, while embracing a range of music, including indie bands, rap, rock, and the blues at full volume. The gals overlap but some prefer the gentler side of colour, pinks and pastels, the love songs. Then we divide into those who mellow out and favour the neutrals – easy listening – and those who prefer more dynamic hues – the complexities of jazz or classical genres. Finally, we get to turn down the volume of whatever it is we are listening to, opting for muted colours or greyed palettes. (Although the elderly are associated with greyed palettes, they often need stronger colours around them to compensate for the yellowing of the eye's lens, which mutes colour perception.) Of course there will always be the funk–loving, full–volume octogenarians like the client who loved the idea of a black vestibule, powder room, and kitchen ceiling. Will I ever part with my reds?

Even though choosing colours can seem like an arbitrary peel–and–stick decision, it is not. We still respond to colours as we have been programmed to do, treating them as carriers of information. Even though, in reality, the colour of your car tells us nothing about it, not its molecular structure, its weight, nor its purpose, we still read the colour as if it did. A shiny silver paint finish makes a car look like it is made of a light metal, like titanium, and built for speed.

Colour speaks to us all the time because approximately 80 per cent of the information we receive is conveyed visually. If I am chatting with you and I am saying yes but shaking my head, you are more likely to register the head signal and discount the verbal one. We think we are governed by our ability to make sound and seasoned judgments but if I were applying for a serious job wearing a pink chiffon dress, the colour and the frothy fabric would trump even the most amazing credentials.

Would you feel confident about your lawyer's abilities if his or her office were pink? Would you be happy to buy life insurance from a man wearing a yellow jacket or one in a bright teal blue? Suppose your blind date showed up and he was in a canary yellow shirt? Or a black one? Would burgundy be better than bright red? Blue might make you most comfortable because it conveys trust and security. White would let you suspend your opinion until you knew him better.

Zara Stender is a colour designer who writes books on the subject. She keeps a record of how colour affects her clients and she researches how the colour she wears affects the way others respond to her. She has found that people trust her when she wears a combination of brown and mid–tone blue: a car–leasing place that she often uses doesn't ask for I.D.; people don't question her opinion. She doesn't wear this combination all the time, though, because she doesn't like the effect it has on her. It makes her feel as if she has disappeared.

Sometimes it is hard to tell if colour affects how we feel or how we feel affects how we feel about a colour. When the National Aeronautics and Space Administration (NASA) studied the way colour could create visual stimulation, volume enhancement, mood shifts, and general relief from prolonged confinement, they found that the effects were not consistent. They varied with individual personality types, with how much colour the person was accustomed to, and with how colours were combined. They found that emotionally responsive or outgoing personality types reacted freely and comfortably with colour. They enjoyed it. Inhibited or introverted types were comfortable with less colour. Detached individuals were less affected by colour around them.

Lüscher was right about our colour codes being tied to nature. We mimic nature's seasonal colour shifts in everything from advertising campaigns to magazine layouts, household accessories, and clothing. Because I live where there are four very distinct seasons, the colour mimicking is particularly pronounced. Just before spring, shop windows and magazine covers sport pastels, especially yellow–greens, the colour of new growth, or pinks, yellows, and mauves, the colour of the first flowers. Summer brings tropicals: turquoise, orange, yellow, magenta – and lots of white. In the autumn, colour starts to hibernate and out come the neutrals and earth tones of the dried landscape along with the orange and ochre of pumpkins and gourds. Almost unconsciously we put away intensely coloured clothing and gravitate toward tweeds and wools that coordinate with the landscape in both colour and texture. In winter, contrasts are heightened. Colour becomes achromatic with more blacks with creamy white contrasts. Accents are jewel tones. It is no wonder Christmas colours are the colour of holly's green boughs and red berries.

Colours look wrong if they are out of sync with nature. I didn't realize that the colour codes applied to nature's own objects until I received a floral bouquet that looked oddly awful. How is that possible? you might ask. Flowers are flowers and we are genetically predisposed to be attracted to flowers. And when you live in Canada, as I do, and it is a cold November day, as it was, what could be nicer than the doorbell ringing and a fellow handing you a box of unexpected flowers? I opened the box. The bouquet was wrong. Outside everything was cold and grey and harsh. In the box, the flowers were soft pastels – pale pink carnations, pale yellow lilies, white daisies, and baby's breath. They were spring flowers in spring colours. They reminded me of an Easter bonnet. I never found it discombobulating in late winter to have tulips or paperwhites in the house. Now I realize that this is because they are not out of season. They are ahead of it. This has an entirely different effect on our psyche. Flowers ahead of the season are the teaser, the warm–up act. They excite us about what is to come. But spring things in grey November, heading toward winter, elicit more of a "Who are you kidding?" response. The bouquet looked as wrong as someone wearing a grey tweed suit with a pair of white pumps. To everything there is a season, even colour.

Because advertisers are in the business of selling, they know they have to time their colours to the seasons. However they also know that bold or surprising colour sells because it triggers an arousal response. When aroused, we are in action and when we are in action we are more likely to do things, like make a purchase. Any salesman knows that overcoming inertia, getting us up off the metaphorical sofa, is the challenge. Once we are up and running, then given the choice between discounting a product or letting us go away and think about it, the discount incentive is the way to go.

One day I was window shopping on Fifth Avenue. In the window of a very pricey ladies' clothing store was a mannequin dressed in a spectacular bright apricot orange. It did its job. I walked in and perused racks filled with black, white, and linen–coloured clothing. Colour was, as my granny would say, the sprat to catch the mackerel.

Colour affects performance. Students who used yellow study rooms got higher grades than students in colourless study rooms. I.Q. tests scores are higher when the exam is taken in pleasantly coloured rooms. Schools that paint their classrooms yellow increase the level of concentration because yellow is a stimulant. (Dr. Harry Wohlfarth, president of the International Academy of Colour Sciences and professor emeritus at the University of Alberta, studied the effects of colour on classroom performance and recommended the three walls the students see be a soft yellow to stimulate learning but the wall the teacher faces be a soft and calming turquoise.)

Packagers and salespeople know that colour affects our judgment. Studies show that orange juice that has its orange colour augmented is perceived as better tasting. Breath mints seem fresher in green packaging. Cleaning products suggest cleanliness packaged in blue and white although red on the label boosts the perception of strength. When pastries are served in pastel shades of every colour, the blue ones are chosen least. Children who eat mashed potatoes tinted blue feel ill afterwards. Sweets don't sell well in green packages because green is perceived as being tart. Cosmetics in brown packaging don't sell well. Magazines with dark green covers sell poorly.

Our instinctive reflex responses are layered with learned ones. And that is why colour psychology cannot always predict what colour will be right. And why what seems wrong isn't always.

When I met Linda, she lived quite happily, so she thought, in a house full of off–white. Choosing the right yellow for her front door was what prompted her to call me. Once we had that sorted, she suggested we tweak the indoor colours. Room by room we made adjustments. We were fairly conservative, with the exception of one room.

I asked that we do her living room last. It was a formal room with good bones of 1930s Arts and Crafts vintage. There was a wide painted brick fireplace, leaded windows, and built–in bookcases. The furniture was pale grey. The overall effect was boring. It was also a dim room, used only in the evenings. She had been thinking of yet another beige but as we discussed the room I noticed that everything she loved, from botanical prints and her grandmother's fancy tea set to the leather bindings of old books, had the same deep raspberry red hue. I knew that she wanted more colour than she thought she wanted. She wasn't listening to herself. She didn't notice the animation and vibrancy she exuded when talking about the things in the room that made her happy.

When I told her that the room was begging to be that raspberry red, she hyperventilated. Then she emitted a nervous laugh, thinking I was pulling her leg. Then it dawned on her that I must be mad. I explained. There was nothing in the room that wouldn't be enhanced by that colour. Red looks great under artificial lighting. It is true that red would bring the walls in but why is that always considered such a bad thing? The room was plenty big enough. Why not make it cozy? Her pale furniture would glow against the deep background. From a decorating perspective, there was no question that red was a great choice. The issue was Linda. Was she ready for the emotional energy level of red? Red is arousing. It is exciting. The change would be huge.

She insisted I give her a fallback choice. Against my better judgment I did. It is her place after all. However, to tip the odds in red's favour, I sent my colour–embracing painter over to quote the job. I knew that if she was still waffling, he might be able to "help" her out. (She was. He did.)

I warned her not to call me right away but to give herself time to acclimatize. A big change elicits a visceral response that takes time to sort out, separating the effect of the colour from that of the colour change. We can't always immediately know the difference between anxiety and excitement. After two weeks, if she didn't love the colour we would worry.

The day after the paint went on she called. It was love at first sight, no adjustment necessary. Her husband loved it. Her sons loved it. Her house, she said, felt like a home for the first time in years. What was most surprising was her emotional response to the red. "I feel nothing but peace in that room now." She was getting the peace of having the colour she needed. She was feeling peaceful surrounded by the most exciting, powerful, and aggressive of colours!

What we have in common is mixed with associations acquired over a lifetime. It is rooted in our culture, climate, and personality. Psychologists and colour consultants can make assumptions about primary colour responses and preferences. These are the foundation on which more specifically tailored colour choices are developed. Knowing how to find the right colours to suit nature and nurture is what makes designing colour so fascinating.

RUTH, THE PAINT LADY

To find out if it is true that changing a colour can change the experience of a place, I flew down to New York to meet Ruth Lande Shuman, a.k.a. The Paint Lady. I had read that she and her organization, Publicolor, were using colour to improve the lives of kids in inner–city schools around Manhattan. These are some of the most hostile urban places imaginable.

The story began when Ruth, a single mother of two boys, was studying industrial design at the Pratt Institute. One of her sons became seriously ill, and Ruth moved into the hospital to be near him. Several of the walls in the ward were painted bright yellow and orange. She could feel the colours lifting her spirits.

Several years later, she discovered how to put colour to work helping others when she transformed Junior High 99 in Harlem as part of New York Cares Day.

Ruth's idea was to brighten the dreary school with feel–good colour. She found a sponsor, Estée Lauder Company, who paid for the paint and sent volunteers to help students paint the hallways and stairwells. In Junior High 99, five hundred gallons of paint were applied by three hundred and fifty parents, teachers, students, and volunteers. The change the colours made to the school, the community, and the attitudes of the students was so overwhelmingly positive that Ruth has been changing lives with colour ever since.

I went with Ruth to her first meeting with students at J.H.S. 193, a high school in the Bronx. We arrived and were on our way to meet with student reps from each grade as the morning bell rang. "The Paint Lady," in a soft, puffy quilted chartreuse green all–weather coat, carrying two very big and very colourful plastic carry–alls full of painted colour palettes, rushed into the spartan brick building as the students were lining up sullenly in dimly lit halls. No natural light penetrated the unappealing fluorescent gloom. Staff members barked, "Settle down" or "Straighten up." By Ruth's standards, this architecturally banal place was a palace, especially compared to Central High in Newark.

Central High was her second project. When she arrived, the school looked like a war zone. Guards stood in the doorways. Graffiti covered the walls. Lockers were broken. Washrooms were vandalized so frequently that the doors were permanently locked and students used the stairwells as latrines. Prisons look more welcoming than that school. The disrepair and the grey walls sent a clear daily message to the students: No one cares!

When Ruth takes on a new school, she sets up a team of student leaders, one or two from each grade. Their first task is colour selection.

That was what we were doing that day in the office of J.H.S.'s loud, bossy, much–loved principal. The student reps gathered, lethargic and aloof, as if animation was not appropriate behaviour. Ruth began, "I need good strong leaders like you." The kids sat up a little taller. Her enthusiasm was infectious. "As part of the paint club, you will be coming after school and on weekdays and weekends for as long as it takes. You can bring friends, parents, brothers, and sisters, but *you* will be my leaders."

With Publicolor's guidance, students select the palette, calculate the paint quantities, map out the placement, and do the painting. The colour is for the public areas like hallways, gymnasiums, cafeterias, and always the front door.

At J.H.S. 193, Ruth pulled out the colour combinations painted onto narrow boards. Students were to put up their hand if they liked one and it went into the next round. She advised them to take their time choosing and to be sure to remember that they were choosing colours to live with and not, as they are inclined to do, think of them as colours to wear. After a slow start, the energy began to fly around the room. Hands went up often. Then they had to pare down their selection to two that Ruth would develop. The entire school would be asked to vote on the finalists so every student takes ownership of the decision.

As the reps headed back to class and Ruth began packing up, the principal expressed a concern. "These kids don't know the power they have as individuals once they start working together. Once you turn them on to this, I know we won't be able to *throw* them out at the end of the day."

After our colour meeting in the Bronx, Ruth rushed off down the F.D.R. Expressway to a morning meeting at a Brooklyn community centre that was desperately in need of colour. By noon she had the go–ahead. She rushed back to her midtown apartment to change into paint clothes before meeting me at the new Publicolor office at 32nd and Lexington. When I walked into the colourful workplace from the grim, grey, fluorescent–lit halls, it was a shock. The walls were all coral orange and two shades of yellow. The floors were two more shades of orange. The tables were an earthy chartreuse. Cupboard doors were multicoloured, a palette used in a recent school project that the staff particularly liked. Computers and telephones are the only interruptions to the exuberant colour scheme.

"Last week these rooms were two white boxes," said The Paint Lady. "This orange wall is one I will change every few months so I can get to know and understand more colours. I hate to keep repeating myself." Her office yellow will stay. "I love warm yellow around me when I work because it gives me so much energy." The phone rings and Publicolor gets the go–ahead to "colourize" sixteen more inner–city schools.

Then the newest member of her paint team arrived and Ruth was off to paint with him. And as she left, I had to wonder if it is her energy that drives her to seek colour or if being surrounded by colour drives her energy. In any case, her colours change lives. Many tell her that even years later the positive effect the colour made to their lives has stayed with them. Some join her growing permanent team.

Colour made school feel more like home. Because kids felt safer and welcomed, they stopped staying away from school. One student said that after the bright colours went on, she felt like she was in heaven. Another said colour made kids friendlier. Groups that wouldn't talk to each other started hanging out together. "We really felt like a family." Students feel a sense of ownership and connection. Graffiti virtually stops. If a student is caught defacing the new colours, they are given a paint brush by a member of the paint team and told to paint out the damage. Money for repairs is allotted to after–school programs. Students say they felt safer, happier, and more empowered. At Central High, violence and absenteeism decreased and test scores in math and reading improved an average of 15 per cent.

In the 1980s Dr. Harry Wohlfarth undertook a five–year study that proved that adding either good colour or full–spectrum light in classrooms improved academic performance and I.Q. scores. Putting both in the room increased them even more.

Frank Mahnke designed the colours for a facility for emotionally disturbed children and adolescents using colours appropriate to the function and their emotional needs. Destructive behaviour diminished almost entirely. Previous changes to the decor had never had the positive effect that resulted from changing the colour. Six years later, even though there had been a continual patient turnover, the behaviour change remained the same. Colour works, according to Ruth, because "if you stimulate their eyes, you stimulate their minds and warm colours convey a sense of safety. Only minds free from fear are free to learn."

I asked her if the bright colours take getting used to. "For kids, never. For adults, sometimes. It usually lasts about two weeks. Then they are fine with it. Everyone needs colour; it just takes adults a little longer to adjust."

INVISIBLE COLOUR, THE MOST IMPORTANT COLOUR OF ALL

LIGHT

Many years ago I was in Paris during a strike of electrical workers. It made getting around difficult as the Metro could be brought to a halt at any time for as long as the strikers saw fit. I decided to walk over to the Louvre Museum and stay there for the day. Because the strike had deterred most visitors, I pretty much had the place to myself. As I wandered through the empty, echoing spaces, the lights went out. I loved it.

The diffuse grey light of a Paris day filtered down from the skylights and everything seemed quieter.

Light is energy. Without the persistent presence of strong, never–changing artificial light, it was as if a white noise had ceased. I wasn't aware it was there until I felt the relief of its absence. In the calm, the paintings were talking directly to me. It reminded me of the theatre director who used to tell his Shakespearean actors, "Don't exclaim on stage. If you want the audience to really listen to you, whisper."

Ideally a work of art should be viewed under the same lighting conditions as it was painted. For most art, that would be in spaces dimly lit with natural light. Art historian John Gage says that if we were to look at art with a pair of sunglasses on, we would get a more authentic lighting level for most paintings. The strike was giving me a more authentic viewing. It was already a thrill to see paintings that I knew so well from art book images in person. It was a double thrill to see them lit *au naturelle.*

One room was dominated by the gloomy turbulence of Théodore Géricault's large *Raft of the Medusa* (1819). Exhausted men struggle to hold onto a flimsy, make–shift raft tossed in the mountainous waves of a stormy sea. Their focus is toward the horizon and their only hope is a ship so far off it is rendered with the tiniest daub of paint. Nearby was another favourite, Jacques–Louis David's (1748–1825) *Death of Marat* (1793), which is now in Brussels. A Christ–like Marat has just been stabbed to death as he is writing in the bath, his slender arm hangs limp over the side, and a white feather pen is falling from his hand, implying we are witness to the moment of death. I was looking at a French painting under French daylight and it was as if I were taken back in time, closer to its maker and the moment of its making.

It would be the perfect day to view Leonardo's *Mona Lisa* (1503–1506) without being rushed along with by a crowd – or so I thought. It was down the hall in a small protective booth, surrounded by a velvet cord.

(Today she is mounted high on the wall behind non–reflective glass in the middle of a large room.) The walls of the room around the booth were hung with row upon row of works by da Vinci and his peers, works that were usually ignored, obscured by the Mona Lisa's eminence. This day was to be no exception. I turned toward the little booth. I walked slowly toward the velvet barrier. My anticipation built. The viewing window was at eye level. I looked inside. The booth's light was out. Inside was total darkness. All I could see was the reflection of my own face, hanging like a portrait in the protective glass. Suddenly those ignored works had much greater appeal.

Light is electromagnetic energy. If we could see energy, we would be aware that everything on the planet – animal, mineral, vegetable, gas, solid, liquid – is pulsating with it. Seeing this vibrating fourth dimension would be a dizzying experience. However we only feel some of it. We sense heat, for example, as energy radiating from the radiator, the fireplace, or the element on the stove. But light seems more like a state than an active phenomenon. We experience it as an ether that surrounds us. I didn't feel it pulsing through the Louvre's skylights that day but light is a pumping energy filled with an invisible spectrum of colour vital for our well–being.

For millions of years, what we didn't know about light's invisible colour content didn't hurt us. Like fish in water, we lived bathed in natural light. It is only in the brief time since we became an indoor species that this changed. We moved out of the sunshine and into our artificially constructed spaces and foolishly thought that because we could make our own light, as much of it as we wanted, whenever we wanted, we had become independent of daylight. We no longer needed sunshine. As late as the 1970s we discovered just how wrong we were.

The sun radiates four million tons of pure energy every second, sending out a whole smorgasbord of electromagnetic energies – X–rays, microwaves, light, radio waves. Light, the small portion of this energy that is visible to us, is what we use to make colour. Only one characteristic differentiates an X–ray from a blue wavelength or a blue wavelength from a green one or a green from any other – size. The smallest wavelengths, cosmic rays, would destroy us if the earth's atmosphere didn't reflect them back into the universe. Slightly larger than the cosmic rays are gamma rays and X–rays – which are still less than a nanometre long. At the other end of the scale is alternating current with wavelengths over a kilometre long, bigger than both telephone waves and radio waves.

The small section of electromagnetic energy that measures between 380 nanometres and 700 nanometres is visible light. This is the only portion of energy we see because it is the only group of wavelengths that match the molecular structure of the human eye. These are the only ones that can be absorbed and turned into sight and colour. Wavelengths a tad shorter than 380 nanometres are ultraviolet. Our eyes can't see them but our bodies still make good use of them to produce Vitamin D. Wavelengths longer than 700 nanometres, our red wavelength, are infrared. We can't see them either, although owls can. Our bodies register them as heat.

All wavelengths of colour race toward the earth's surface at the same speed, the speed of light. But the earth's atmosphere is like an obstacle course full of tiny floating particles of dirt, dust, pollutants, and water molecules. Longer wavelengths with slower frequencies, like yellows and reds, have an easier time avoiding obstacles because they move forward with long strides. The short wavelengths, like blue, have a higher frequency. They have to oscillate quickly, run like crazy, to keep up. Blue wavelengths travelling along next to reds are like dachshunds running beside greyhounds. All that frantic back and forth leg movement means the small dogs are much more likely to hit, trip, or bump into something. When blue wavelengths hit something, as they are more likely to do, they get thrown off course, *scattered,* giving the sky its blue. With less and less blue left in the light as it reaches the earth's surface, it starts to look warmer and "sunny."

Scattering is called the *Tyndall effect* because in 1869, John Tyndall figured out that the shorter the wave, the more likely it would be to get bent off course, refracted. Besides making the sky blue, the Tyndall effect puts the iridescent blues and greens into the feathers of birds like budgies, kingfishers, and peacocks. It makes frogs green. Light hits their colourless transparent cells and is bent or refracted. This is *interference colour,* colour made of light.

Most of nature's white – snow, swan feathers, orchid petals, and polar bear's fur – is made the same way. White occurs when all wavelengths are equally refracted. (The transparent "white" fur of polar bears acts like a solar panel funnelling light down to their black skin where it is absorbed and becomes heat. When they are waiting for a seal to come out of an ice hole, they sometimes cover their black noses to complete their white camouflage.)

When the sky is white and not blue, it is because airborne molecules of water, sand, and snow in the atmosphere are large enough to bump all wavelengths off course. The red of the setting sun is light's last hurrah. It has travelled its farthest as it dips over the horizon. Ironically, we get the reddest sky, the most spectacular sunsets, when there is an abundance of air pollution (or volcanic dust) in the atmosphere banging the red survivors off course at last.

We mistakenly think of light in terms of quantity or volume and not content or colour. We tend to think it goes to one place, our eyes, to serve one purpose, vision, so the flick of a switch gets us what we need. But light goes to another and equally important place, our body, and serves another vital purpose, fuelling it with energy. We are plugged into light like a lamp into a socket. Light's energy is sent, via the hypothalamus and the pineal gland, to the spinal column. It triggers nerve impulses full of information that are sent out via the bloodstream to act on our tissues and organs that govern the release of hormones. Our bodies need light, not just of a certain quantity, but of a certain quality. Just as a car runs better on good fuel, our bodies run better on good light. And, like the air we breathe and the food and water we consume, the difference between good quality and bad is content. Good light has all colours present in balanced amounts. The best colour is sunlight.

John Ott (1909–2000), who pioneered time–lapse photography, found this out in 1950 when he was working on *Cinderella* with Walt Disney. Walt Disney was watching the scene in *Cinderella* where the pumpkin grew and transformed itself into a carriage. It occurred to him that it would be interesting to use the newly invented time–lapse photography to make a film showing pumpkin seeds growing into pumpkins. It could be just as fast and the effect just as fantastical. He asked the cameraman to apply his new technology to making a film called *The Secret Life of Plants and Animals.*

Ott planted pumpkin seeds under a skylight in the studio basement. To speed things up, he augmented daylight with over thirty fluorescent lights. The vines grew quickly. Then Ott noticed something strange. The female or pistil–producing flowers withered as soon as they matured. The male pollen–producing flowers were fine but useless without the females. The shooting schedule was put back a year. More seeds were planted. This time, because his supplier was out of the normal cool white fluorescents, Ott used ones of a slightly different colour. The seeds grew into vines. The female plants did fine. The males started out well then died prematurely.

Ott decided to take a closer look at how changing the light changed what happened to the plants. He put several under a microscope and began filming the movement of their chloroplast cells under different lighting conditions. Under natural daylight, they moved around in an orderly fashion. When it was dark, they rested. When ultraviolet was removed, as it is under ordinary fluorescents, they became sluggish and clumped to one side. Under red light, some moved normally. Some invented odd short cuts while others stopped moving altogether. Under blue light, the same thing happened but the short cuts started from a different place. Normal light restored normal movement. Ott was discovering that varying the light waves, or colour content of light, had a huge effect on living organisms.

Ott started to study the effects on rats and mice. Under artificial light, males had to be removed from the cage before the arrival of a litter because of their aggressive and cannibalistic behaviour. Under natural lighting conditions, the males stayed and took on their normal paternal role. Mice living under light high in pink were more prone to cancer. Chickens living under artificial lighting produced fewer eggs, lived shorter lives, and had cholesterol levels that were 25 per cent higher than chickens exposed to lots of natural light. Cows kept under artificial light were 15 per cent heavier and produced less milk.

You would think these findings might have given us humans a bit of a wake–up call but for decades no one paid any attention. The scientific community was convinced that we had evolved free of light. Over time, our pineal gland, a mammal's major light processor, had shrunk to the size of a pea. This is remarkably small compared to the pineal gland of all other mammals. It suggested that perhaps this gland, like the appendix, was a vestigial organ.

When it gets dark, the pineal gland, our light switch operator, signals the body to release melatonin. This makes us sleepy. When light returns, it shuts off the release of melatonin and we are energized. The shift from light to dark sets our internal clock, our circadian rhythm, encouraging us to sleep and wake in unison (teenagers exempted). But experiments that subjected people to extended and contracted periods of light and dark indicated that light had no effect. Those tested showed no shift in the production of melatonin and consequent sleep patterns. However, there was a big flaw in the testing. It was done using artificial light. In 1980, psychiatrist Dr. Alfred Lewy proved that artificial light has to be bumped up to five times ordinary room levels for the body to register it as anything more than darkness.

It is hard to imagine thinking we are not affected by light. Anyone who has experienced jet lag knows our body hates to be wrenched from light's rhythm. Anyone who gets sluggish and miserable when the days are shorter and happy and energetic on a bright sunny day knows light's effects. NASA has found light therapy was better than sleeping pills for resetting the biological clocks of astronauts who needed to rest by day and work by night.

SAD, Seasonal Affective Disorder, a psychological depression caused by a lack of sunlight, affects up to 6 per cent of people, more in northern climates where days are short much of the year. SAD sufferers get depressed and sleepy and crave carbohydrates. Basically their bodies are trying to hibernate. Extending their "daylight" with special full–spectrum lights acts as an anti–depressant. We are all potential SAD sufferers who feel happier and energized by walking on the sunny side of the street or leaving wintry climates for sunny holidays.

The detrimental health effects of being cut off from natural light appeared in the Industrial Revolution of the eighteenth and nineteenth centuries. Across Europe and America, many of the children who worked in sweat shops got a crippling disease called rickets. They became weak, their joints malformed, and their pelvises misshapen. Rickets is caused by a Vitamin D deficiency. All that they needed was exposure to ultraviolet wavelength, a short daily dose of sunshine.

Ultraviolet, the colour missing from most artificial light, is the wavelength we fear in sunlight. But UV facilitates the Vitamin D production our bodies require for absorbing the

calcium to make strong bones and teeth. We can never eat enough shellfish, mackerel, swordfish, and other Vitamin D–rich foods to replace our need for sunshine. Just fifteen minutes of noonday sunlight on the face and the back of the hands gives us a good daily dose.

The lighter skin of people living in northern climates is an adaptation enabling them to absorb sunlight that would be blocked by more protective dark skin. A reasonable amount of sun on even pale skin builds up protection from bad ultraviolet rays while its full–spectrum light gets our systems working as they should. Fear of too much UV exposure has caused us to throw out the baby with the bathwater, with the result that osteoporosis has become a hidden epidemic among the house–bound elderly. A large percentage of pregnant mothers are seriously deficient in Vitamin D and their newborns begin life deficient too. Rickets in children is making a comeback. Staying out of the sun to avoid skin cancer contributes to higher numbers of people dying annually of colon cancer in North America than in more tropical climates or places where more time is spent outdoors. Add to this the increased number of cases of other cancers, including breast cancer and prostate cancer, that adequate Vitamin D from UV would help prevent and a hit of sunshine makes sense.

In ancient Greece, hospitals had outdoor areas for light therapy. In 1860, Florence Nightingale noticed that patients on the sunny side of the hospital wards did better than those on the dark side. In the 1950s, a British nurse discovered that jaundice in newborns was cured by their being in the sunlight coming in from an open window. Since then jaundiced babies have been given phototherapy treatment instead of complete blood transfusions to cure the condition. Different wavelengths affect different parts of our bodies in different ways. Full–spectrum light is the balanced colour diet that meets all needs.

Without all of sunshine's invisible colours energizing our bodies, we become as sluggish and listless as cows that don't get out of the barn. Even the best artificial light cannot compare with sunlight. I love the fact that just lounging in the sun has many of the same benefits as a workout or going for a jog! It decreases the resting heart rate, the blood pressure, and the blood sugar while increasing our energy, strength, and endurance. Sunshine boosts our blood's ability to absorb and carry oxygen and is a great stress reliever.

> My advice to anyone who is renovating and considering how to apportion their funds is to make light the priority. Never, never, never skimp on light. Light animates a room and everything in it, including us. Light pays back every single day. Having good light is like getting a built–in energy booster.

Architect Christopher Alexander and five others who wrote *A Pattern Language,* the bible on what makes a space work, state that people always gravitate toward rooms filled with lots of natural light especially if it comes in from more than one direction. They are happy there and content to stay longer. I found this to be true when I was writing an article about an interesting house tucked discreetly in a back lane in downtown Toronto. It was designed by a professor of architecture at the University of Toronto and built for himself and his wife. It was one large interior space with a few upstairs rooms that looked like they were suspended in mid–air and reached by a cabled bridge system. As the architect gave me the tour and explained his process, it was clear he took great pride and delight in all his carefully considered details and his novel solutions to design challenges. The house was a showcase for his design aesthetic. The most impressive feature was the expansive glazed south wall with a view of an intimate little courtyard garden with lush plantings, a water feature, and a city panorama beyond.

The day I went back with a photographer to shoot it for the story, the morning sun poured in through these windows. The architect was away and his wife was with us. As the photographer packed up his equipment, I asked her what it was like to live in such an unusual space. She said the awkward access to the upstairs rooms took getting used to. The bathroom was not entirely private. But none of the idiosyncrasies or features of the place bothered her except for one: the light. It didn't matter how much light came in through the vast expanse of the south window wall. "When it only comes at you from one direction," she said, "somehow you always get the feeling that you are living in a cave." Recently our paths crossed. They are no longer living in the house.

Light can make or break a place. A room with good light needs very little else to be beautiful. For one thing, it does not need colour. Colour is light's understudy and always second best. It may seem odd that a colour designer would, given the choice, always choose daylight's invisible colour over colour we can see, but that is because daylight holds every colour. Why pick one when you can have them all?

LIGHT – IT'S WHAT'S INSIDE THAT COUNTS

I recently wrote an article about why I hate and don't willingly use energy-efficient lighting. Needless to say, some readers took umbrage, like Sue, who wrote, "I certainly would never hire, nor want to read design advice from a person who couldn't work with fluorescent light – it has been around long enough and is used in so many applications that a self-proclaimed colour expert should be able to successfully work with its few shortcomings. I'm not being stoic by using CFL (compact fluorescent lamps) bulbs. I'm using better options . . . because it's necessary."

The issue is: better in what way? The light from a good old incandescent bulb is aesthetically pleasing but comes from a heated filament. Almost 90 per cent of the energy is lost as heat, not light. Sue is right. This is wasteful. Halogen bulbs use the same tungsten filament but the halogen gas and their small, tight, glass capsules make them better but not best. But we like the warm light they give because it mimics sunlight and firelight. We are biologically accustomed to light that gets cooler as it brightens and warmer as it dims. And in my experience, colours picked in daylight usually look good warmed up at night so most of us have happily built colour palettes using these two compatible systems. They suited our decor and our psyche.

Fluorescents are up to ten times as energy efficient. But (big but) a certain amount of this energy efficiency is lost when they are used in bulk quantities, set at levels that are too bright, left on too long. Some flicker, some buzz. They contain small amounts of hazardous mercury. Most have a start–up time lag and can, at best, only be set low or high, not dimmed. Most emit an unpleasant greenish–grey colour we associate with institutional lighting although some are closer to the colour of incandescents. All artificial light has colour content, measured on a scale called the colour rendering index (CRI) and, compared to daylight, it is usually unbalanced. The colour content of most fluorescents feeds our body the junk food of lighting.

In the 1970s, John Ott improved fluorescent lighting options by developing "daylight" or full–spectrum fluorescents to end what he called "malillumination" of unbalanced artificial lighting. Together with the Environmental Health and Light Research Institute, he studied the difference it made to children in windowless Grade 1 classrooms. Two rooms had normal artificial lighting and two had full spectrum. Time–lapse cameras filmed the classes at random times. The results showed that children in the classrooms with the standard bad lighting were more restless, tired, and irritable. Their attention lapsed. Where the lights were changed to full spectrum, there was marked improvement. Students became less hyperactive and more able to focus. Students in the full-spectrum-lit classrooms also had one-third fewer cavities because Vitamin D-producing UV was not deleted from the lighting. Full-spectrum makes fluorescents better functional lighting, but how many places actually pay the surcharge to use them? People who still think light is about getting lots cheaply might think about the difference between white bread and multigrain.

Even with improved colour, fluorescents emit the wrong *kind* of light. It is not crisp like a sunny day but diffuse like a cloudy one. It gets depressing. In the 1980s, the University Eye Clinic in Munster, Germany, found that people who spent most of their day under regular fluorescent lights had higher levels of our stress hormones. When the endocrine glands that pump out cortisole become exhausted, we are more susceptible to colds and illness. The West German government restricts the maximum distance that employees can be from a window and the amount of fluorescent lighting allowable.

I wonder if Sue finds the broad light of her CFLs "unnatural" at home in the evening when she wants to bring her lighting levels down to read a book and relax but can't. I have tried to work with fluorescents and here is my problem. Fluorescent light, no matter how inexpensive and energy efficient, besides looking and feeling bad, completely messes with any colour palette ever conceived using daylight.

Colours are changed by the colour of light bulb so if you work under fluorescents you might want to dress under them too. If not, those trousers that looked black when you left home might look navy when you got into the office. This phenomenon is called metamerism.

A client once called me to say the colour of her bedroom looked nice in the day and not at night. Would I please come

> back and sort it out. I was really surprised because it was a colour I knew well. I went over and it looked fine. Then she turned on the pot lights over her bed. It looked harsh. As I was working out whether that wall should be over–painted in a slightly softer version of the colour to compensate, I noticed her paint cans. Her painter had colour–matched "my colour" in a different paint. The ingredients were different. It colour–matched in daylight but metamerized, went off on its own direction, under artificial light. All she needed was to paint the wall with a coat of the right paint.

People like Sue feel it is worth making the switch to use CFLs. Others know they are a stopgap and want to go straight to LEDs (light emitting diodes), which are even more energy efficient, contain no mercury, and last "forever." But they are wonky too. Their white light is bluish, and the intense pinpoint beam they emit is not diffuse enough for most residential situations. Even as Christmas tree lights, they don't sparkle but merely sit like sullen bullets of colour. So LEDs are better for architectural lighting, light effects, dashboards, small appliances, and under–cabinet lights. It will be exciting when organic LED lighting, flexible sheets, can be used as luminous wallpaper or as microscopic dots that can be painted on any surface. I am sure the riddle of good and efficient light will soon be solved. In the meantime, I don't think I am being irresponsible by sticking to my incandescents and halogens. I will use CFLs in utility areas where they belong. I will dim or turn my lights off whenever possible. Others may be more stoic and try to get used to the unnatural light of CFLs but as it took millions of years for us to adjust to a warmer and varied light, I am not optimistic.

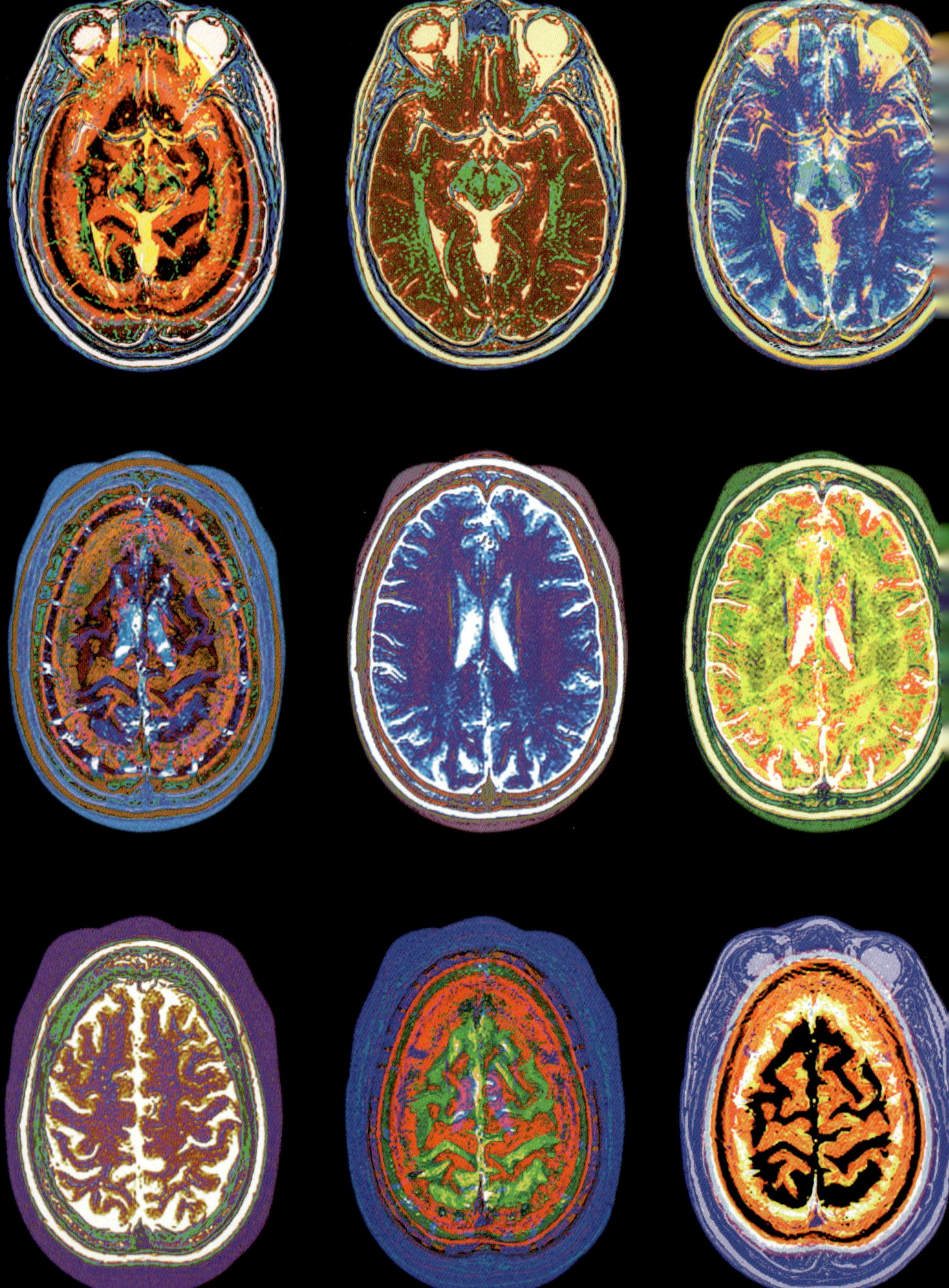

THINKING MAKES IT SO

COLOUR PERCEPTION

When I was a child I used to ask my father the usual stream of "what if" questions. What if you could be any animal, what would you be? What if you could go beyond infinity, where would you be? He was a doctor so I included questions such as "What if you had to choose between being deaf and being blind, which would you choose?" He preferred to be blind and that surprised me. For me, blindness would be like being put into a dark cupboard, for him deafness was the more confining. His love of music might have been part of his choice. He explained that sound lets you experience the world in 360 degrees. Sight only lets you see what is in front of you. Hearing, in his opinion, kept you in a more three-dimensional space, connected to the layers of life, near and distant, foreground and background. I wasn't convinced. Being deaf, he explained, would be lonely. It would restrict you to vision's claustrophobic tunnel. And then what if you closed your eyes?

I have always considered myself a visual person but the more I learn about the idiosyncrasies of how we see and the limitations of what we see, the more I have come to appreciate his point of view. Seeing is a weird business. Knowing something about how it works has taught me how it can be tricked. Working with the idiosyncrasies of how we see colour opened up a whole realm of possibilities in my work.

Until the end of the twentieth century, we had no real idea how we see and particularly how we see colour. Only in the 1970s, when science could finally pinpoint what brain cells were doing individually, did the complexities of how we see start becoming clearer. But, for most of us, what goes on is still a complete mystery.

If you were to describe how you see, based on how you experience it from inside your head, you might say it is like looking through a picture window or an oval like an old–fashioned diving mask. The reality is that we see everything via two tiny holes in our eyes but we experience it as if we use one big Cyclops eye.

We think we see the world around us instantly, fluidly, effortlessly. We sense no boundaries between ourselves and what we see. There is the world in glorious Technicolor. And *bam,* it's right inside our head. However, this simple skill is hugely complex. Seeing, particularly seeing colour, is so unimaginably different from the way it feels that revealing the mystery might be like Dorothy drawing back the curtain in *The Wizard of Oz*.

At school I avoided science. But when I became fascinated with colour, and what it is and how we see it, the brain became a frontier I had to cross. I needed some answers. Clients have often found it hard to understand my colour strategies. It seems to them that what I suggest is not always normal or logical or the way their painters do things. However, if they suspend their scepticism, the most seemingly radical notions end up looking perfectly, and often inconspicuously, right. Even their painters agree. But how could I explain it in ways that were more objective and authoritative than a feeble "Just trust me"?

Colour was to me like wine is to a connoisseur. In the beginning there is red, white, rosé, and sparkling, but the palate keeps expanding. Soon Australian Pinot Grigios taste different from the Italians; the chardonnays worth drinking become the ones beyond the budget. Knowing about where wine is made and when and how adds nuance to the tasting experience. Between sip and swallow comes an expanded savouring as the flavour explodes in the mouth . . . radiates out across the taste buds . . . and rounds out to a 360–degree fullness. It takes its time to finish, like a last note when the pianist's foot lingers on the pedal. Red becomes inadequate to describe Burgundies and Beaujolais. Good or bad doesn't fully describe flavour, and the vocabulary expands into the realm of robust, delicate, fruity, peppery, light, thick, velvet, peaty, with better high notes or low.

Colour is like that. When I collaborated with Shelley, a friend and interior designer, one of the great pleasures was our shared enthusiasm for colour. She might say: "I am doing a dining room Lime–onade. The accent is Savannah Grass. What accent colour would you use for the wall behind the buffet?'

"Dark aubergine."

"Like this?" And she would open her file and there would be that same colour!

Even whites were interesting.

"Gulls Wing trim would be nice with French Linen walls."

"No. That's too pale and yellowish. How about Eiderdown?"

"Oh yesssss!" And then we purr like two people taking that first sip of a brilliant Pinot Noir.

For me, one–room–one–wall–colour was at times too restricting. One white for all ceilings and trim throughout a place, too flat–footed. Stopping and starting colours in odd places or using more colours than usual became my norm.

I did a rather colourful design plan for a big Victorian home and just as my client and I were finishing up, her partner came home. She said cheerfully that she would be happy with anything we chose because the only thing she was firm about was ceilings. They were all to be white and the same one. My client and I looked at each other. "Well," I said, "they are light but I have coordinated the ceiling tones to the wall colours, but suit yourself." A few weeks later the partner called with a colour question. I asked how the painting was coming along and she started to laugh. "It's the ceilings," she said. "Today the painter is back doing the last one according to your plan. I am a complete convert."

The mystery and magic of how we see is not taught at school. There we get vision's boring stuff. It's usually in a chapter called "How the Eye Works." And if you can keep awake long enough, it says: Light passes through the cornea. The cornea focuses light into an image that passes to the lens. The lens fine–tunes the focus, making adjustments for distance, and passes the image on through the pupil, the little hole circumscribed by the iris. From there it crosses the vitreous humour, the soft jelly that fills the eyeball. It lands light data onto our retina and, voilà, we see. Easy. Just like a camera.

If seeing were as straightforward as taking a picture, it would raise the questions: Where is the film? Is there a projection screen in our brain that runs images? And if so, how do we see them? But we don't see with our eyes. They are our receptors, not our processors. They might take the picture but they don't develop the film. Eyes receive the necessary visual information for seeing but we don't know what is in front of us until the information, like a parcel, gets opened up and sorted – brain work. To say we see with our eyes is as accurate as saying this book was written by my laptop. In conversation, when someone makes a point we say, "I see." We don't mean "I hear what you just said." We mean "I have just processed what I heard you say and the penny has dropped." "I see" means "I understand." We are blind if we see but can't perceive. Seeing is understanding and understanding is the domain of the brain.

Besides, if our eyes did the seeing, then any blind person gaining sight would be ecstatic. It would be like the blind pauper in Sunday school Bible stories. All newly sighted people would simply open their eyes and see – a dream come true, a miracle! In reality, a blind person who gains sight often becomes depressed, frustrated, and, even, suicidal. Our eyes receive the data and send the information to the brain. But in the case of a blind person gaining sight, the brain hasn't got a clue what to do with the bombardment of new stimuli. The brain that has previously deciphered the world without this channel on gets overloaded with new and confusing signals. It struggles to cope. The visual information goes to the brain, but the brain has no visual experiences stored for quick reference so vision gets bogged down. A blind person gaining sight does not have an easy time because the eye–brain wiring needed for sight is in place at birth but, unless it is quickly activated, learning will never come naturally and easily.

Richard Gregory in *Eye and Brain: The Psychology of Seeing* tells the story of a fifty–two–year–old blind man he calls S.B. who lived an active and happy life until surgery enabled him to see. Face recognition, an innate skill if activated at birth, was always difficult. Things that were not part of the world of touch, like his reflection in a mirror, the moon, and the concept of distance, were perplexing. He could see objects but did not know how far away they were. Any distance beyond arms' length was a mystery. If he looked out of his window, he had no idea how far below him the ground was. It could be five feet. It could be twenty.

But the hardest blow was colour. The world looked so drab compared to the world of his imagination. He craved the bright colours he had always thought would be there. (I think that we are born with a propensity to the bright colours of Gauguin or Matisse, the ones that have often been called primitive, the ones we love in childhood.) He began seeing what was wrong more than what was right. Gradually he became more depressed and inactive. Seeing required such an overwhelming effort that three years later he decided he could bear it no longer. Life was no longer worth living.

We see easily because information sent from our eyes to our brain is combined with past experience and memories of things seen before and stored by the brain so it can make snap judgments about what it is currently seeing. If htis wren't the csae tehn we wuold nto be albe to raed thsi. Somehow we can still make sense of the jumble because we fill in from what we already know. Sometimes mistakes are made, which is why we are startled and jump at the sight of a moving dust ball, a bent stick, or our child's woolly mitten as if they were spiders, snakes, or a mouse. We can be surprised by things in our peripheral vision before we realize they are not a threat. We see before we perceive so we get the frisson of recognition, a fast feeling of knowing, when we spot someone we think we recognize in a crowd. Then our slow system snaps to attention and works out that it only looks like cousin Sarah.

We don't register all that we see. What gets our attention is often things that are either unexpected or somehow relevant. We can pass by hundreds in a crowd, deep in thought, seeing without seeing, but if one person walking by is half–naked, is unusually tall, or is cousin Sarah, we do a double take. We notice. We are not being rude when we look at something out of the ordinary. Our brain spots something different, and it gives us a wake-up-and-process-this alert. We analyze and file it for future use. Vision is not lazy. It is selective. (An orthodontist notices teeth and I notice colour.) This is so we can hear ourselves think, plan the day, or walk and talk without bumping into things or being hit by a car (the deeper we are in thought the blinder we are). When we look up a new word, think about buying a car, or start planning a holiday, these things move into the "new" or "noteworthy" categories. All of a sudden, related things jump out at us: "perspicacious," Passat wagons, and Peru ads are everywhere. Were we blind before? No. These were not important before.

Because we skim what is old and grab onto what is new, a new wall colour is obviously major news. It sets off a neurological alert. Our stored image of place has to be reprogrammed. There is no such thing as too much colour but I learned the hard way that there can be too much colour change. Not recognizing this led to one of my biggest colour mistakes.

Gordon asked me to design a colour plan for the lower level of his office building. He wanted to make the long, dreary, windowless pale grey halls more interesting to attract better tenants. On previous jobs I had found him very open-minded. This time I would push a bit further.

On one side of the long narrow hallway I suggested big blocks of colour – burgundy red, terra cotta orange, tan, and ochre. Everything else was neutral. The tenants found the colours overwhelming.

The curious thing was that the most vociferously negative response came from the fellow who ran a copy shop. Ironically, in his copy shop, every surface was orange. Not a pumpkin. Not a terra cotta or a melon hue. The laminate that covered every surface was capital O orange. He was so acclimatized to his own vibrant colour that it was as invisible to him as beige. But confront him with colour where he wasn't accustomed to it and his response could only be described as aggressively negative. Putting strong colour into what had been a colourless space was the visual equivalent of feeding someone a plate of hot Mexican food when they usually ate pabulum.

To Gordon's credit (or his need to make the most of his paint investment), he rode the complaints and left the colours on. Now I would love, as an experiment, to paint the halls back to their original pale blue–grey anaemic tone. I would like to find out whether the tenants' sense of loss would be greater than their relief. I suspect losing the colour, once they were used to it, would be as big a colour shock as getting it. Often colour is not upsetting, change is.

The same principle of economy – spot the new and ignore the old – applies to all our senses. My kids always know when their grandmother has arrived for a visit because the minute they walk into the house they smell her. It is her perfume that they smell. She has worn the same scent all their lives. After a short time, her perfume becomes barely noticeable. It isn't that her perfume stops smelling. It is that we stop noticing.

Smells, like colours, are not put on earth for our sybaritic pleasures. They are functional and advise us on the proximity of food, sex, toxins and dangers. No matter how much we might like to wallow in the scent of oils and unctions or Grandma's perfume, unless they bring news, unless they change, they are as good as gone. Whether it is sautéed onions (a smell I love), Grandma's perfume, or fresh manure, our brain grabs the bulletin then moves along on the high–speed treadmill of processing information. Survival allowed no time to lie back and smell the roses or the onions.

To save time, familiar things are stored in groups or patterns called *schemata*. Common things like chairs, trees, the living room, or the drive to work are stored there for quick reference. Like faces in a crowd, we see them without noticing them. The brain's chair category knows what chairs have in common. It holds onto the essence of chairness so when we see a chair, we fast–track past what is the same – four legs, seat, and so on – to get to what is different about the specific chair.

Entire scenes and settings once integrated as schemata are not forgotten but filed away. If you go back to the place where you grew up many years later, you are flooded with associated memories because seeing the place triggers that place's schemata. The file is retrieved and opened. Out pops the name of your teachers and chums, school yard games and rhymes, and the day your friend fell off a bike. It is no coincidence. It is efficient filing. The same brain strategy means we remember the lyrics to an old song but only as it is playing or we realize we have seen a movie but only once the DVD is in the machine and the opening credits are rolling. The forefront of your mind has limited space so things are pulled forward only when relevant.

Seeing everything every day would make us crazy so we file our rooms as schemata so we can come home, sit down, plan the evening, review the day, read a book, and listen to music. We are freed to spot new information – the painting is crooked, the furniture has been moved, someone's sweater is on the chair, sh–, the stereo is missing! Changing a wall colour is a brain jolt, one that translates into panic or excitement, depending on our personality and our ease with change. Colour is held responsible for the emotional turmoil but change is the culprit. Leave that colour there long enough and it won't matter what colour it is, it will become visual white noise. (Interesting that sound we don't hear is white noise.) We hear the air conditioner go off, not when it's running. Babies presented with the same colour – any colour – again and again lose interest. Present them with a new one and they perk up again. Colour, whether it is red, green, or blue, like sound or smell, perfume or manure, becomes barely noticeable once it's been around for a while.

If sight uses what we know and patterns we have stored, I sensed that I could design colour plans that took advantage of our quick–take seeing. Like walking through a crowd, we take things in with broad strokes. Survival data is more important than decorating details. Based on a few million years of colour practice, we make snap assumptions that colour never lies; it only informs. As long as colour mimics the brain's expectations in some fashion, then everything is okay. We can cheat the brain in the most amazingly useful ways.

One brain assumption is that at a corner the two surfaces look different, one lighter than the other, because of the way the light is hitting them. This is very handy. I can change a colour to a lighter or darker version of itself and no one will spot the trick. Why would I want to? Because in an open plan, I can make a colour darker where I want things to be cozy, and lighter where I want to give a more open feel, by shifting the hue wherever two planes meet at an angle. Also, in many homes it is nicer to make the upstairs hall a lighter version of the lower hall colour to compensate for the fact that it is usually smaller and we want it to feel spacious. Psychologically, we like to feel less weighed down as we move upward. A lighter colour gives the sense of an airier space. It feels more relaxing.

If the brain is doing so much seeing, what exactly are the eyes seeing before the brain kicks in? German physicist Hermann von Helmholtz said that if we were sent the human eye by an optometrist and asked to try it out, we would send it back saying that it was faulty and in need of improvement.

If we see what the eye sees turned into an eight–foot–square poster, it would look a bit like this: upside down and back to front because our eye lens is like a camera lens. Two–dimensional, divided into pixels and only a very small section in focus – less than four square inches out of the sixteen square feet! Even there either the foreground or background would be in focus, not both. Colour within this four–inch patch would be excellent but it would start to fade farther out from the centre. At the outside edges of the image, there wouldn't be much colour at all. On either side of the image would be a small hole, a blank area, our blind spot. And your nose would be a blurry blob at the bottom edge of the image, which would be at the top since everything is upside down. (You can check that your nose is in the picture by closing one eye at a time. The brain didn't think it necessary to erase the nose from this one–eyed view as it isn't one you are going to use for much.) In short, what your eye sees is a mess.

In addition, we would have to switch the lights on and off about fifteen times a minute. Even thinking about blinking makes you blink. You are blacking out this page every few seconds. We don't notice, unless I keep mentioning it, because our brain edits out such useless information. Like breathing and salivating, blinks are just housekeeping and not informative. The brain also conveniently turns off when vision is in between jobs and we move our eyes from one object to another. When we are stationary and want to look at a moving object, we have to target it by blurring the background and holding it in focus on our retina.

Our eyes have another oddity. They cannot stare at something that does not change. This is why staring competitions are so hard. This is why, if you fix your eye on one word of this page, it will blur then disappear. Without a tiny movement of the page or your eye, it all goes blank. Eyes do their job – grab a visual reading – and need to move on, which is why, unconsciously, we constantly make saccades, little movements, to refresh our eyes so they see again.

On their own, our eyes may seemed flawed but together with the brain they make an amazing team. Eyes are actually an outgrowth of the brain that evolved down and forward but are still connected via the optic nerve. They have improved a lot since the time when they were primarily just motion detectors.

Frogs' eyes haven't advanced beyond this early stage of development so they can only see flies, their main source of sustenance, as they fly by. Frogs could be surrounded by an ocean of dead flies and starve to death not knowing they were right under their noses.

The fovea, a small area of the retina, lets us see clearly but only things in our direct line of vision. Everywhere else our vision is not much better than a frog's – bad with colour and shape, good with motion. Kids playing hide–and–seek know instinctively to freeze to be less visible. Peripheral vision is fine for letting us know if a double–decker bus is coming our way but we still turn our eyes to *see* it. If anything around us moves, we automatically shoot a quick look, catching it in our little bit of clear vision. We are not even aware of these involuntary eye movements. So for players in the middle of a match at Wimbledon, a perfectly still elephant would be less distracting and more invisible at the side of the court than a fidgeting ball boy.

Our eyes are hugely sophisticated pieces of equipment. Of the three million messages that are sent to the brain every second, two–thirds come from the eyes. Each eye contains more than a billion cells, including about 127 million photoreceptors. Keeping everything in good working order and well fuelled requires healthy eating habits. Eyes are nutrient–guzzlers. They are greedy for vitamins and minerals and use up to 25 per cent of our total intake. They need twenty times as much Vitamin C as our muscle joints. They need more zinc than any other organ. And to do their work they use a third as much oxygen as our pumping heart! We should think about what our eyes need the next time we, or our kids, are tempted to skip fruits and vegetables in favour of fries and a Coke.

The meeting point between the external and internal world is the retina, the surface at the back of the eye. Light waves enter via the rods and cones. But news of the outside world can't be taken in whole. It has to be absorbed in tiny bits. Millions of photosensitive cells can absorb only the smallest possible unit of light, a *photon*. Breaking down our image into photons is like knocking down a sandcastle that has to be reassembled one grain at a time. It should take forever, yet we can look around as quickly as we like and grab images of the world in a fraction of a second. The brain, amazing as it is, does need a moment to reassemble the view so we can't look up from this page and pan our surroundings in one fluid take. We might think we can. Our brain *wants* us to think we can. It would be unpleasant to be aware of our tunnel vision, aware that we see clearly only in that four–inch square in the sixteen–foot poster image. It would not be a comfort to know we see only by grabbing and catching the world one chunk at a time in that tight area of focus while letting memory fill in the blanks.

We think we see like a camera panning a scene but we really see like a baby learning to walk. We visually grab an object, hold it until we see it, then move over, and grab another. That visual grab is the beat that our brain requires to get and process the millions of swallowed photons. The jump or saccade between objects is, like blinking, something the brain edits out so that we think we see fluidly. If you try to pan you can't. If you sit in a moving car or train and try to look at the scenery without visually grabbing tree to tree, telephone pole to telephone pole, object to object, your brain freaks out. It signals your body for help and your body tells you to stop immediately or get carsick.

Once the upside–down and back–to–front image information absorbed as millions of photons enters the rods and cones, we see the world in full colour, right? Not quite. The light waves are not, strictly speaking, coloured! They are raw material from which colour will be made. We call these waves red, blue, and green but they are more accurately described as long, medium, and short. Eyes take in size signals and *translate* them into colour codes. Colour is made in our head.

To enter a cone or rod, light waves have to find one that fits its size, like the right hole for its key. Infrared and ultraviolet wavelengths find matching receptors in some animal eyes but not ours. Where there is no fit, no molecular do–si–do, there is no entry, no sense of colour.

Cones work best when there is lots of light. They process it in three sizes of wavelength: long – the red, orange, and yellow end of the spectrum; medium – yellow–green information; and short – the blue to violet colour range. Every cone responds to every wavelength of light a little but most emphatically when they catch wavelengths in their area of specialization.

We don't see all colours equally well. In our peripheral vision we have more blue cones so we see blue better peripherally than red and green. This matches nature, where most blue is in wide expanses. On our fovea, we have the reverse arrangement – plenty of green and red cones and very few blue ones because there are fewer blue objects under our noses.

Unlike cones, rods are extremely sensitive. Daylight is too bright for them. When there are too many photons clambering to get in, rods become *saturated* and shut down. They let the cones take care of business until the hordes diminish. When it gets dark or you stick your head into a cupboard, the cones can't see a thing and the rods take over. Rods favour green–blue wavelengths but they really aren't colour fussy. Their photosensitive pigment, rhodopsin, lets in any colour wavelength – a photon is a photon to a rod. Rods see tonally and work like a one–colour printing of a full–colour image. All colour information goes in but because it is processed with one ink colour, the image comes out in perfect tonal clarity but with no colour truth. It isn't the colour of light that interests rods, it is brightness. They map areas of light and dark.

Rods outnumber cones about six to one and spread out across the retina to give us good peripheral vision at night. When we lived as nomads in nature, it was more important to spot something moving on the periphery than to know what colour it was.

Rods take time to kick into full gear, which is why we trip over the people sitting on the aisles when we arrive late at movie theatres and concert halls. Actors waiting in the wings for their cue to go on stage in the blackouts between scenes often close one eye to keep their rods primed for the dark while the other handles bright lights. This way they don't bang into the scenery in the blackout and aren't totally blinded by the lights coming on at the top of the scene. (I find this actor's strategy of having one eye primed for darkness and the other for light is also very handy for getting to and from the bathroom at night.)

Many city dwellers are often not aware that they have two kinds of vision: *photoscopic* vision, full–colour daylight vision handled by the cones, and *scoscopic,* no colour vision, handled by the rods for night or when we stick our head into dark places. Colour–blind nocturnal vision seems unimportant now but once upon a time, in our hunting and gathering days, things were very different. At twilight, the transition from light to dark, we were aware of cones shutting down for the night and rods getting ready for their shift because during that twenty–minute period, we noticed the warm colours darken and the cool colours that rods prefer brighten slightly. It was last call for shelter. If we weren't there already we'd better use this fleeting blue–green glow to hunker down or the odds were we'd become a tiger's dinner.

This cones–to–rods transition is called the Purkinje shift because it was Czech physiologist Jan Purkinje who observed it in 1819. He was such an avid gardener that he rarely stopped for the day until he could hardly see a thing. He noticed just before he had to pack up his trowels and pruners that the colour of his flowers did very weird things. The red, yellows, and oranges turned black as their leaves and stems started to glow.

Only once have I ever managed to take in the Purkinje shift because there is a streetlight beside my garden and I am rarely threatened by night predators. But one evening at dusk I was sitting at my desk when my son, Blake, walked by and stopped. He looked in and turned on the lights. I asked him to turn them off as he leaned against the doorway and chatted. While I listened I enjoyed observing the day's last light, the one we have usually obliterated with that flick of the switch. As it got darker, I watched the red wall beside Blake go dark. I glanced over at the lime green and off–white colours in the rest of the room. The shift from colour vision to black and white began. There was a point when I was not sure if I was still seeing colour or only adding it in from memory's assumptions. And then the red was definitely black and the scene was undeniably colourless. Blake turned on the lights.

That we could make our vast array of colours using only three–colour processors hadn't occurred to anyone until, in 1802, Thomas Young (1773–1829) stumbled on the idea. Young, who was the first to describe astigmatism and decipher Egyptian hieroglyphs, mentioned it as an aside in a lecture. Few paid much attention when he surmised that if colour printing, which had been invented in 1722 by Charles Le Blon could make full–colour prints using a three–colour process, perhaps the eye worked the same way. Eyes, Young said, could not be set up like ears. Ears have thousands of thin hairs, cilia, each one vibrating in response to a specific frequency. There is room in the ear for all these cilia because knowing *what* a sound is is more important than knowing *where* it is. If we need to locate a sound, we try to see where it is coming from. With colour we need to know what *and* where. There is not enough real estate on the eye to have a receptor for every possible colour on every part of the retina ready to pick up every pinpoint of the visual field. The eye developed a more economical system than one–to–one resonators for getting what–where spatial acuity.

Colour vision, as Young concluded, is the product of three primary "colours" or resonators, set like tuning forks, to vibrate to light in a particular part of the spectrum. He had hit the nail on the head a hundred and fifty years before science and technology could prove him right. Hermann von Helmholtz tweaked the concept half a century later and got half the credit. Today it is known as the Young–Helmholtz theory.

The retina is not vision's landing pad. It is more like the departure lounge. At this point the eyes have gathered colour information accurately. Like nerds who dot their i's and cross their t's, eyes are as precise as spectroscopes. They register light signals but they do not translate them. The brain will gather information together using a process that is more creative than accurate. It interprets colour news extracting what is useful but making us less accurate judges of colour. Using tricks like colour constancy the brain stabilizes colour and how light and dark things are. We can be happily reading or chatting and not notice the book's pages turn amber in the light of the setting sun or the fact that the room has gone dark because everything goes amber or gets dimmer to the same degree.

The brain does not think it necessary to see millions of colours. Living in nature did not require matching dye lots or coordinating fabrics and paint colours. We can see millions of

variations only when we compare things side by side, like holding a paint chip next to a tile. It is an odd fact that if we hold colours up and away from their context, our ability to see different nuances of colour is reduced from millions to thousands. Subtleties are impossible to retain. When helping clients pick colours, I have to keep comparing, moving colour chips around the room, and holding them next to different objects so I can begin to know the colour of a colour. How much blue is in this soft blue–grey pastel? How much yellow is in this yellow? Or pink in this white? The only way to know is to compare them to other hues. Then and only then can we see subtleties. The difference between an experienced colourist and a novice is not that we can see the subtleties without comparing; it's that we know we can't.

If I stick a big red balloon in front of your eyes, the "red" cones can't just swallow a bigger mouthful of red. A photon is their limit. Speed becomes their solution. At the sight of the red balloon, the long wavelength cells that were taking things easy, popping out a signal once or twice every few seconds, speed up to a rate of 1,000 per second. It is like switching from firing a single rifle shot to letting loose a barrage of machine–gun fire. Signals are the same size. Their quantity indicates a red balloon filling your POV. The size of wavelength tells us what colour; speed tells us how much.

The signals shoot across synaptic gaps, and dendrites are there like a root system waiting to suck them up into *bipolar* and *horizontal* cells. These next cell layers pool the information and send it on to the *amacrine* cells, which ignore colour and detect movement. Information we need superfast for reflex actions, like blinking and ducking, skips stops like this one entirely and are sent express to our brain.

At every stage, vision processes things in priority sequence. We duck or blink to protect ourselves from things before we recognize what they are. Unconscious seeing, seeing without knowing, is faster than conscious seeing. It is like pre–seeing and is called blind–sight. People who have only blind–sight have perfectly good eyes, but damage to parts of their visual cortex means they are not aware of what they see or even that they do see. Like us, they could duck a tree branch but we work out afterwards that it was a branch and the blind–sighted would not know what you were talking about. They can reach for a pencil or catch it if it were suddenly tossed at them but only through touch could they know it is a pencil. The blind–sighted share our fast–track express visual path so they see, but theirs is like a dead end so they cannot perceive.

The next stop is the *ganglions.* Deliveries from 130 million photoreceptors are transferred to only one million ganglions. Obviously this comparatively short–staffed cell layer has to do a fair bit of info integrating. Exactly what was going on there was a complete mystery until the 1950s when Stephen Kuffler, at Johns Hopkins University, was researching cat's eyes. Shining light of different colour or intensity on cat's eyes seemed to trigger no response at the ganglion layer. Cells were as unresponsive as when the cats were in darkness or asleep. One day as Kuffler was winding down his efforts, something surprising happened when he pulled a slide with a pinhole in it out from his microscope. As he removed the slide, the tiny shaft of light being dragged across the cat's ganglion cells triggered a huge response. When he pushed the slide back in, he noticed that a different set of ganglions reacted strongly. If he moved it up or down, still others fired. Kuffler had discovered the ganglion specialty: small bits of information. To the ganglions, big is boring and repetitive. There are not enough of them to keep responding to what is basically the same information. "Red balloon over here. Red here too. Red here. And here. And here. Yeah. Ditto. Red. Red . . ." Instead, the twenty different kinds of ganglion specialists respond only to light in their specific area of expertise, things like dark spots on light backgrounds, light spots on dark backgrounds, light going off or light going on, colour. Many are movement specialists. Just like a cat's, our ganglions see by detecting edges but only when the edge is at their specific angle or colour of expertise.

Ganglions ignore the body of the balloon like they ignored Kuffler's big diffuse light or his coloured light, because they assume anything within those edges is the same. Rather than responding to light in general, they pick out the smaller features within light's information. It is like outlining a shape on your computer monitor and then pressing the "fill–in" command rather than colouring each pixel. The ganglion strategy with redundant signals is to say, "All right, you, at the borders, give us the coordinates. The rest, hold your fire until something different comes along." When the balloon moves, a new set of cells picks up the edge information and fires away so we can track it, see it.

But if we see quickly and presumptuously *and* if we see by using edges, what might that mean for interior colours? What the ganglions reveal is why colour is not tiring but the edges that divide one colour from another can be. Lots of colours mean lots of edges. Reduce the number of colours and not necessarily the amount of colour and things calm down. The brain floats across colour in a way it cannot float across colours. Coloured edges are how we distinguish one thing from another and how we sense their size and placement in space. This is the basis of contrast and camouflage in the natural world. Things that want to be seen are colour–contrasted and stand out from the background along clear edges. Things that want to hide blend so edges disappear or are less obvious to a busy brain.

Lots of edges make colour clutter. The clutter can be reduced by matching the walls to the main colour of the furniture or the reverse, matching objects to the wall. I often suggest the former, using colour in the walls to reduce colour clutter in the room. In my dining room, I upholstered the extra chairs in red to camouflage them against the walls rather than matching them to the dining room set. Because they blend in, the room appears less cluttered. In my living room, the fireplace mantel looked too short for the tall room. To stretch it to the ceiling, I painted the wall above the mantel the same dark aubergine brown in the same sheen as the wood. Judging colour by its edges is a handy way to manipulate the eye–brain to see the wood and paint as one tall thing. In my upstairs hall there is a large built–in bookcase. The hall is narrow. To make the bookcase disappear, the sides are camouflaged by painting them the yellow of the wall. Everything across the front is light wood. The whole thing looks very slim. Camouflage is handy.

When designing colour plans, the brain's ways let me manipulate size, shape, and space, simply by paying close attention to where I add or subtract edges. To make a short room taller, I take an approach that my clients find counterintuitive. I put the wall colour or a similar one on the ceiling. By deleting the horizontal edge that divides the two, the height becomes unnoticeable rather than emphasized.

A short room is also made taller by an accent colour on one wall that stops before it reaches the corners. The edges of the colour give the illusion of a slimmer and taller wall. Shifting the colour change away from the corner also softens and curves them. They become a less obvious secondary edge.

If I want a tall room to seem shorter, then I stop the wall colour at whatever seems like the right room height and bring the ceiling colour down to meet it. The ceiling seems bigger and the walls shorter. The brain does not require any fancy bit of trim; a coloured edge is enough to establish where things stop and start.

Edges can improve the shape of long skinny halls. A long wall can be shortened by painting a section in a contrasting colour. The new edge divides one wall into two shorter pieces. Length is diminished and at the same time, height is added.

To make a narrow space wider I add a different colour to one side. This cuts it off and separates it from the rest. The box is broken apart. The tunnel effect disappears. A feeling of width is added. My long skinny Victorian house is yellow on one side of the main hall. The rest is off–white (except for a block of orange). No one has ever asked about it. Not only do they not seem to see anything wrong or odd, they don't see it at all. They feel it.

Brains have more important things to focus on than the logic of colour placement. We are free to use as much or as little colour as desired, letting edges and not wall dimensions set the parameters.

Ganglions may have encouraged me to use colour more freely but to be exceedingly careful about edges. I have a huge respect for the power of the edge. Edge fatigue is why I dislike decorative bits and pieces of colour. Colour should not be tossed and sprinkled about, not peppered across upholstery, wall tiles, and borders. Contrasting colour should rarely be used to emphasize windows and trim. I caution anyone who is contemplating the high contrast edges of a black and white checkered floor. Coloured outlines, coloured details, coloured patterns all keep the ganglions busy and require restraint and care to get a good balance and not an overloaded buzz.

The brain is not stupid when it skims past things. It pays attention when it senses something is not logical. A coloured circle or a few curvy squiggles added to a wall would have the ganglions grabbing the edges and sending the news upstairs for processing. The brain would wonder what the devil was going on. It would work hard to make things make sense. Not so the vertical lines of a colour block going from roughly the floor to the ceiling. These sit within the realm of the expected. They signal a corner of a wall or the edge of a panel or any "normal" thing. As long as the colour obeys a loosely defined and stored premise, our brain floats gullibly over the trick.

When it comes to processing colour, the ganglions don't use the red–green–blue set–up of the rods and cones because they are not dealing with light. At this point the signals are electrical and they are processed by three teams: black–white, green–red, and blue–yellow. Each ganglion cell is designed like a two–ring, two–colour target. They are called *opponent cells* because, like a couple that should get a divorce, what turns one part of the cell on turns the other off. A red balloon has them cancelling each other's signal *except* where a tiny bit of red is small enough to hit one part that is red positive and green negative and not the part that is the reverse. That would be at colour edges. Where signals indicate that the edge of the red balloon meets blue sky, one part of the cell responds and the other part stay oblivious so a signal is fired.

In 1875 German physiologist Ewald Hering (1834–1918) observed that vision probably used six colours in three pairs. New scientific investigations of colour–blindness seemed like proof because colour deficiencies are normally red–green or, less commonly, a blue–yellow. Afterimages, or *simultaneous contrast,* also appear in the same complementary pairs. The afterimage of a red object is teal green, for a blue object it is yellow. The afterimage of black objects is white and vice versa. Furthermore, Hering noticed that no colour contained any of its complementary colour. There is no reddish–green or greenish–red, no bluish–yellow or yellowish–blue.

This is not what anyone wanted to hear. The world was just coming around to the Young–Helmholtz three–colour theory so Hering's ideas threw a spanner in the works. Much later science proved them both right. The cones worked on the three receptor system, and subsequent stages were organized according to Hering's opponent pairs.

The ganglions do what–colour–where mapping and send the information all the way down their long axons, the optic nerve, super–highway to the brain. A million axons squeeze together into this tight bundle for the journey. But, as vision is never as straightforward as it seems, the journey goes backward to go forward.

The rods and cones are not sitting on the surface of the retina like bristles protruding from a brush, catching light and sending signals toward the back of our head. They are at the very bottom of this heap of these cell layers *and* they are facing away from the light and toward the brain! So now the signals have to be sent backward.

Light hitting the retina has to pass through the tangled web of cell layers, like running through a dense forest, before it even reaches a rod or a cone. Some doesn't make it, which is why most of our field of vision is a complete blur. Our small area of visual clarity is thanks to the fovea or macular. Like a clearing in the woods or a bald patch on the retina, the fovea has no cell layers on top of it. To make the most of this little piece of prime real estate, cones make themselves as skinny as possible to squeeze on board. Chubbier ones scatter themselves more spaciously on the rest of the retina. There are no rods there because they don't like the direct light.

By the time light that finds its way through the mesh of cell layers is absorbed, processed, and compressed into the optic nerve, signals have worked their way right back up to the surface of the retina. The optic nerve has to return in the direction from which it came. In its wake it leaves a blind spot, the hole in the retina that has no rods and cones.

Because the ganglions are good at filling in, they just paste in a little information from neighbouring areas so we don't notice. This process, called completion, is why we are not aware of our blind spots.

You can see your blind spot if you close one eye and hold a pencil with an eraser or a Q–tip in front of the other. Slowly move the pencil or Q–tip to the side, keeping your eye still. At about 18 degrees out, the tip will briefly disappear and reappear again.

Optic nerves are straightforward transporters of goods. They meet up once, at the optic *chiasma*, and switch half their shipment. Information about the right field of vision from both eyes gets put together in the left optic nerve and goes to the brain's left hemisphere. Information about the left field of vision from both eyes is loaded onto the right optic nerve heading to the right hemisphere. As often happens, small parcels of urgent information are fast–tracked to our body via the thalamus for reflex actions. The rest carries on into that mysterious three–pound organ, our brain.

It is odd to think that the human brain, the most sophisticated processing mechanism ever created, was considered, by even the most sophisticated civilizations of the past, to be a useless piece of grey, wrinkly pulp, a worthless blob. Because the brain is bloodless at death, they reasoned it couldn't possibly hold the human spirit. Mind and soul were thought to be located elsewhere, either in the stomach, liver, gall bladder, or, most commonly, the heart. It is the heart that beats harder and faster at times of strong emotion or strenuous effort – it must, therefore, be at the core of our existence. And so Egyptians, who preserved all the important organs of the deceased in special containers, sucked the brain out through the nostrils and threw it away.

Even a few decades ago, what we knew about the mysterious workings of the brain was about as sophisticated and useful as blood–letting. When the activity of a single cell could be measured then we could figure out where things were really happening. Even though we know what cells are busy and when, we still can't figure out how their actions all come together as our experience of the world. We know what and when but not how. The brain remains complex and perplexing.

We do know that inside our head is a place where the sun don't shine. Unlike Egyptian pyramids, there is no system of long tunnels with reflecting mirrors set at the ends to bounce light around curves and corners and on into our deepest core. Visual information received as light must morph itself into *electrical impulses,* the language spoken by the brain.

Electrical impulses are what the brain uses to "see." The head has no film, no projection screen, and no inner eye, only millions and millions of mini–electrical signals acting like an elaborate contrapuntal Morse Code. All of our senses turn their data into binary code and send it along their specific routes through the central nervous system to the brain and, as if by magic, all the data converges and we get our cohesive experience of the world. In the farthest reaches is a place the size of a small bean, and it is there that many of those signals are turned into colour.

Each optic nerve delivers its information to the *lateral geniculate nucleus (LGN),* the brain's landing pad. The cramped shipment of signals spreads out through the LGN, which is layered like a birthday cake or a club sandwich in six layers. Many layers process information about the same spot in the image but some cell layers skip the details in favour of speed. Some pay attention to colour. Signals are sent forward for visual processing or to the body for immediate action; some go in circles.

Bright colours do not make soothing background colours because, unlike neutrals, they are part of the information

that gets fast–tracked to our limbic or old brain as survival essentials. In nature, bright colours were never to be ignored so they get speedy delivery to the reflex action and emotion centres.

No wonder bold colour is used relentlessly by advertising companies to attract and alert us. These are the colours that some blind people imagine the world to be full of. These are the colours that all children love and can't get enough of. These are the vivid hues you imagine if I say the word colour or the ones clients often fear I will impose on their peaceful lives. For colour–lovers the sight of bright bold colours can feel like the hit of something vital to our core that we can't get enough of.

Gauguin and van Gogh felt that colour in a portrait conveyed the sitter's personality and presence as much as an accurate likeness. On walls they reveal much about the personality of those who inhabit the space. Bright colours are used freely by indigenous people the world over because they are more in touch with nature and deep colour instincts than the average urban dweller. Because bright and joyful colours are so tied to emotions and emotions are so hard to control, these are the colours that throughout history, from the Reformation's sumptuary laws to Afghan rules about burqas, repressive regimes try hard to eliminate.

The lateral geniculate nucleus sends signals on to the *primary visual cortex*. You might be thinking, "At last we have arrived at our final destination!" Early in the twentieth century, Swedish neuro–pathologist Salomon Henschen (1877–1930) thought so and he called it the *cortical retina,* the brain–eye. Henschen felt that what the eye registered was not tossed back from the retina to the brain, willy–nilly. And he was right. He thought it went to this eye–brain area, the end of the road, and vision clicked in. And he was wrong. Instead, one hundred billion nerve cells end up swapping signals from thousands of other neurons without ever landing in one place.

The *primary visual cortex,* also called the *striate cortex* because its layers resemble stripes (V1 for short), is at the back of our head and as close as we get to the end of the road. The cortex, from the the Latin for bark, is the thick, lumpy outer layer of the brain. It is divided into the left and right hemispheres. Information from each side of our body is shipped to the same processing areas but on the opposite side of our head. The cortex developed during a recent brain growth spurt about fifty thousand years ago. It wraps our older more primitive brain, the workhorse that handles unconscious activities like reflexes, breathing, moving, body functions, and emotions – fundamental jobs – without ever having to be told what to do or bothering us with the details.

The *primary visual cortex* tackles visual information in sections like a patchwork quilt. The cells of the V1 are an army of two hundred million cells, divided into over forty kinds of specialists, ready and waiting to grab information from a mere 1.5 million LGN cells. There are specialists in edges at a specific angle or motion in a certain direction or luminance or depth. Until recently, no one could figure out where the colour experts were hiding. In the LGN, almost 10 per cent of cells were colour oriented but in the primary visual cortex colour–processing cells were nowhere to be found. Then in 1981, David Hubel and Margaret Livingstone stained a section of the V1 with dye. Previously invisible colour cells showed up as spots scattered throughout the layers of the V1 like a bad case of acne. Hubel gave the small colour–specific clusters of cells the remarkably unscientific name *blobs.*

V1's specialists work side by side on their particular patch, paying no attention to their neighbours. Because V1 works piecemeal if it is partly damaged, only the part of the visual field represented in that small patch disappears, like a missing puzzle piece, from the finished image. Everything else remains intact. If the V1 is severely damaged, then it doesn't matter how good the eyes are, we are blind.

The patches that get information from the fovea are blown up to super–size. It is as if the V1 is doing to foveal information what medieval artists did when they depicted Christ or the Virgin Mary: they make them billboard huge compared to everything else, ensuring they grab our attention.

If the patches are worked on independently, where does the image finally get stitched together? As it turns out, the primary visual cortex is not Henschen's eye–brain, final destination. Wrapped around it like the suburbs around a city centre is the *association cortex,* a group of specialists each with its own department, each on its own piece of cerebral real estate. There is the department of movement, the department of form recognition, the department of face recognition, even a department of hand recognition. And, in an area the size of a bean, there is the department of colour. This is where *potential colour,* electrical impulses about light wave information, is changed, for the first time, into our experience of *colour* and the balloon under your nose that triggered a long wavelength response is experienced as red.

In the association cortex, all of the departments are, as their name implies, associates, team players. They get the V1's processed patches via its assistant, V2, which clumps them together into bulk shipments. Then they compare notes with each other and they compare what is coming in now with what came in previously. Unlike the cells in V1, they are not launched fully fledged specialists at birth. At birth they are like a new library with lots of shelving that immediately begins to acquire books. They build up a repository of information through experience. Here vision is no longer the passive "accident of light on the eye" Newton described. It becomes, as Goethe suggested, an active and subjective process, what Helmholtz called "an act of judgment." We actively participate and connect the dots. Vision is fleshed out, perception occurs, and colour is made.

If one of the departments in the association cortex is damaged and ceases to function, the others carry on with business. We see the image but without the damaged department's contribution. Without our motion detector working, we can't cross a street or pour a cup of tea easily. Without our face recognition department up and running, we wouldn't know our kids in family photos, our parents if they showed up at the front door (except by voice), or our own face in the mirror. We would see a nose, eyes, and a mouth but whose would be a complete mystery.

In the story by neurologist and author Oliver Sacks, *The Case of the Colour Blind Painter,* we learn what happens when V4, the bean–sized colour department, doesn't work. A painter, known as Mr. I, suffered from *cerebral achromatopsia,* total colour–blindness. His V4 area was damaged, probably due to a small stroke so he stopped seeing colour even though every other part of his visual system was doing its job.

We might assume that what the painter saw was like a black and white movie, which, in the scheme of things, would be sad but not horrendous. But Mr. I felt depressed and suicidal. It wasn't just that everything looked colourless, that skin looked mouse grey and very unappealing and that mustard looked dirty white and identical to mayonnaise or that jam and ketchup were equally black. It was the wrongness of it all. Food looked dead. Blacks looked cavernous. Shadows looked like crevices, making driving difficult because he kept swerving to avoid what he thought were holes in the road. Whites glared yet appeared dirty. Clouds were often invisible against a blue sky. Yellows and blues were dirty white. Reds and greens were often black but it depended on lighting. He lost all subtle gradations of tone. Everything was in high contrast like an over–exposed image put through a bad Xerox machine a few too many times. It was hard to see anything that wasn't set off against a contrasting background colour. Flowers disappeared into foliage. His own brown dog was visible against the sidewalk but blended into shrubbery.

It wasn't just a black and white world where everything was shades of grey. It was a world in which even those greys were not stable. Everything fluctuated. Changes in light or lighting altered his palette of greys. Red, though usually black, became pale in the warm light of the setting sun. Turning on a fluorescent light made all the greys in the room shift. What Mr. I lost by not having a functioning V4 was colour but also his mental colour–stabilizing mechanism, *colour constancy*. We see these same shifts but mentally block them out. Without this editing, everything shimmered or, as Mr. I described it, looked molten.

Colour processing done before the V4 is pre–chromatic. It is literal, like a spectroscope. The V4 tinkers with the information by comparing the colour now to the colour before and computes what it thinks is the "real" colour, the colour in colour–balanced daylight, deleting the lighting effects that Impressionist painters tried so hard to see. In Mr. I's world, light's flux was not deleted so he didn't have the "normal" stability of a black and white movie but a world of tonal chaos.

Mr. I finally made peace with his new reality. Slowly he forgot what he was missing, colour's associations, memories, and emotions. He not only forgot how it looked but he forgot how it felt. Sunsets stopped looking wrong and started to develop a new magic. He started to enjoy their shimmering monochromatic shifts. Gradually things were re–jigged in his brain and he was able to settle into his pulsating, colourless norm.

Reaching V4, our colour maker, is not like hitting pay dirt. It is as far as we can go but it is not at the end of a road. There is no end. V4 sends and receives information and continues looping it forward and backward, making more and more interconnections. It sends lots of colour information off to the *superior collis* in our limbic or old brain, the destination that already received fast–tracked colour information and where feeling is added to seeing.

The brain is a symmetrical organ but there is more neural wiring between the brain's right hemisphere and the emotion centres than from the left, so creative types, right–brain thinkers, tend to be more in tune with colour. Whenever feeling drives colour decisions, the choices tend to be brighter and bolder. When feelings are put into check by more rational thinking, the opposite occurs. Too much thinking and too little feeling can lead to the sad stories like the one about a colleague, Bruce, and the colour that got away.

Bruce succumbed to second–guessing, the killer of all good colour intuition. He was buying a Citroën C3 Pluriel, a.k.a. *trois chevaux*. This was not a get–to–work–and–back–in–the–rigours–of–the–changing–Canadian–seasons kind of car. This was a sporty little number for jaunts near his home in the countryside in the south of France. This was for picking up baguettes and wine, taking in the sights, and visiting friends. As he went off to the dealer his wife said, "Get something colourful."

When he got there, all the brochures and promotional material for the car featured it in a beautiful orange. For anyone who thought orange was not beautiful, the images were seductively clever: orange car against orange sunset, orange car against amber fields or golden city light. Somehow orange became more appealing with each image. Bruce felt the thrill of the orange. It was calling him. It tempted him like the devil saying, "It is not a sin to cut loose and set your inner child free. It is not a sin to follow your bliss. Bruce, choose orange or be damned."

The problem is that Bruce hesitated. He thought about it. He tried to rationalize it. The head is never as colour–free as the heart. The more it tries to make sense of colour the less it does. Colour will always be umbilically connected to our emotions and those who trust their emotions trust colour. So the more Bruce thought about it, the less inclined he was to embrace orange. When his wife heard the car approach, she looked out the window. Up the drive came the shiny new *trois chevaux*. Much to her disappointment it was silver.

Silver is the automotive equivalent of no colour. Black is to clothing and neutrals are to walls what silver is to cars – the no–statement statement. Bruce would be the first to admit that he bought what seemed appropriate. So it came as a surprise to him that doing something right could feel so wrong. He knows there is a side of him that keeps pining for the orange, keeps accusing him of not being bold enough or free enough to have chosen it. He knows he will always miss that extra spark of pleasure, that added value, that bigger bang for the buck that could so easily have been his. The freer we are with our feelings the freer we are with colour.

We never get to be Dorothy, pulling back the curtain to reveal a Wizard of Oz, a man at a machine. Perception is just a lot of binary code streaming at different speeds to and from hundreds of departments in our body and our brain without meeting up in one place. We can watch a baseball player swing the bat and hit the ball. We don't need to know that the sound of the ball against the bat travels more slowly than our image of it. We aren't aware that even in our image the colour, the motion, and the form recognition are sorted in different departments *and* at different speeds. We aren't aware that we don't see in real time but in time mysteriously bound together in the brain. Our senses combine data the way we combine the sounds of different instrumental parts into a unified piece of music. Just as we make Beethoven's Fifth out of oboes repeating a short phrase, with violins taking up the melodic line while cellos bring in the harmony and the percussion section goes into a syncopated rhythm, our integrated experience combines a multitude of flowing "micro–consciousnesses." Sound, shape, colour, and motion unite. The batter hits a home run. We experience that nano–beat, the present, as an accumulation of nano–presents, anticipating the future using experience from the past.

Thanks to the idiosyncrasies of how the brain sees and how it doesn't, I am free to ignore or bend all the old colour rules, the ones that assume that we see with our eyes and that our eyes are very critical experts on decorating do's and don'ts. The higher brain regions of the cortex and the old, fast, emotion–centre limbic brain deal with colour in ways that have nothing to do with the rules that guide most house–painters.

Sometimes I am asked if I have ever had a client I couldn't help. There have been one or two. And they have something in common. They couldn't let go and trust. They were unable to bend or to try anything outside their comfort level. They knew what made sense and what seemed crazy. They relied on their left brain where everything is supposed to be logical, not knowing that this area of the brain is inexperienced with colour. It lacks the right brain's extra colour–emotion connections. It lacks the old brain's fast, intuitive colour responses that are tied to emotion and survival. For them colour will always be about things like paint. For everyone else colour, like a good wine, starts to open up and expand into a fuller experience. Even if it is hard to find the words to explain why, they know when harmonies look good and feel even better.

red
blue
orange
purple
green
red
blue
orange
purple
green

red
blue
orange
purple
green
red
blue
orange
purple
green

Don't read these words. ***Say what colour they are.*** The brain's priority system puts reading a word – its meaning – over how it looks. When the two match, describing the colour of the word is easy. When there is a contradiction it takes more time and concentration. This interference in reaction time is known as the stroop effect after American psychologist John Ridley Stroop (1897 – 1973) who wrote about it in 1935. Like switching from automatic pilot to manual, directing our attention by inhibiting one response to perform another takes effort. It makes us appreciate how skillfully the brain does things without "our help."

HOT OR NOT? HOW TRENDS ARE BORN

Whenever I give a talk about colour I am invariably asked about colour trends. When clients ask what colour's hot and what's not or what is the new or latest colour, frankly, it used to drive me nuts. Colour is colour. It isn't ever in or out. Then I realized that while colours don't go in and out of fashion, colour combinations do. This is why colour palettes evoke different eras and different cultures. Colour combinations from the 1940s tended to be much drabber than those of the fifties, which were different from the wilder sixties. Pastel pinks and apricots with teal looks Tex–Mex eighties. An African palette is different from a Scandinavian one. In my theatre designing days I used colour combinations to help establish time and place because each has a colour zeitgeist, a flavour of its own.

Now, instead of silently cursing the dreaded "trend" word as I nudge would–be followers of fashion to focus on their own taste and their own rooms, I have started to pay more attention to trends. In fact in my small way I suppose I contribute because I joined the Color Marketing Group.

This colour–trend forecasting organization was started in 1962 to bring colour cohesiveness to the chaos of choice. Its aim was to help manufacturers produce carpet, textiles, and other products in colour ranges that would not only reflect current popular taste but would also be compatible with each other. Twice a year I go to conferences to discuss, with a few hundred other colour people from many industries and countries, just what colours will be strong in the future and why. This is what goes on behind the scenes.

Members are divided into two general categories: Contract Colours, which are colours geared to commercial markets, and Consumer Colours, colours geared to residential use and consumer markets. Sub–categories include sports and recreation, communications, automotive, fashion, and home. In workshop sessions, about fifteen people from complementary industries – paint, carpet, and textile manufacturers; other designers or furniture company reps – sit around a table for a day, each presenting a particular shade of colour or colours that we see causing interest. We are not bringing in what colours are selling but what will be selling in the future. We also try to understand what is driving the change socially, politically, or artistically.

What we do not do is sit around looking at colours trying to come up with some new and different ideas and then voting on the ones we like. We do not arbitrarily decide that maybe a lime or chartreuse would be a fun accent colour this season and that teal should take a permanent vacation. No. We are more like a big antenna picking up signals that are out there; in essence, picking up your signals and bringing them to the table.

Our mission is to clarify and distil them into useable colour information. What we do with that information is what will be exciting.

After each member has presented, the colours go up on a display board and the fun begins. We must reduce all the colours to the most representative eight or nine. Opinions are diverse and the debate can get heated. In the last few years, the decisions have become increasingly complicated because it isn't just a colour that matters but how or where it is used. Is orange going into the kitchen? Is black being used for faucets?

White was hot at the Prague conference in 2006. Members from a Japanese motorcycle company told the group that their most powerful bike, the kind I imagine being ridden by a big, beefy, bearded, leather-clad, and tattooed tough guy, was not just coming out in the usual black or dark burgundy – for the first time ever, it was going to be available in translucent white. Someone remarked that glossy translucent white was big at the Milan Furniture Show due to the iPod effect.

With increasing frequency, a colour's finish is what makes the colour interesting. Bold colour hit cell phones one year and by the next the news was special effects – sparkles, pearlescent, or interference finishes that change colour with the viewing angle. What we called Root Beer was a dark brown emerging in the automotive category that had to be metallic, a glossy finish but with depth and a very fine sparkle effect. Root Beer was not just brown. It was a colour "lit from within."

Kitchen people notice if kitchens are getting more colourful, if wood finishes are going darker or lighter, warm or cool, if grains are subtle or strong and used vertically or horizontally or if in Italy cabinets are going beyond glossy to glassy. Colour is not just colour any more.

Before each conference, I procrastinate. The idea of "hot" colours seems so arbitrary. The truly shocking thing is that once I get into it, I always have a colour epiphany. It is as if a colour jumps out at me and berates me for ignoring it even though it has been trying to get my attention for quite some time.

Black was one such epiphany. It jumped out, swamping me with its presence. Black was going to be everywhere. I thumbed through stacks of magazines to see if it was coming. Page after page after page advertised products on clean strong backgrounds of black, and not just the usual things – watches, cars, champagne, perfume, and white sofas. Black had infiltrated the land of white – kitchens and bathrooms. Even black sofas were against black! Within the year I noticed Waterford was making crystal goblets in black, Swarovski was making black crystal chandeliers, Mooie produced the Carbon Chair, a Victorian wingback chair with black leather tufted upholstery and a black enamelled frame. I opened a British design magazine and it showed black rooms in San Francisco, London, and Paris and an eight–page spread on black. I know we often see what we are looking for but this went way beyond that.

At the conference I did my show–and–tell to the group. They seemed surprised until I laid out my story in visuals. Next came the last presenter in our group, a young product developer for Target stores. He revealed his three colour heavyweights. And to everyone's surprise one of them was black.

The colour picks from each industry's workshops are pooled. Over the course of the next day, an inner circle of colour consolidators debates and discusses and edits the results down to the final finalists. It is interesting to take a look at the workshop boards all lined up prior to editing. Invariably there is one colour that keeps popping up like a weed, often in several categories. It might be in Home, Fashion, and Communications. One year it was turquoise, another, magenta. Recently it was hits of an acidic citrus yellow–green. What is it in the collective unconscious that makes us crave that particular hue?

Colour trends used to start out in fashion and percolated down into home decor over a year or two. Now it can be almost simultaneous. In the past, choosing a colour was a huge commitment for a manufacturer, and a colour mistake spelled disaster. Consequently, the more expensive a product and the longer it was to last, the more conservative its colour range had to be. This reinforced the notion that expensive things are colourless. Cheap things are colourful. Now, at the CMG conferences, there is a lot of buzz about mass customization and advances in technology that facilitate short runs and quick colour turnaround. Even cars and carpets that, in the past, had to be ultra–conservative have started unleashing amazing colours. Colour is becoming less an indication of price and more an indication of attitude.

Change is refreshing, and trends inspire new possibilities and a craving for change. A recent trend was bold greens, and I had to smile when I saw a pair of Mies Van der Rohe lounge chairs, in grass green. Mies, who hated colour, would roll in his grave. His chairs in black or white leather have always been the icons of quality and good taste in hundreds of high–end corporate spaces. If it can be given a colour spin, then maybe colour is no longer just for things juvenile or cheap.

So in answer to the question what is the new hot colour, it is not a question of what–colour but what–colour–where–and–how–and–with–what–other–colour–and–in–what–finish that makes colour new. No wonder everyone's interpretation of a colour trend will be unique. Colour trends are not what a good designer forces into his or her work, but I confess they occasionally find a way in on their own. And so the year that black was the big thing for me was the year more of my clients "coincidentally" seemed to want or need black. When it was greens, greens crept into projects in delightful ways. Maybe the importance of trends is to keep us all, designers included, open to new ideas. Trends are like an infusion of fresh air that finds its way into our work, our home, or our wardrobe if it is one that suits. It can sail by unheeded if not. If an interesting colour combination resonates, it will just happen to come to mind and seem like the right thing for the right place – right here, right now.

GOING HOME

For me it was a big deal. Years after I decided to make colour my career, I was asked to give a talk on colour at IDEX, the Interior Design Exchange, a trade show for interior designers and architects in Toronto. Many in the audience would be design experts. Tickets sold out and the talk was moved to a larger space. It felt like an affirmation that what I do, colour, is important.

After my initial enthusiasm over the opportunity to talk about my favourite subject came the terrifying reality that I did not know what to say. There are so many sides to colour, so many ways to slice the pie. Where would I begin? I agonized and I procrastinated and, when there was only a week left before the show, I panicked. Why had I ever said I would do the talk in the first place?

Design professionals would already know that caring about colour and using it well is not a frivolous pursuit. But would they know that it is so essential it evolved into our DNA, and that seeking beauty and being attracted to things that are good for us is a survival instinct.

Interestingly, what looks good to us *is* good for us. Women are attracted to tall, well–toned men, with symmetrical bodies who would make good hunters. Men like well–upholstered women who would make good gatherers and childbearing types. We have an aversion to spiders, snakes, heights, darkness, and the smell of food that's gone off – things that aren't good for us – but we crave natural sugars and sex. Long, shiny hair is attractive because it is a sign of good health over a long period. Our taste hasn't changed much since the Pleistocene era.

Aesthetic, from the Greek for "to perceive" is about *how we see*, not *what we see*. Beauty requires familiarity. Call me conditioned, but I married a man with the wavy, brown hair and blue eyes that ran in my family. Art and music familiar to our culture tends to be what we find pleasing. When colours are familiar and tagged with positive associations, we enjoy them. A happy childhood in a yellow house can incline us to yellow; a miserable childhood would produce the opposite effect. Designers have to find choices that accommodate our innate responses combined with those we acquire through experience and association. Red on the walls might overpower someone accustomed to neutrals but make my client Linda, my daughter, Caroline, and me content and happy. But colour experts would already know that.

My anxiety about my IDEX talk built. It was crazy. Why not just start at the beginning and talk about kids, the true colour experts? Colour is always so easy for them. Have you ever come across a child who worried about colour and ever second–guessed a colour choice? My sister, an artist, described watching small children paint. With enthusiasm and confidence they pick up a brush and dive into colour. And they paint with carefree alacrity. When a piece is finished, they put down their brush or they pick up a fresh sheet of paper and off they go without hesitation. (That they knew when their painting was finished was almost as startling to my sister as the confidence with which they began.)

Children are instinctual colour users because they are still in touch with their natural colour smarts. Colour is one of our first tools for deciphering the world. At the beginning of our lives there is a short window of time when we organize everything by colour first and shape second. In an experiment to test this, young children are given triangles, squares, and circles in red, yellow, and blue. They are asked to sort them into groups. Up to the age of three or four, children group them by colour, not shape. Older children sort by shape. Adults either sort by shape or look confused and ask for more information. But no adult ever organizes the multicoloured shapes into groups by colour – ever. As we become more analytical and less instinctive, colour takes second place to shape and stays there forever.

Children are intuitive colourists because they follow their feelings and emotions. Hesitant intellect develops at the expense of fearless instinct. We are born colour confident, we get colour confused. When I was beginning my colour practice, my son, Blake, then seven years old, reinforced for me how colour–clever kids are. I was asked to pick a colour for the home office of our friend Gillian. She wanted "the colour of a brown paper bag" because it would be toasty warm and earthy casual. Onto her wall I taped half a dozen large chips, all tans. Then I put up a burnt orange. Gillian looked surprised. "Don't panic," I said. "It is just that from your description of how you want the room to feel, the pumpkin colour might work. See how the idea settles."

That night I was sitting at my desk contemplating Gillian's palette options and wondering which would be the best. I asked Blake as he was passing by to give me his opinion. (Kids love to give their opinions and I always find them refreshingly honest and decisive.) When I asked what colour he thought best, to my amazement, rather than picking one he liked, he said, "Best for what?"

"Gillian's office," I replied. Still he did not choose. With a kid's uncanny wisdom he asked, "That would depend on how she wants it to feel." (Not "look," "feel.") Kids are so much better at colour than most grown–ups! "Warm and friendly," I said and he pointed to the pumpkin. By the next day Gillian had reached the same conclusion. When the room was renovated years later, the architect called me and asked for the colour number. Gillian was not ready to change her pumpkin walls.

What happens to all this wisdom? Knowing colour is ingrained but knowing how to use it gets lost in rules and over–rationalizing. Our intuitive colour–confident bubble bursts as we thwart our fast and best colour responses.

Before we are even aware of colour, our brainwaves and our nervous systems are affected. Nothing in our few generations spent adapting to built habitats is going to shift these ingrained genetically encoded responses. Colour organized the world so we knew things fast. Green was trees and grass, sky was blue, and approaching stripes in orange, black, and white meant time to run for it.

There is a surprising amount of strong colour in nature. Grass, plants, leaves of every size and shape are a shockingly strong green. But imagine a room dressed in those greens. How odd that outside they are like wallpaper, the background against which we notice more significant things! A Martian landing on the earth might find it a commodious enough place to live except that with all those wacky greens everywhere it would be like having one big migraine. We evolved with nature and her colour schemes – in nature there are no colour mistakes.

We know what colours look good if we tune in to our natural colour wisdom by paying attention to our primal self and what it tells us. If we ignore its opinion, it will keep up a low–level nagging: "I really don't like that yellow." "I am very tired of all these wishy–washy neutrals." "We need a change around here." The more we listen, the easier colour gets. Giving our animal self what it wants has such a positive effect that it can feel like falling in love with all that surrounds us. Colour can be part of building a good relationship.

Love and colour. My talk had to link them because that is essentially what good colour is all about. It is the magic spell, the abracadabra, that turns the ugly toad into a handsome prince or brings the bad, misshapen, forlorn–looking space to life and makes it beautiful.

I might mention Leslie. She was not in love or even infatuated with her new house when she called for help several years ago. She was close to tears. She and her husband had two small children and they needed to be near parents who were going to help with babysitting. This would have been fine if Leslie had not consequently found herself the proud owner of a house she hated in a location that was less than her dreams.

We spent a morning designing a colour plan that put drama (red) into the insipid hall and fun (apple greens) into the living and dining rooms. We gave each bedroom its own soft tone, and as we progressed Leslie wrote down additional decorating ideas (for example, put a window–sized opening in the wall between the windowless kitchen and the dining room so the two spaces "talk to each other").

A few weeks later she called to say thank you and to share her excitement. The work was done and she was thrilled. The effect of the colour was cheaper and faster than therapy and a lot easier than moving. It felt as if every inch of the house was "her." Leslie was in love with it and was completely happy there.

Colour's most important attribute, now that our life does not usually depend on it, is the way it feels, and colour should feel like comfort or pleasure, it should feel like home. We know home when we experience it because, for better or worse, feeling at home is the one skill at which we are all experts. Even before we can walk and talk, we have a very finely tuned sense of when a place is safe and welcoming. In the millions of years we spent as nomads on the savannahs, life depended on knowing. We were constantly setting up temporary abodes in new settings without the luxury of time to waste on unsuitable spots. We had to be experts in recognizing a potential home when we passed it even if we were also doing other things at the same time, such as hunting and gathering. We have held onto this primal insight.

I wanted to tell designers and architects that our work needs to acknowledge and cater to this ancient savannah skill. It is the foundation for good design and the reason people say they know they want to buy a particular house or rent a certain apartment as soon as they walk through the door – even before. We know which schools will be good for our kids, which workplaces we feel good about, and whether a restaurant feels right instantly. If we get a positive emotional response, we then go on to work out why.

Years ago I convinced my husband that we should sell our home and buy a bigger one (even though for him home was a comfy chair with a good reading light). I didn't know then that we judge a place with our savannah mechanisms, I just knew that colour, fresh–cut flowers, and a spray called French Country made my place feel really nice. So, it seems, did everyone who came through the door, and the house sold for well above the asking price in one weekend in the middle of winter.

Real estate agents may not realize that we are using animal instincts and seeking savannah characteristics but they certainly know that first impressions are the deal maker or breaker. With nomad smarts, we evaluate any new setting in seconds. Smell and colour response lead the way. We are more likely to be swayed positively by the smell of baked cookies and lovely colours than a firm roof. We will be negatively influenced by kitty litter odours and dingy wall colour even if the plumbing and wiring are in great shape. Vendors are advised to de-clutter to make the space look bigger and to add strategically placed fresh fruit and flowers because, like Constable's landscapes, if we manipulate a setting to look like the savannah, it will look more like the universal idea of home.

Many of the essential feel-good ingredients have been bred out of our buildings. I help many clients deal with truly awful spaces – unintelligently conceived, poorly appointed, and often exceedingly expensive.

We are sensual creatures too often cut off from the essential characteristics of our original home, a place full of movement, change, colour, texture, and variety, too often starved of the stimulation that kept us mentally refreshed and alert. We get trapped in hotels, condominiums, and office towers with too few colours and textures, too little natural light, and too many straight lines.

At work many have to suffer from bad lighting, windows sealed in the name of energy efficiency (the building's and not ours), controlled air (in the city where I live, on the hottest days of summer, offices, theatres, and shopping malls are filled with people wearing jackets and sweaters to avoid pneumonia). Sick Building Syndrome does not exist where fresh air and variable and colour-filled sunlight come in.

Static spaces dumb us down. Stimulating the senses keeps our brain up and running and on its toes. Neurons work best when they are active, processing and prioritizing sense information on multiple tracks. How fit our brain stays depends on the kind of workout it gets.

Dr. Marian Diamond at the University of California in Berkeley found that rats of all ages grew bigger brains in a stimulating environment. Brain size diminished in an impoverished one. Even old rats gained brain power with stimulation. Our brains are a use-it-or-lose-it muscle that needs a rich environment to reach full potential.

Colour must not be dismissed as a personal taste issue but rather deployed as a functional necessity in interior environments. In 1976, Swedish environmental psychologist Rikard Kuller studied what happened when six men and six women were placed in a colourful and complex room and in a grey and sterile one. The grey room triggered faster heart rates and a feeling of stress and boredom (men even more so than women). In a colourful space, no such negative effects were experienced. Unfamiliar colourless settings lead to unwelcome introspection – think doctors' and dentists' offices, high schools, and offices. Colour welcomes and engages us.

In 2006, Kuller found that for the just under a thousand workers in diverse areas from Argentina, Africa, Britain, and Sweden, "mood was consistently better for those in a more colourful work environment."

Caring about our physical setting is caring about ourselves. In *The Experience of Place,* Tony Hiss describes a 1956 experiment done by environmental psychologist Abraham Maslow and his colleague, Norbett L. Mintz, to find out how a physical setting affects our mood, our behaviour, and our judgment.

With the help of Maslow's wife, three rooms at Brandeis University were decorated for the experiment. One was "The Beautiful Room." It had a big window, comfy furniture, soft lighting, art, books, and a nice rug. Another was "The Average Room," and it was tidy, clean, functional, and office–like. Then there was "The Ugly Room," which was dirty, cluttered, and painted battle–ship grey. (Unfortunately there was no mention of the wall colours used in the beautiful and average rooms.) The overhead light had a torn shade. A mattress and box springs leaned against one wall.

Volunteers sat at a table in each room and supervisors asked them to look at a series of photographs of people to decide if they looked vibrant. In the beautiful room, volunteers said yes. In the ugly room, they said no. The photographs were the same but faces appeared tired and displeased. The negative setting fostered negativity in the participants. But what was even more interesting was that in the functional room the responses matched those of participants in the ugly room.

Maslow and Mintz discovered the same thing also happened to the supervisors. They were hired to do the interviews but were not told the purpose of the exercise or that they were being studied too. The supervisors' behaviour varied with the room. In the ugly room, they were more irritable, impatient, and curt. They rushed the interviews and complained of fatigue and boredom. In the ugly space, they judged every aspect of their experience as negatively as the participants in those rooms judged the people in the photos.

And again, to the surprise of Maslow and Mintz, the supervisors' response in the average room were the same as in the ugly room. Places that meet only our pragmatic needs feel as bad as dirty, disorganized, and dysfunctional ones. Aesthetically pleasing "extras" are functional essentials. Functional minimalism, no matter how neat and tidy, is as draining on our psyche as squalor. Novelty and complexity keep us alert. Colour and aesthetics engage us intellectually and emotionally and make us feel complete. We can live without them but we cannot thrive. Beauty is tied to survival.

We know this but don't usually articulate it. Complaining about how a place looks can seem silly, fussy, and personal. But in fact, we also don't talk about it because colour and aesthetics are handled by our senses and our right brain and neither likes to verbalize. Feelings, not words, are their mode of communication. They take the measure of a place holistically. We get a quick thumbs-up or thumbs-down. The more methodical and sequential left brain can work out why but it is usually busy with other things in its own areas of expertise. Besides, why take time to put into words what we already know?

After the Maslow–Mintz experiment, not one of the people attributed their grumpy and impatient behaviour or their negativity to the space they were in! Imagine how many millions of people are like that – made grumpy every day by bad or merely functional places but never laying blame on the place itself. Now think of the positive effect that good colour and attractively appointed rooms and offices could have on the behaviour and attitudes of every impatient and negative employee and employer, student and teacher, hospital patient and nurse, child and old person, none of whom blames their banal surroundings for their negativity or lethargy. (My advice is this. If you go for a job interview and the place is ugly or purely functional, suggest going somewhere nice for coffee. You will seem better if the place is!) We are not a fixed fact, like a table or a rock. We are part of a fluid relationship with place.

The first book in English on architecture was written in 1642 by a poet, art connoisseur, and English ambassador in Venice, Sir Henry Wotton (1568–1639). Quoting from Vitruvius, he wrote that good architecture has three essential qualities: commodity (it functions), firmness (it is made to last), and delight. It is delight, the pleasure to be gained from seemingly superfluous extras, that keeps our minds alive and engaged, our bodies refreshed and alert, and our sense of well–being restored.

Good places function well but they also invite our participation, make us feel we are in a give–and–take relationship and that our presence makes a difference. It can be as simple as being able to open a window, turn off a light, display photographs, hang art, and pick a wall colour. A Toronto design firm, HOK, found that just asking employees their opinion about how an office renovation should look brings a 2 per cent increase in productivity when the new offices are complete. Just asking! Acting on those recommendations increases this to between 10 and 15 per cent.

When choosing colours for public areas or communal spaces, designers, like everyone else, can find it almost impossible to get consensus. It is controversial because we really are all colour experts. We all have opinions and none is the same. But avoiding colour to offend no one, conversely, pleases no one. It is better to work through the inevitable comments and criticism than to avoid colour to avoid controversy. We get used to any colour.

This was true when I did a colour plan for a huge warehouse. It was being turned into offices, and I was asked to break the vast space up into work zones with colour. I used neutrals but punctuated key places with hits of strong colour and I used red on the vast ceiling to bring it down and warm the place up. A week later I got a call to say that everything was working well with the exception of one colour. Would I come and suggest a replacement for the yellow–green used in a small amount in part of the front reception.

I was too busy to go right away. Two weeks later the manager apologized when I arrived. He had meant to cancel the meeting. In the interim, the least favourite colour had become, to his surprise, everyone's favourite. We get to know a colour and it ceases to be the enemy. The absence of colour is what makes the strongest statement. It is the colourless we–are–not–talking–to–you silence that feels hostile in perpetuity.

Perhaps during my IDEX talk I should show slides of a school where I used colour, not just to make it look better but so it would function better. My kids' grade school had a jumble of almost identical hallways. When I showed the kids the before photographs of the halls, they didn't know one from another unless there was a give–away clue. "Oh, that is my teacher's coat on the hook so that is the hall on the second floor near Anne's classroom." Because colour psychologists have found that young children like warm, clean colours and that cool colours are an acquired taste, the long hall next to the junior classes became a sequence of orange through hot pink to citrus yellow. For the hall by the senior classrooms I suggested apple greens, aqua, turquoise, and periwinkle blue. Each stairwell had a signature colour on one wall. When it was finished, everyone seemed to enjoy the transformation but the colours also made clear markers. Teachers could say, "Go to the French room downstairs at the end of the orange wall." No one got lost. The principal's only regret was that they hadn't done it sooner.

To talk about the benefits of good colour and savannah–like design would mean mentioning green architecture and the work of American William McDonough. He is the Al Gore of architecture when it comes to preaching environmental responsibility. He believes in cradle–to–cradle patterns of consumption that eliminate waste entirely and sustainable building practices that are a celebration of the interdependence with living things. In 1995 his firm, William McDonough and Partners, applied their intelligent, nature–inspired design to a 295,000–square–foot glass and steel plant for furniture manufacturer Herman Miller. And the effect of a design that taps into the use of natural light (full–spectrum colour at its best), fresh air (operable windows), and diversity (curves, for one)? A 25 per cent increase in productivity, which amounts to a profit increase of $50 million a year. Not bad for a building that cost $15 million total. And, as often happens in many McDonough–designed workplaces, employees that leave to take higher paying jobs usually return. The trade–off, dealing with a bad building, just isn't worth it.

In my talk I could share my observations about companies and developers. It seems to me that those who recognize our animal need for colour, texture, variety and, if possible, a bit of savannah greenery tend to be confident, innovative, and successful. Their buildings become communities. In Toronto, 401 Richmond Street West, a hundred–year–old warehouse a city block long that contains 200,000 square feet of rental space, is filled by small businesses and art galleries. The building's old bones and aging architectural elements were respected and incorporated into the interior renovation. Art by contemporary local artists enliven the less interesting new walls that divide the building into offices. The entrance hall is old brick and one vibrant red wall. The hall leading to the thriving bistro with home-cooked smells is painted magenta. Every floor has a different colour on its landing.

Is it a coincidence that a place that cares about colour and pleasing detail also has a nursery school in the central courtyard, a huge garden on the roof, a newsy notice board, an interactive website and a constant waiting list for rental space?

My talk would have to include some present-day colour heroes such as Edi Rama, a pushy, opinionated guy who likes to wear coloured socks and funky ties and has been elected mayor of Tirana, the capital of Albania, for three consecutive terms (so far). When he was first elected in 2000 the city was ugly and run-down. With a Bruno Taut-like conviction that nature and colour could heal his city, Rama reclaimed thousands of acres of parkland and green space from illegal squatters. Then he planted thousands of trees and installed street lighting around the city. But the most shocking difference was made with colour. The façades of shabby, grey buildings of the post-communist regime are being painted with lots and lots of happy hues. Apartment buildings, civic buildings, shops are turning red, yellow, peach, orange, blue, and green or all of the above.

Rama uses colour to unite communities in a common good. Neighbours paint together, not just on their own place. Bulldozers move away rubble and fill in muddy ditches so orange buses can move around the city that colour is healing. Rama says, "Tirana will become a city where people will want to live; chroma will restore what has been lost and be the catalyst for change in a city that was dead."

I would also mention England's Banksy, the superstar of graffiti artists. Vandalism is a protest from urban disenfranchised against hard and hostile cityscapes but graffiti, part of the protest, is at its best an urban art form with the same benefits as Rama's colours.

The elusive Banksy has taken on one of the ugliest walls in the world, the security fence between Palestine and Israel. His goal, he said, was to make "the most degrading structure into the longest gallery for free speech and bad art." Although verbally abused and shot at, he continued to stencil a picture of a little girl holding a bunch of balloons that seem to be elevating her up the wall and paint a cheeky *trompe l'oeil* image of a big hole broken through the wall revealing a tropical paradise on the other side.

Banksy has honed his graffiti fame and his artistry to such an extent that his gallery paintings fetch hefty sums. *Bombing Middle England* sold in a Sotheby's auction for one thousand pounds and *Space Girl and Bird,* for three times that. So now when any of his graffiti is whitewashed from buildings, the loudest protest usually comes from the owners. Banksy was among the graffiti artists who was invited to cover the walls of the underground parking for the Swiss embassy in London with colourful murals seven years ago. It was to be temporary but the embassy realized it was a huge improvement and Banksy will stay.

Pablo Aravena made the documentary *Next: A Primer in Urban Painting* about graffiti around the world and says, "My thesis was these are important artists who will be remembered. Spending time with them was the equivalent of hanging out with Impressionists in Paris cafés. . . . If I had money, this is the art I would be decorating my house with and not van Gogh."

Graffiti artists represent the opposite extreme from my colour–inhibited clients. They take their colours and work fast and work big, risking life and limb to participate in their setting and to express themselves and if what they achieve is erased the next day they live with it. I spoke to a Toronto artist named Trik who said his biggest, fastest piece was forty feet across and two storeys high and thrown up in four hours.

I know I should not connect this to clients who take months to contemplate adding one quart of a colour to some part of their house but I do. There are times when I go into a home that is so held back and repressed that I would gladly take a spray can and scrawl over the hall wall, "Let's just have some fun right here!!! Right now!!!" I think every home should have a graffiti wall, a constantly changing outlet for self–expression, even if it is on one side of the stairs to the basement. Why don't parents let kids do what they want to their bedroom walls? Some of the most creative people I know had that freedom when they were teenagers.

My daughter wrote to me about San Francisco's Mission Hill area where colourful graffiti has turned a district divided by gang turf wars into a neighbourhood. It began in the 1970s when one woman painted a mural on her garage door in the back alley. Soon more and more people did the same. Today an organization called Precita Eyes brings children to the alleys to learn from the murals about their culture and social issues such as violence, war, love, AIDS, consumerism, and recyling. Professional artists join in to paint with children. Juvenile delinquents, some who had been in trouble for doing graffiti, are encouraged to use their talents to paint legitimate murals to raise awareness of issues such as drinking and driving. The walls of Caesar Chavez School (a school that has some deaf students) are covered with colourful murals. Nice, wrote Caroline, that a school for deaf children would be so visually stimulating.

Kids kept tagging one mural that was painted with very dark browns and greens. Finally the mural painter redid it in bright colours. The tagging stopped. Caroline's tour guide said, "Our solution to solving the problem of graffiti would be to paint the whole city!"

Banksy was quoted in *New Yorker* magazine as saying, "Imagine a city where graffiti wasn't illegal. A city where everyone could draw wherever they liked, where the street was awash with millions of colours and little phrases. . . . A city that felt like a party where everyone was invited, not just the estate agents and the barons of big business."

Taut and Rama, Banksy and the ladies of Mission Hill, they all use colour to get rid of the animosity between person and place. Ruth Lande Shuman and Publicolor uses it to turn around daily life for kids in run-down schools.

There was so much to tell about colour that I had no idea how to tie everything together into a single talk that was suddenly only two days away. And that was when it came to me. I was driving home from a consultation at a paint contractor's house. He had said that when I spoke about colour or responded to how nicely his colour chips looked together it was as if I were in love. I said that maybe I was. Driving away was when the key theme flashed across my brain like a welcomed text message. "Colour," the message went, "is . . . like . . . sex." And the talk began to write itself.

And what I said was: You don't have to be taught colour to figure it out. Sometimes the less you are taught the better it is. You don't have to learn it in school because everything you need to know, you know already. You are born with all the colour wisdom you will ever need. Colour smarts is part of your biological makeup. Like falling in love, you know what appeals. No one tells you. No one but you knows what looks good to you. You know it because you don't think it; you feel it. What you love is what you love, whatever that looks like.

You can be walking along the street one day and clasp your eyes upon a beautiful person or a particularly attractive red wall and feel throughout your being that you would just love to take them home. Others might not notice what you have found so stunningly attractive or, if they do, they might not agree. That does not matter in the least. People, places, and situations just feel right – or they don't, instantly. Seeking that beauty, discovering that passion, being in love is good for us.

Physical settings are no different than the people in our lives. They are the company we keep. For better or for worse, we are part of these relationships. They can support and empower us or, like any bad relationship, hold us back, drag us down, and prevent us from being our happiest and most productive selves. They are not to be ignored.

Colour is changing Tirana. Colour is changing dysfunctional schools and community centres into places of learning and community. Colour helped turn Dave's student room into a home and his friendship into a romance.

But trusting our colour feelings can take some coaxing. When I begin working with a new client and I ask them what colour they were thinking of for a room, they sometimes respond rather petulantly, "If I knew that I wouldn't have called you, would I?" It often surprises them to discover how much they do know and how opinionated they can be. We confuse not knowing colour with finding it hard to make paint choices. By ignoring rules and letting our heart lead the way, we may never return to the easiness of the colour–filled Eden of childhood but we just might get a whole lot closer.

Colour's mysteries and magic will never be fully understood. But that doesn't matter because these are only the extras. You know colour. Trusting your instincts is all that is needed to engage with it.

To respond to it with the conviction of a lover,
the confidence of a child
and the wisdom of millions of years.
Then colour, like a companion,
will make you happy.
and bring you home.

COLOUR TERMS

Colour: Often used as a synonym for hue but colour is considered a broader term. Colour encompasses hue (red, green, blue, etc.), appearance (finishes like metallics), and value (lightness and darkness, tones and shades).

Hue: The red, green, blue, etc. dimension of colour.

Saturation: The amount of colour in a colour or the amount of pigment compared to medium in a paint mixture.

Chroma: A synonym for saturation.

Shade: Variations of a colour that are darker than the pure colour.

Tone: Variations of a colour that are lighter than the pure colour.

Value: Degree of lightness and darkness of a colour.

Tint: Pure colour added to a base colour or the result of adding a bit of pure colour to a base colour.

PIGMENTS

Azurite: Blue with a hint of green that turned green when mixed with water so not good for frescoes.

Indigo: Deep blue from indigo plant, usually used as a dye.

Lake: Transparent dye, usually red, yellow, or blue; made from berries and plants, has a tendency to fade.

Lapis lazuli: Ultramarine; most vivid and expensive blue, made from ground mineral.

Malacite: Green pigment with a bluish tint made from carbonate of copper.

Minium: Red–orange pigment made from lead.

Ochre: An earth pigment ranging in colour from yellow to red and brown.

Orpiment: Bright yellow, popular in the sixteenth century, made from arsenic.

Realgar: Reddish–orange pigment made from arsenic.

Smalt: A blue pigment made of ground glass, less intense than ultramarine and less costly.

Vermilion: Cinnabar; a strong red pigment from the mineral mercuric sulphide.

Ultramarine: Pigment made from ground lapis lazuli; the most expensive pigment after gold.

TECHNIQUES

Cangiantismo: Painting using contrasting colours placed side by side to give dimension to objects and to increase the range of available colours by optical colour mixing at a time when physical mixing was forbidden.

Chiaroscuro (pronounced key–aro–skuro): Painting in high–contrast tones that reduce colour and add theatrically strong lighting effects that are set against a dark background.

Sfumato: Painting in mid–tone colours to reduce contrast and softening or blurring the transitions between one colour and another.

Unione: Painting with colours of the same or similar value and intensity, unmixed and without darkened shadows, to give an even, over–all colour effect that is not misty or blended like sfumato.

Fresco: Pigment is mixed with water and added to wet plaster. Lime in the plaster bonds with the pigment, making it long lasting.

Egg tempera: Pigment is mixed with egg yolk, egg white, or both and water.

BIBLIOGRAPHY

Alexander, Christopher, Sara Ishikawa, and Murray Silverstein, with Max Jacobsen, Ingrid Fiksdahl–King, Shlomo Angel. *A Pattern Language: Towns, Buildings, Construction*. New York: Oxford University Press, 1977.

Ball, Philip. *Bright Earth*. New York: Farrar, Straus and Giroux, 2002.

Baars, Bernard J. *In the Theater of Consciousness*. New York: Oxford University Press, 1997.

Batchelor, David. *Chromophobia*. London: Reaktion Books Ltd., 2000.

Bell, Quentin, and Virginia Nicholson. *Charleston: A Bloomsbury House and Garden*. London: Francis Lincoln Ltd., 1997.

Benyus, Janine M. *Biomimicry*. New York: Quill, William Morrow, 1997.

Blackmore, Susan. *Consciousness: An Introduction*. New York: Oxford University Press, 2004.

Botton, Alain de. *The Architecture of Happiness*. London: The Penguin Group, 2006.

Barrow, John D. *The Artful Universe*. Oxford: Clarendon Press, 1995.

Brebner, John. *Environmental Psychology in Building Design*. London: Applied Science Publishers Ltd., 1982.

Calloway, Stephen. *Twentieth–Century Decoration*. New York: Rizzoli, 1988.

Colquhoun, Alan. *Modern Architecture*. Oxford: Oxford University Press, 2002.

Cumming, Robert, and Tom Porter. *The Colour Eye*. London: BBC Books, 1990.

Dawkins, Richard. *Unweaving the Rainbow: Science, Delusion and the Appetite for Wonder*. Boston, New York: Houghton Mifflin Company, 1998.

De Wolfe, Elsie. *The House in Good Taste*. New York: Then Century Co., 1913.

Evans, Dylan. *Emotion: The Science of Sentiment*. Oxford: Oxford University Press, 2001.

Faulkner, Waldron. *Architecture and Colour*. New York: John Wiley and Sons, 1972.

Finlay, Victoria. *Colour: Travels through the Paintbox*. London: Hodder and Stoughton, 2002.

Garfield, Simon. *Mauve*. London: Faber and Faber, 2000.

Gage, John. *Color and Meaning: Art, Science and Symbolism*. Berkeley and Los Angeles: University of California Press, 1999.

Gage, John. *Colour and Culture: Practice and Meaning from Antiquity to Abstraction*. London: Thames and Hudson, 1993.

Gimbel, Theo. *Healing Through Colour*. Saffron Walden, U.K.: The C. W. Daniel Company Ltd., 1980.

Greenfield, Amy Butler. *A Perfect Red*. New York: Harper Perennial, 2005.

Gregory, Richard, L. *Eye and Brain: The Psychology of Seeing*, 5th edition. New Jersey: Princeton University Press, 1997.

Hall, Marcia. *Color and Meaning: Practice and Theory in Renaissance Painting*. Cambridge: Cambridge University Press, 1992.

Hesselgren, Sven. *On Architecture*. Bickley, U.K.: Chartwell–Bratt Ltd., 1987.

Hiss, Tony. "A Need for Home." *The New York Times*. May 6, 2007.

Hubel, David H. *Eye, Brain, and Vision*. New York: Scientific American, 1995.

Hughes, Robert. *Nothing If Not Critical*. New York: The Penguin Group, 1990.

Hines, Thomas S. *Richard Neutra and the Search for Modern Architecture*. New York: Rizzoli, 2005.

Horsefield, Margaret. *Biting the Dust*. London: The Fourth Estate Ltd., 1997.

Inghilleri, Paolo. *Light Fields*. Artemide, 1996.

Kakuzo, Okakura. *The Book of Tea*. Rutland, Vermont: Charles E. Tuttle Company, 1956.

Koren, Leonard. *Wabi–Sabi for Artists, Designers, Poets and Philosophers*. Berkeley, California: Stone Bridge Press, 1994.

Liberman, Jacob. *Light–Medicine of the Future: How We Can Use It to Heal Ourselves Now*. Sante Fe, New Mexico: Bear & Company Publishing, 1991.

Linton, Harold. *Colour in Architecture*. New York: McGraw–Hill, 1999.

Mahnke, Frank H. *Color, Environment, and Human Response*. New York: Van Nostrand Reinhold, 1996.

McDonough, William, and Michael Braungart. *Cradle to Cradle: Remaking the Way We Make Things*. New York: North Point Press, 2002.

Pastoureau, Michel. *Blue: The History of a Colour*. Princeton, N.J.: Princeton University Press, 2000.

Porter, Tom, and Byron Mikellides. *Colour for Architecture*. London: Studio Vista, 1976.

Rybczynski, Witold. *The Look of Architecture*. New York: Oxford University Press, 2001.

Rybczynski, Witold. *Home: A Short History of an Idea*. New York: Penguin Books, 1989.

Riley, Charles A., II. *Colour Codes: Modern Theories of Color in Philosophy, Painting and Architecture, Literature, Music, and Psychology*. Hanover, N.H.: University Press of New England, 1995.

Ruegg, Arthur. *Le Corbusier's Polychromie architecturale and His Colour Keyboards from 1931 and 1959*. Basel: Birkhauser Verlag Publishers, 1997.

Savage, George. *A Concise History of Interior Decoration*. London: Thames and Hudson, 1966.

Sekuler, Robert, and Randolph Blake. *Perception*, 4th edition. New York: McGraw–Hill, 2002.

Sharpe, Deborah T. *The Psychology of Color and Design*. Chicago: Nelson–Hall, 1974.

The Study and Application of Color in Extraterrestrial Habitat. Texas: National Aeronautics and Space Administration, Johnson Spacecraft Centre.

Torrice, Antonio, with Rosalie Logrippo. *In My Room: Decorating for and with Children.* New York: Ballantine Books, 1989.

Thompson, Evan, Adrian Palacios, and Francisco J. Varela. "Ways of Coloring: Comparative Color Vision as a Case Study for Cognitive Science." *Behavioral and Brain Sciences,* 1992, 15:1.

Varichon, Anne (Translated from French by Toula Ballas). *Colours: What They Mean and How to Make Them.* New York: Harry N. Abrams Inc., 2007.

Williamson, Samuel, J., and Herman Z. Cummins. *Light and Colour in Nature and Art.* New York: John Wiley and Sons, 1983.

Wilson, Edward O. *Biophilia.* Cambridge, Mass.: Harvard University Press, 1984.

Wolfe, Tom. *From Bauhaus to Our House.* New York: Pocket Books, 1981.

Wright, Angela. *The Beginner's Guide to Colour Psychology.* London: Kyle Cathie Limited, 1995.

Wright, Ronald. *A Short History of Progress.* Toronto: House of Anasi Press, 2004.

Wright, Mary and Russel. *Guide to Easier Living.* Salt Lake City: Gibbs Smith Publishers, 1950.

INDEX

IMAGE CREDITS

iii: Chicago, Aida Fry; viii: Graffiti behind the Drake Hotel, Janice Lindsay; 5: Caroline and Dave, Janice Lindsay; 6: Akiko's Apartment, colour by Janice, Janice Lindsay; 8: Venecia Game Reserve, South Africa, Janice Lindsay; 20: Birds and boots in Kensington Market, Janice Lindsay; 24: Turquoise hut near Fugitives Drift, South Africa, Janice Lindsay; 36: African greenery, Janice Lindsay; 41: Gertler's kitchen, Janice Lindsay; 42: Daybreak over Indian Ocean, Janice Lindsay; 56: Salvador Dali sofa in Paris, Janice Lindsay; 64: Paul Edmondson/Getty Images; 78: Finlay in blue goggles, Janice Lindsay; 86: Polyptych, Lorenzo Monaco/Art Resource; 103: MIT, Rem Koolhaus, architect, photo by Janice Lindsay; 104: Mary's room, Janice Lindsay; 110: Michael Duernickx/Getty Images; 130: Reuven and Raluca's powder room, Janice Lindsay; 136: *Rembrandt with toque and gold chain*, Art Resource; 157: Sue's striped skylight, Janice Lindsay; 158: Flaking wall, Aida Fry; 164: *Exposition Universelle de Paris, 1889*/Corbis; 166: Todd Gipstein/ Getty Images; 182: Mauve wall in Prague, Aida Fry; 188: South African foliage, Janice Lindsay; 202: Thailand's guard of honour, Chaiwat Subprasom/Reuters; 208: Claude Monet, *Haystacks (Effect of Snow and Sun)*, 1891, Art Resource; 228: Gertler's living room, Janice Lindsay; 234: James MacNeil Whistler, *Nocturne in Blue and Gold: Old Battersea Bridge, c.1872–5*, Art Resource; 253: Kandinsky swatches; 234: African bowl, Janice Lindsay; 262: Villa Savoye, Le Corbusier, architect, photo by Brian Pirie; 264: Hall to MOMA toilets, New York City, Janice Lindsay; 301: Getty Museum, Los Angeles, Richard Meyer, architect, photograph by Janice Lindsay; 302: Anne Coban's dining room, designer, Janice, photograph by Janice Lindsay; 309: White textures, My Showhouse Room, Janice Lindsay; 310: Itten's colour wheel; 324: Silk threads, Janice Lindsay; 332: David Muir/Getty Images; 349: Blue house in San Francisco, Janice Lindsay; 350: Inner City School, courtesy of Publicolor; 356: Vancouver sky, Aida Fry; 368: Chelsea Hotel, New York, Janice Lindsay; 374: Don Farrell/ Getty Images; 409: Stroop Effect; 410: Based on an image of Audrey Hepburn on the Set of "Breakfast at Tiffany's"/ Corbis; 416: Musée Quai Branley, Janice Lindsay; 434: Colour contemplation at the Chelsea Hotel, Janice Lindsay.

ACKNOWLEDGEMENTS

Thank you to all my clients. You make my work and my life a fascinating adventure. Each one of you has taught me much about colour and without you there would be no book. Thank you to the authors and experts whose research was my guide: John Gage, who probably knows more about colour history than anyone, Christopher Ball, who knows more about the history of pigments, Simon Garfield, the authority on chemistry becoming our key colour maker, and David Hubel who guided me through through the mysteries of our grey matter.

I am grateful to Frank Mahnke for his insights into the psychological and physiological effects of colour and for teaching me the important lesson that, as a colour designer, no colour choice should be arbitrary or only decorative.

Behind every good woman are great allies. Thank you to my first agent, Bruce Westwood for getting the ball rolling and Samantha Haywood for keeping it rolling. Thank you to my first editor, Chris Bucci for getting me through many a long inning and to Susan Renouf, who came in as the closer. Without her editorial acumen and decisive ways, I would probably be writing this still.

Thank you to good friends who at various times and in various ways gave me the encouragement needed to keep going – Ian Proud, Martin Manning, William Saunderson–Meyer. Thank you to my Colour Marketing Group buddy and friend Aida Fry for sharing not only her passion for colour on our travels but also her images. Thanks to my sister, Caroline Hart and my friend, Lorraine Greey, not just for their enthusiasm and kindness but for giving me so many happy and productive writing escapes. Thank you to Joanna Gertler, John Plank, and Richard Longley, insightful readers all. Thank you to my husband and the real writer in the family, David Macfarlane, the person who first thought of this book, endured its long incubation, and always encouraged me to use my own voice. Thank you to our children, Caroline and Blake. They are wise, fun, empathetic, and always a reminder of what is important in life when one might otherwise be distracted.

And finally my greatest thanks go to my mother, Molly Lindsay–Kent, an avid reader, honest critic, zealous spell–checker, and the most colourful person I know. I hope I have been blessed with inheriting a small portion of her love of people, her curiosity, and her enthusiasm for life. Even as one of six kids, I remember her as my most attentive listener. Sometimes that is the best gift we can give another. Without listeners, we tell no stories. Mum was, however, not the most patient champion of this oeuvre. And so, in answer to her perpetual question, "Why don't you just get on and finish that damn book of yours?"

Here it is – at last!

Thank you.

Thank you all.